Checking Presidential Power

A central concern about the robustness of democratic rule in new democracies is the concentration of power in the executive branch and the potential this creates for abuse. This concern is felt particularly with regard to the concentration of legislative power. *Checking Presidential Power* explains the levels of reliance on executive decrees in a comparative perspective. Building on the idea of institutional commitment, which affects the enforcement of decision-making rules, this book describes the degree to which countries rely on executive decree authority as more reliance may lead to unbalanced presidential systems and will ultimately affect democratic quality. Breaking new ground by both theorizing and empirically analyzing decree authority from a comparative perspective, this book examines policymaking in separation of powers systems. It explains the choice between decrees and statutes, and why legislators are sometimes profoundly engaged in the legislative process and yet other times entirely withdrawn from it.

Valeria Palanza is Assistant Professor in the Instituto de Ciencia Política, Pontificia Universidad Católica de Chile. Her research interests focus on issues of democracy, institutional arrangements, and the legislative process. Her most recent publications appear in *Comparative Political Studies, Revista de Ciencia Política,* and *Legislative Studies Quarterly.*

Checking Presidential Power

Executive Decrees and the Legislative Process in New Democracies

VALERIA PALANZA

Instituto de Ciencia Política,
Pontificia Universidad Católica de Chile

CAMBRIDGE
UNIVERSITY PRESS

CAMBRIDGE
UNIVERSITY PRESS

University Printing House, Cambridge CB2 8BS, United Kingdom

One Liberty Plaza, 20th Floor, New York, NY 10006, USA

477 Williamstown Road, Port Melbourne, VIC 3207, Australia

314–321, 3rd Floor, Plot 3, Splendor Forum, Jasola District Centre, New Delhi – 110025, India

79 Anson Road, #06-04/06, Singapore 079906

Cambridge University Press is part of the University of Cambridge.

It furthers the University's mission by disseminating knowledge in the pursuit of education, learning, and research at the highest international levels of excellence.

www.cambridge.org
Information on this title: www.cambridge.org/9781108427623
DOI: 10.1017/9781108573580

© Valeria Palanza 2019

First published 2019

Printed and bound in Great Britain by Clays Ltd, Elcograf S.p.A.

A catalogue record for this publication is available from the British Library.

ISBN 978-1-108-42762-3 Hardback

For Gael

For Gael

Contents

Figures

Tables

Acknowledgments

This book started as my doctoral dissertation at Princeton University, where I was fortunate to coincide with an extraordinary group of scholars and friends who made that portion of this journey both intellectually challenging and socially delightful. I am especially grateful to my advisors, John Londregan and Nolan McCarty, for having provided instruction, criticism, and support. Each read numerous drafts, provided healthy doses of doubt, and contributed uncountable suggestions from substantive to editorial. In that process, they shaped me into a scholar and the dissertation into something more interesting than what it might have been without their backing. Jonas Pontusson was also an exceptional mentor who provided valuable criticism, suggestions, and advice at key moments of the writing process. Chuck Cameron raised great questions at an early phase, which led me to shift my focus to a more interesting problem, and his suggestions that came later led me to make a better book.

Outstanding scholars contributed in different ways to this project, either through direct feedback or by providing examples of scholarship that helped shape how I think about political problems. As a doctoral student, Chris Achen, Doug Arnold, Scott Ashworth, Nancy Bermeo, Brandice Canes-Wrone, Joshua Clinton, Kent Eaton, Kosuke Imai, Adam Meirowitz, Tom Palfrey, Grigore Pop-Eleches, Joshua Tucker, and Deborah Yashar each influenced parts of this work. The National Science Foundation funded Summer Institute for the Study of the Empirical Implications of Theoretical Models offered a stimulating intellectual environment, and Skip Lupia and Daniel Diermeier provided insights to methodological questions that shaped this dissertation in important ways.

Along the way, participants at diverse fora at Princeton University, the University of Notre Dame, the University of Illinois at Urbana-Champaign, CIDE Mexico, the Pontificia Universidad Católica de Chile, Universidade de Brasília, and Universidad del Pacífico in Peru, among others, raised challenging questions that improved the quality of this project. Will Barndt, Sarah Bermeo, Maria Bernedo del Carpio, Rachel Beatty Riedl, Sarah Chartock, Ian Chong, Chris Darnton, Shana Kushner Gadarian, Amy Gershkoff, Ezequiel Gonzáles Ocantos, Frances Hagopian, Stu Jordan, Jaime Kirzner-Roberts, Jennifer Lieb, Noam Lupu, Scott Mainwaring, Quinton Mayne, Carlos Meléndez, Andrew Owen, Cynthia Sanborn, Prerna Singh, Mariela Szwarcberg, Martin Tanaka, Maya Tudor, and Samuel Valenzuela provided insightful comments. Noam Lupu was very supportive when I finally decided the manuscript was ready, and he deserves special thanks. Special thanks also go to Javier Corrales, James Kim, Monika Nalepa, Illan Nam, Matt Winters, Cesar Zucco, and Scott Wolford for carefully reading and commenting on early drafts. I thank Cecilia Martínez-Gallardo for her insights and for providing support at different stages. At an early conference presentation, Eduardo Leoni's question shifted my focus to a more interesting problem, for which I thank him.

I thank Octavio Amorim Neto, Ernesto Calvo, Argelina Cheibub Figueiredo, and the folks at The Brazilian Center of Analysis and Planning (CEBRAP), Monica Pachón, Carlos Pereira, Tim Power, and Lucio Rennó, for facilitating access and discussing their datasets. Early in the process, Constanza Figueroa-Schibber in Argentina and Helena Martins in Brazil provided research assistance, as did Eduardo Aguilar Colque, Samuel Castro, Carlos Gallardo, Esteban Torre, and Ricardo Silva in Argentina, Brazil, and Peru. Later, in Chile, I received valuable assistance from Natalia Jara, Nicolás Díaz, Gustavo Díaz Díaz-Romero, Christian Parada, Sebastián Umpierrez, and Cristóbal Sandoval. Benjamín Muñoz, and Giancarlo Visconti provided outstanding assistance in Chile, and both were key during the final phase as well. I completed the book thanks to the invaluable assistance of Benjamín Muñoz, and I thank him especially.

As with many comparative endeavors, this project led me to conduct research in several countries: Argentina, Brazil, Chile, and Peru. It benefited from the insights of scores of legislators, presidential staff members, Supreme Court justices and staff members, a former president, and senior political advisers in Argentina, Brazil, Chile, and Peru. I am especially grateful to the scholars and government officials who generously assisted me in my research in numerous ways, and to those who made some of those interviews possible. I thank Universidad de San Andrés in Argentina, the CEPPAC at Universdade de Brasília in Brazil, the Centro de Investigación at Universidad del Pacífico in Peru, and Universidad Adolfo Ibañez in Chile, for providing institutional affiliation and stimulating intellectual environments. In Argentina, special thanks go to Carlos Acuña, Mariela Barresi, Gabriela Catterberg, Analía Villar, Hilda Kohan, and Ana Mustapic. The Dirección de Información Parlamentaria provided constant assistance with data, for which I am most grateful. In Brazil, I am especially thankful to Leany Lemos, Antonio Octávio Cintra, Camilo Negri, Arlindo Fernandes de Oliveira, Gilberto Guerzoni Filho, Benício Viero Schmidt, Lia Zanotta Machado, and my dear friend Juliana Amoretti. Work in Brasilia was easier thanks to the support of Henrique de Oliveira de Castro and Sonia Ranincheski. David Samuels and Diana Kapiszewski each provided tremendously helpful advice and contacts in preparation for the different trips that I made to Brasília. During the fieldwork I carried out in Chile as a graduate student, Cristóbal Aninat, Gregory Elacqua, and Patricio Navia were most helpful and generous in sharing their deep understanding of Chilean politics, insights of specific relevance to my project, and very valuable contacts. I am also most thankful to Hernán Larraín Matte and others at Universidad Adolfo Ibañez, and to Andrés Allamand for facilitating my affiliation. I thank Eduardo Morón for facilitating my affiliation with Centro de Investigación de la Universidad del Pacífico (CIUP). Special thanks to my good friends Mariana Llanos and Eric Magar, who generously shared experiences and provided support and advice throughout the years.

Financial support for this project came from numerous sources over the years. I am most grateful to the Graduate School at Princeton University. The Institute for International and Regional Studies and the Program in Latin American Studies provided funding for research travel, and additional funding during the writing stage was generously granted by the Research Program in Political Economy and the Mamdouha S. Bobst Center for Peace and Justice, each housed at Princeton University. Thank you to Gayle Brodsky, Danette Rivera, Monica Selinger, and Helene Wood for their cheerful support during those stressful graduate school years. The Kellogg Institute for International Studies allowed me to take a step back and think broadly, and I thank Dan Brinks, Frances Hagopian, Rodney Hero, and Scott Mainwaring for their support and encouragement.

I am grateful for two research grants from Chile's national research committee, the Comisión Nacional de Investigación Científica y Tecnológica,

FONDECYT Project No. 11100174 and FONDECYT Project No. 1140974; additional funds came from the Millennium Nucleus for the Study of State and Democracy in Latin America (RS130002), of the Millennium Scientific Initiative of the Ministry of Economy, Promotion, and Tourism of Chile.

Work at the Instituto de Ciencia Política of the Pontificia Universidad Católica de Chile has provided abundant motivation and challenges. David Altman and Andreas Feldman provided friendship and intellectual encouragement from the very beginning and through the hardest times, and each has marked my time at ICP; along with my colleagues Rossana Castiglioni and Helena Olea, their families have become part of my own.

An outstanding group of women has provided support and intellectual inspiration in work and life: My colleagues at UC, Cassandra Sweet, Julieta Suárez-Cao, Marisa Von Bulow, Carmen Le Foulon, Francisca Reyes, Umut Aydin, Lorena Oyarzún, and Ximena Illanes, and friends from different walks of academic life, Rosario Aguilar, Laia Balcells, Analía Béjar, Clarisa Béjar, Daniela Campello, Carla Carrizo, Rossana Castiglioni, Gabriela Catterberg, Carolina Daroch, Carolina De Miguel Moyer, Marcela González Rivas, Mariana Llanos, Mariely López-Santana, Milagros Nores, and Elsa Voytas. Mariana Chudnovsky and Marina Hondeville have been indispensable in work and life.

I am especially grateful to the group of scholars I met at CEDI/Universidad de San Andrés. My work has been influenced by ideas discussed at CEDI's weekly seminar, and I thank Mariano Tommasi, Pablo Spiller, and Mark Jones for their enduring intellectual influence on my work. N. Guillermo Molinelli was an outstanding mentor who is greatly missed. A portion of the data used in the chapter on Argentina is taken from the book co-authored with Guillermo Molinelli and Gisela Sin. I thank José Cheibub, David Doyle, Shane Martin, and Guillermo Rosas especially, for their encouragement. I thank Gisela Sin for her unconditional friendship and support both inside and outside of academia.

I am particularly indebted to Sara Doskow at Cambridge University Press, and to two anonymous reviewers, whose comments helped me improve the manuscript and better convey the argument. While I am grateful for all contributions, any and all errors are my own.

Finally, I mention my personal debts of gratitude. My uncle Juan Barresi, probably the brightest and most generous individual I have known, and also a political scientist, has been an inspiration. My gratitude to him is beyond words. I thank my parents, Augusto Palanza and Norma Barresi, for having trusted my judgment even when they did not share my choices; I am a stronger and wiser person thanks to them. The sound of my brother's laughter has always reminded me that life should not be taken too seriously, for which I thank him. I thank Juan Pablo and Mariela for having teased me enough that I can easily laugh at myself. I thank my aunt Ana Maria for having provided a much-needed example of light-hearted enthusiasm. Ximena Castrataro, Ivonne Jeannot, and Marina Hondeville have been there through thick and thin. I thank my grandparents and Lukas for so much love. Jorge Lotito's words of wisdom remain today as ever in my heart. Thanks to Vero, for her silent support and for bearing the distance so bravely. Thanks to my friends at Princeton, in Argentina, and all other places, for keeping me sane.

My deepest gratitude is to my son Gael. He has been my sunshine and an anchor to the truly important things in life as I worked to finish my dissertation and painstakingly turn it into a book. I took many hours from him to put into this book, and I can only hope that the choice made sense. I thank Rodrigo for being with Gael when I could not and for providing encouragement throughout. I thank Alejandro for reminding me that life lasts only two days, and can be easily enjoyable.

Abbreviations

CDA	Constitutional Decree Authority
DNU	Decretos de Necesidad y Urgencia (Decrees of Necessity and Urgency, Argentina)
EC32	Emenda Constitucional 32 (Constitutional Amendment, Brazil)
HCDN	Honorable Cámara de Diputados de la Nación (Chamber of Deputies, Argentina)
ICI	Institutional Commitment Index
MPV	Medidas Provisórias (Provisional Measures/Decrees, Brazil)
SC	Supreme Court
STF	Supremo Tribunal Federal (Supreme Court, Brazil)

I

Introduction

A Choice of Paths behind Each Policy

Executives in new presidential democracies have concentrated great influence over the legislative process, often to the extent of excluding the legislative branch from the process. Many have been granted constitutional decree authority, and they use this prerogative accordingly. Often, however, unconstitutional decrees, i.e., decrees that violate the wording of the constitution, are enacted. The consequences of such violations are not uniformly tolerated. On occasion, supreme courts strike down decrees, other times legislatures react and overturn decrees by way of statutory legislation. Rarely, executives are threatened with impeachment. Most often, however, decrees simply stand.

This book is concerned with the role of checks and balances in the legislative process, especially in countries where the effects of institutions cannot be taken for granted. It approaches the problem from an unusual point of entry: the choice of legislative instruments; specifically, the choice of decrees versus statutes when enacting policies. The question I ask is: Under what conditions should we expect policies to be passed by congress instead of executive decree? What determines this choice? I argue that the choice is a function of (a) the allocation of legislative prerogatives across the branches of government, (b) politicians' valuation of those prerogatives, and (c) external agents' valuation of policy. This explanation captures the importance of institutions by taking into account the way institutions structure interactions. It also acknowledges that the mere existence of a rule is not sufficient to predict outcomes.

This caveat introduces the notion of institutional commitment, which I define as the politicians' willingness to defend their decision rights from encroachment. By bringing in external agents, I place the onus of putting policies on the table on external actors who are vested in specific policies and wish to see them prosper.

The main contribution of this book is to shed light on the complex process behind the enforcement of checks and balances. It puts forth the notion that the existence of rules imposing checks on executive behavior is worth nothing if the actors in charge of imposing constraints on the executive do not act to do so. It goes further to outline the mechanisms leading to politicians' willingness to enforce limits on the executive, by means of exercising and enforcing their own decision rights. Those mechanisms are associated with the value politicians assign to their decision rights, which, in turn, is associated to their expectations regarding how long they will remain in their posts and what benefits they derive from their tenure. In sum, the book highlights the utility to legislators, other politicians, and the polity as a whole, of enforcing their decision rights. In doing so, they strengthen the institutions they embody, and endow them with added value. By the same token, it reveals the conditions under which enforcement is more likely to occur and when one should not expect it to emerge.

This introduction proceeds as follows: In the remainder of this section, I present an example of a failed policy. I argue that the policy was enacted by decree due to a blunt miscalculation that ultimately led to its demise. The example illustrates many of the dynamics that I model in Chapter 2. Section 1.2 presents a review of the various literature on law making and decree authority that shape the questions and approaches in the present work. Section 1.3 engages with the debate surrounding explanations of decree authority, questions prevailing assumptions, and presents the shift in assumptions guiding this book. Section 1.4 presents a brief introduction of the theory put forth in Chapter 2. Section 1.5 provides a roadmap of the remainder of the book.

1.1.1 A Miscalculation

In March 2008, Argentine President Cristina Fernández de Kirchner enacted a decree raising taxes on agricultural exports. In an attempt by the administration to ride on the commodity boom of 2008, it increased the tax on agricultural exports by implementing a movable rate designed to rise with international price increases.[1] The infamous tax, established through Resolución 125/2008, became known as *Retenciones Móviles*. Its enactment gave way to the country's worst wave of sustained strikes in many years, placing the economy on hold and putting on display the political muscle of organized agricultural interests.

Given the will to enact a tax on agricultural exports, the question becomes whether to do it by statute or decree. The first path acknowledges congressional decision rights over the process by which policies are decided, while the second does not. On this occasion, the president overlooked the forces at play and chose to enact the policy by decree.[2] The choice was made with no apparent consideration of the interests and influence of farmers, a traditionally powerful group in Argentina.

What happened during the next four months provides a unique opportunity to observe the interplay between political actors and external agents regarding policy enactment. Immediately after the decree was issued, farmers went on strike. The agricultural sector brought its resources to bear on the conflict, and the strike, initially intended to last only a few days, was extended again and again, showcasing the weight of opposition to the policy. In a form of mobilization that has become common in Argentina, the strike took to the roads and interrupted transportation of goods (foods and others) almost entirely for weeks. By March 19, the media referred to the strike as the largest ever conducted by farmers (*La Nación*, 19 March 2008).

Apparently seeking to fight this battle in the public arena, on March 22 the president addressed the country, requesting farmers to cooperate and participate in negotiations. That same day, the *Union Industrial Argentina* (UIA, representing industrialists), also admonished farmers to reconsider their stance. Of course, this was more than a rhetoric battle; by March 25 there was widespread concern about the disruption in the supply of basic foods. In the next few days, the country broke out in *cacerolazos*.[3]

---

[1] The mobile index would move with the price of commodities, increasing as the price of commodities increased, and decreasing when prices went down.

[2] For the sake of clarity, note that this decree was an administrative decree, not a *Decreto de Necesidad y Urgencia*, the type of decree allowed by Constitutional Decree Authority in Argentina. The dynamics that it spearheaded, however, are well suited to illustrate the interaction of influential actors and politicians when deciding policies.

[3] A form of public demonstration that became popular at the height of the 2001 crisis, in which predominantly urban-middle class demonstrators bang pots and pans to show discontent.

On April 2, farmers put the strike on hold to enter negotiations with the government. Unsatisfied by what the government offered and empowered by the success of their mobilization efforts, farmers went back on strike. Toward the end of April, the Minister of Economics, Martin Lousteau, resigned under the weight of the administration's failure to put an end to the seemingly endless tug of war. June was plagued by *cacerolazos* carried out by the urban middle class, which was infuriated by the lack of basic foods and the apparent paralysis in negotiations, and which blamed the government for their misfortune.

While the executive showed no signs of caving, on June 11 the Supreme Court declared that it would rule on the constitutionality of the decree. Almost immediately, only a week following that announcement, the executive sent a bill to Congress requesting an up or down vote on the tax. Farmers applauded the move, called off the strike, and moved into Congress, where they spent most of the next 30 days in consultation with legislators and their provincial allies. Exactly one month later, on July 17, Congress struck down the bill, putting an end to the long conflict. The status quo was re-established.

This narrative is intended to illustrate the confrontation between the branches over the enactment of policy in a case where the stakes were clearly high; had the stakes been low, the decree may have passed unnoticed. It shows external agents confronted over the policy (farmers opposing the tax, the UIA on the opposite sidewalk), and how powerful farmers invested their resources abundantly in support of their interests, ultimately getting their way, through congress. The narrative is largely at odds with the perception of Latin American presidents being able to legislate unchecked, empowered by the lack of horizontal accountability (O'Donnell 1994). Admittedly, the mayhem caused by the mobilization described above does suggest that conventional democratic instruments of representation are disrupted (Machado et al. 2011), as one would expect in delegative democracies. However, one cannot overlook the intervention of the supreme court and congress in settling the issue.

Clearly, as the growing literature on Latin American legislatures strives to demonstrate, the executive does not rule alone. In fact, this book finds motivation in the puzzle posed by the opposite scenario: even weak Latin America congresses enact laws, often, important ones. Once and again, the ever-powerful presidents portrayed in the literature are left to stand by while bills go through the congressional procedure for approval. Why not simply rule by decree? How can we explain the enactment of statutes where decrees are so readily available?

Furthermore, what explains the variation in the responses to these questions across cases? While Argentina, Brazil, Chile, and Peru have very similar institutional arrangements, careful analysis of the details of their legislative processes reveals stark differences in the way actors in each country come to policy decisions. Each of the four countries is endowed with constitutional decree authority, yet we observe that decrees are practically never chosen to legislate in Chile, whereas Argentina, Brazil, and Peru enact decrees routinely.

1.1.2 Decree Authority and Levels of Reliance on Decrees

In recent times, democracies around the globe have increasingly resorted to policymaking by executive decree. The third wave of democratization has been haunted by questions regarding the quality of the new democracies, often casting doubt on the very meaning of democracy in specific settings. Among the problems leading to the debate is the fact that these democracies have increasingly chosen to endow their executives with constitutional decree authority (Negretto 2009). Although Latin American democracies provide well-known cases of this approach to decision making, countries in other regions have also made indiscriminate use of decrees; Russia and Nigeria are two notorious cases that exemplify the extensiveness of the phenomenon.

Consequently, executive decree authority, usually identified with authoritarian regimes and dictatorial modes of decision making, has become an integral component of many developing democracies. Amid public reactions that range from utter outrage to indifference, the phenomenon has captured the attention of pundits and laymen alike, and much has been written on the topic since the onset of the third wave of democratization in the 1970s. Scholars analyzing third-wave democracies were quick to note the problem and to dismiss it as an authoritarian legacy, which the "consolidation" of these regimes would overcome.

Yet given the continued centrality of decree authority in democracies around the globe and its impact on policy, understanding the determinants of the choices leading to the use of decrees over statutes constitutes a long-postponed priority in our discipline. It remains that, despite frequent use of decree authority, policies are enacted through congressional statutes constantly. And although many countries have established constitutional decree authority (CDA, following Carey and Shugart's (1998) terminology), even where presidents are perceived to be very powerful, there is huge variation in the extent to which they use the prerogative.

The incidence of congressional statutes is just as puzzling in certain institutional environments as we might find the frequency of decrees to be in others. If policies may be easily enacted by executive decree, why would some go through congress at all? In response, I have already referred to legislators' interest in the process, but why should we expect *variation* in the outcome?

The rules governing the approval of decrees and statutes are certainly a determinant, yet many decrees that blatantly breach constitutional rules are enacted and sustained for years. The fundamental reason, I argue, is that politicians' valuation of their decision rights varies. It varies across countries, and it varies across policy areas. I refer to this as varying levels of *institutional commitment* among legislators and Supreme Court justices. I expand on the notion of institutional commitment in the next two chapters.

1.2 POLICY, LAWMAKING, AND NEW DEMOCRACIES

1.2.1 Lawmaking and Checks and Balances in US Politics

The legislative process in separation of powers' systems has been analyzed most frequently and intensely within the scenario of the United States. Given the difficulties inherent to comparative endeavors, theorizing on the determinants of the legislative process in separation of powers' systems in general is, to a large extent, influenced by our knowledge of the US case and by US congressional politics (Mayhew 1991; Krehbiel 1998; Shepsle and Weingast 1987, among many others). The role of the executive in lawmaking, as analyzed by the US politics literature, is restricted to that of a veto player who intervenes in the process and can affect outcome policies given its formal prerogatives (Krehbiel 1998; Cameron 2000; McCarty 2000; McCarty and Groseclose 2001). Some of the most influential comparative work shares this basic framework when studying the executive and other key institutional players in the policymaking process (Tsebelis 2002). An insightful approach is that taken in Sin's (2015) book, where she proposes that given the effects of rules on outcomes, actors look across the branches not only when deciding policy but most importantly, when deciding the rules that will later affect policy choice.

While students of comparative politics have learned a large amount from the approaches and insights of US politics, important caveats are needed regarding the assumptions made by this literature and the extent to which they may be transported to different settings. Scholars have been aware of these difficulties. For example, a fairly uncontroversial adjustment has affected the basic reelection motivation, a guiding assumption in rational-choice US politics. This motivating assumption has been translated as progressive ambition, that is, a motivation to advance one's career through either reelection or any alternative career path (Schlesinger 1966; Rohde 1979; Samuels 2002).[4]

Additionally, although with valuable exceptions in recent times, mainstream work in US politics does not consider most legislative prerogatives held by the president as part of the law-making process *per se*, but rather as part of the intrinsic role of the executive during the implementation of policies. Within American politics, the participation of the executive in the implementation of policy emerging from the legislative process has been analyzed from the perspective of legislative delegation, with emphasis on the role of congressional decisions in that respect. This gave way to the initiation, over two decades ago, of a line of research that was guided by questions regarding legislators' capacity to ensure that their policy decisions do not deviate from their intended goals during the implementation process. Landmark contributions to this literature include McCubbins, Noll, and Weingast (1989); McCubbins and Schwartz (1984); Epstein and O'Halloran (1999); and Huber and Shipan (2002), among others. However, given the inadequacy of some assumptions when transported outside of the United States (and of other developed democracies), substantive conclusions of the literature are of limited direct applicability in different political scenarios.

Yet, for all its contributions, US politics has paid comparatively less attention to the executive's prerogative to enact decrees. Valuable work breaks ground in this terrain as it shifts focus from congress to the executive and places emphasis on executive orders and how these interact with congressional decision rights (Mayer 2001; Howell 2003; Lewis 2003; Canes Wrone, Howell, and Lewis 2008). This shift of focus is more in tune with mainstream approaches to non-US presidential systems.

---

[4] Likewise, the US literature most usually assumes that the executive and Congress direct policy preferences, which are entrenched preferences that do not change with political moods or external preferences. Direct preferences are perhaps associated to ideology, beliefs, or political identification. This is another assumption worth re-thinking in the Latin American context, where policy preferences seem to be quite unstable. This book assumes politicians' policy preferences are indirect, derived from those of other actors. I develop this notion later in the book.

1.2.2 The Legislative Process from Various Perspectives

The analysis of the more conventional aspect of lawmaking, via congressional statutes, has been less extended outside of the United States. One of the most ambitious works on lawmaking and policy change in comparative perspective, contributed by George Tsebelis in 2002, seeks to establish bases for the comparison of political systems independent of the type of regime (in the author's words: non-democratic, presidential, or parliamentary) or party system, some of the most commonly used standards for comparison. He suggests that a fundamental characteristic of the policy process is policy stability, which is, in turn, determined by the preferences of veto players. Tsebelis' analysis of veto players in comparative perspective is a landmark contribution to the field, and some of the insights there have influenced the analysis I present in this book. Tsebelis argues, "It is the constellation of veto players that best captures policy stability, and it is policy stability that affects a series of other policy and institutional characteristics" (2002, 5). I agree with Tsebelis on the count that the institutional structure is fundamental. We must focus on those institutions that are of relevance to the legislative process if we are to gain leverage over the determinants of policy change and policy stability. However, Tsebelis' work does not provide guidance to determine under what conditions players are effectively veto players, that is, which institutions are of relevance and why. In other words, what explains variation in outcomes when we are confronted with polities that show identical structures in terms of veto players? Or, more bluntly, what makes a player a veto player? The framework presented here, which builds on the work of Diermeier and Myerson (1999), seeks to provide an improved tool to uncover the determinants of policy stability and its opposite: change.

Furthermore, Tsebelis makes a strong assumption when stating that people participate in a political system to promote their policy preferences. This is sometimes the case. But this book argues that other motivations may guide participation. What if politicians lack direct policy preferences, and simultaneously have only indirect links to their constituents?[5] The consequences of presuming that these politicians will make policy decisions constrained by the same factors that shape those with direct policy preferences or close monitoring by constituents can greatly mislead our conclusions. This implicit assumption in Tsebelis' (2002)

---

[5] By indirect links to constituents, I refer to the link promoted by electoral rules. Majoritarian systems favor a more direct link between constituents and voters than does proportional representation, for instance.

work leaves some political systems out of the parameters of his analysis. By contrast, this book provides guidelines to establish which actors are veto players (or, more specifically, under what conditions we can expect actors to be effective veto players), and it also establishes that actors' preferences are not primordial but are indirectly derived from other actors' preferences.

Guided by a related concern for policy stability, Spiller and Tommasi (2007) seek to unveil the determinants of policy in Argentina. Their work ignited the study of the determinants of policymaking in a series of countries in Latin America, providing a framework for analysis that emphasizes the details of institutional arrangements and the importance of the effects generated by these institutions when they interact. The study of policymaking in a series of Latin American countries following the general framework put forth by Spiller and Tommasi (2000, 2007) was compiled into a volume published by the Inter-American Development Bank (IADB) (Stein et al. 2008), and traces the characteristics of policy and policymaking in a number of countries to specific traits of the institutional setting in each.

Moving away from the question of policy stability and toward studies of legislative politics *per se*, considerable analysis and theorizing have been advanced regarding the role of different congressional institutional arrangements. However, the record is uneven with respect to testing those claims. Work along the lines of Mayhew's (1991) contribution to our understanding of the law-making process in the United States, which provides broad-ranging characterizations of law enactment and inter-branch relations in the context of this country, largely does not exist for other countries. Furthermore, the next step, which requires advancing from the single case to carrying out such projects in comparative perspective, is a daunting task that has barely been undertaken.[6]

Studies of country cases are most common for good reasons, as they provide a well-grounded point of entry to our understanding. In this line, valuable contributions are made by Alemán and Calvo's (2010) analysis of executive influence in the legislative process in Argentina, Calvo's (2014) book on the characteristics of law making when presidents lack majority support in Argentina's fragmented legislature, Londregan's (2000) volume on Chilean legislative institutions, Londregan and Aninat's (2006) analysis of the law-making process in Chile, Hiroi's (2005) analysis of the dynamics of law making in Brazil, or Zucco's (2009) analysis of the

---

[6] Saiegh (2011) is a noteworthy exception.

effects of ideology on legislative behavior in Brazil. Tsebelis and Alemán's (2016) recently edited book stands out in this line of work, with different authors undertaking aspects of the law-making process and focusing on specific countries.

Contributions have been made that analyze the process of approval of specific laws or particular policy areas (Llanos 1998; Etchemendy and Palermo 1998; Stein et al. 2006). Palanza and Sin (1997) analyze law-making in Argentina from the perspective of executive bargaining with provincial parties. Pereira and Mueller (2002) focus on bargaining between the branches for the budgetary process. These analyses are highly informative of the specific dynamics and transactions in place for those specific cases, and provide valuable insights to broader processes, but they are not intended to reach generalizations regarding the legislative process in comparative perspective, with the exception, among the works cited here, of Stein et al. (2006).

On the other hand, more specific aspects of the process have been analyzed comparatively. For instance, while theorizing on veto bargaining in comparative perspective, Magar (2001) advances a broader analysis of law-making in Latin America, with focus on legislative vetoes. Our theoretical understanding of the executive veto prerogative in Latin America is advanced in Tsebelis and Alemán (2005). On the topic of decree authority, Negretto (2004) compares Argentina and Brazil, and Alemán and Pachón (2008) analyze conference committees in Chile and Colombia. A large literature of this kind exists, and the references provided here are but a small sample.

Sebastián Saiegh's book *Ruling by Statutes* (2011) stands out in its broad comparative approach to law making. Saiegh's work is interested in explaining policy creation and change, and it approaches the topic from an understanding of legislators as strategic actors, highlighting that while partisan and constituency-related considerations are important, so is the notion of vote buying. While Saiegh's interest and approach are close to those of this book, he focuses entirely on statutory law making and excludes policy enactment by decree altogether. As a measurement of the executive's legislative success, to dismiss that some presidents enact huge amounts of legislation by decree seems to miss an important part of law making by presidents.

Finally, links between the judiciary and the legislative branch have received relatively little attention in the academic literature until quite recently. Despite valuable contributions, such as the work of Murphy (1964), Epstein and Knight (1998), Gely and Spiller (1990), Spiller and

Gely (1992), Epstein and Segal (2005), and Clark (2011), the study of judicial politics has been scarcely developed until recently, both in comparative perspective and regarding the United States. The implications of judicial politics for the law-making process, however, are apparent. Also in the Latin American context, judicial politics are widely understudied, although specific experiences, such as that of Argentina, have captivated the attention of scholars in recent years (Iaryczower, Spiller and Tommasi 2002; Chavez 2003; Scribner 2004; Helmke 2005; Kapiszewski 2005, among others). More recently, a valuable contribution by Helmke and Ríos Figueroa (2011) advances this agenda. In this book I incorporate the judiciary as a key actor affecting the law-making process. In this respect, my work resembles the approach taken by Kim (2007), who incorporates the judiciary as a fundamental actor in his model of decree enactment.

1.3 DELEGATION OR USURPATION?

If not through direct analysis of decree enactment, the US literature briefly reviewed above set the stage for the debate on decree authority outside the United States. This debate encompassed two perspectives: on one hand, unilateral action theory, linked to the work of Moe and Howell (1999), Mayer (2001), and, analyzing Brazil, Cox and Morgenstern (2002); on the other hand, "delegation theory", attributed to the collective efforts of McCubbins and Schwartz (1984), McCubbins, Noll, and Weingast (1989), Kiewiet and McCubbins (1991), Epstein and O'Halloran (1999), and Huber and Shipan (2002) among others. "Unilateral action theory" suggests that the president seizes opportunities to impose her policy preferences whenever political or contextual conditions allow it. This approach carried considerable acceptance during the early years after democratization in Latin America, when dire economic crises seemed to enable presidents to snatch decision-making power. Delegation theory argues, instead, that what appears to be usurpation of congressional power is really deliberate delegation by congress: often legislators give up their decision rights under specific circumstances, among other reasons, to avoid responsibility for unpopular decisions.

Beyond US politics, executive decree authority has attracted significant attention due to its salience across presidential systems around the globe. A milestone contribution to our understanding of the use of executive decrees was made by Carey and Shugart's (1998) edited volume, which presents some initial theorizing and extensive analysis of various country cases. The volume's main challenge was theorizing the determinants of executive decrees and presenting evidence of the existence and use of decree authority in comparative perspective.

Influenced by the debate between delegation theory and unilateral action theory, Carey and Shugart's (1998) volume remains the most expansive collaborative contribution to our understanding of how executive decrees are used in different countries. There, Carey and Shugart distance themselves from previous work by emphasizing that the predominant usurpation interpretation of decree authority had been overstated, arguing instead that where we see decrees, legislative interests are not necessarily marginalized. Either as part of or in direct dialogue with Carey and Shugart's work, a wealth of studies on the topic emerged and continues to grow. These contributions include: on Argentina, Maurich and Liendo (1995), Ferreira Rubio and Goretti (1998), Magar (2001), Alemán and Calvo (2010), Kim (2007); on Brazil, Figueiredo and Limongi (1997), Power (1998), Amorim Neto and Tafner (2002), Amorim Neto, Cox and McCubbins (2003), Pereira, Power and Rennó (2005 and 2008); comparing Argentina and Brazil, Negretto (2004); on Chile, Scribner (2002); and on Peru, Schmidt (1998). These studies all undertook the analysis of decree authority, presenting novel data, interpreting reliance on decrees, and proposing explanations. This literature is reviewed in greater detail in Chapters 4 and 5.

Remington's (2014) recent book on the use of decrees in Russia brings attention to the topic in the context of a region less present in comparative analyses of institutions until recently. His work also deserves special attention, given its breadth. It highlights that the problem of reliance on decrees by executives is not a problem of Latin American democracies alone, but one closely associated to polities where institutional roles are in flux. Remington shows trends over time regarding how different partisan scenarios in congress and in the political context affect levels of reliance on decrees in post-soviet Russia. He theorizes that reliance on decrees is a function of the institutions in place (rules), partisan preferences, and the political context.

Together, this literature has advanced our understanding of decree authority in many aspects. It has reasserted that congressional actors are not as quiescent as they were once assumed to be (O'Donnell 1994). It has acknowledged that the use of executive decrees must be analyzed *vis à vis* the use of congressional statutes, and not in isolation (Carey and Shugart 1998; Amorim Neto and Tafner 2002; Amorim Neto 2006; Pereira, Power and Rennó 2005 and 2008). It has brought into consideration the effects of changes in the rules (Power, Pereira, and Rennó 2008).

It has expanded the breadth of our analyses by including all branches of government (Kim 2006). We have learned that specific legislative prerogatives cannot be analyzed in isolation, but need to be addressed within the entire set of legislative prerogatives across branches (Shugart and Carey 1992; Amorim Neto 2006). Perhaps most importantly, in striving to explain the use of decrees, but falling short of providing consistent and broad explanations, this literature has highlighted the necessity of developing a solid theoretical foundation to guide our understanding of the phenomenon, and make clear predictions that we can test against data.

1.3.1 Prevailing Assumptions

Despite the many contributions of the established literature, I claim that it has misconstrued the strategic environment of decree enactment. A set of general assumptions are prevalent in the literature on the use of executive decrees in Latin America that misguide us and lead to problematic hypotheses and conclusions. One such assumption is that the executive is at the heart of all decisions to enact policies. This construction, I argue, confounds an observational regularity (i.e., executive activity) for its cause, and assumes that the executive is effectively at the center of lawmaking. In most of this work, the executive is not only the main actor, sometimes she is the sole actor.[7] This is most remarkable when it occurs alongside explicit acknowledgments that we must look beyond the executive to understand lawmaking. For instance, Sebastián Saiegh, in *Ruling by Statute* (2014), highlights the importance of including the legislature in strategic considerations for the enactment of policy, yet surprisingly only analyzes statutes proposed by the executive, suggesting that the only ruler of relevance is the president. And while a reasonable justification of the assumption is that in some cases the executive is in fact the only actor held responsible for policy choices (Zucco 2009), it would be wise to acknowledge that this is not always or exclusively the case.

Another such assumption is that legislatures are only marginally relevant. Several interrelated reasons are given: electoral incentives, lack of professionalism, lack of technical support, lower appeal of legislative positions *vis à vis* executive posts, and others. Remarkably, the assumption often goes hand in hand with the proclamation of the need to bring legislatures into our analyses (Jones et al. 2002). In practice,

---

[7] Throughout this book, I refer to the executive with feminine pronouns and legislators with masculine pronouns.

this understanding is trumped by the observation of weak institutions, and any evidence to the contrary is swept under the carpet rather than explained. In the end, the proposal to include legislatures becomes trivial as they are simultaneously minimized in their role by research design. Despite valuable exceptions (chiefly, Calvo 2014), the norm is for legislatures to be assumed to be weak. Siavelis (2006), for instance, speaks of Chile's exaggerated presidential system and weak legislature while also claiming that the country "embodies the best of representative democracy and consensus politics in Latin America" (Siavelis 2006, p. 34). He attributes this success to a set of informal institutions, which, in turn, emerged thanks to the country's strong formal institutions. One is left to wonder what role congress plays in this account, as it seems to unfold in spite of congressional weakness. The literature assuming weakness does not inquire further into the comparative question of the observed differences in levels of weakness, or the effects emerging from the presence of prerogatives that legislators may choose to use or not use.

This choice in the hands of legislators, which I assume to be at the core of institutional weakness (and strength) is brought to our attention by literature focusing on transaction problems affecting political institutions. This literature lends insight to the origins of some of the difficulties impinging on legislatures and legislative behavior. Work by Weingast (1989) points to the transaction costs facing legislatures due to inter-temporal problems affecting these collective bodies – among them, the difficulty to bind future members to current-day agreements and the difficulty to commit to promises made to constituents. Weingast's work moves us to consider short and long-term incentives, and how institutions, by shaping those incentives, can diminish transaction costs. It motivates this book by suggesting that inter-temporal costs are at play when we observe violations to legislative decision rights and variations in levels of institutional commitment. In this tradition, recent work by Gary Cox (2016) analyzing England's Glorious Revolution of 1689 highlights the process through which a weak legislature chose to become strong, a choice of great consequence not only for the rule of law but also for the establishment of policy.

A third assumption is that decrees can be analyzed in isolation from other legislative tools, in particular congressional statutes. More recently, this bias evolved into an understanding that whenever a decree is enacted, a choice has been made not to use statutes. This constitutes an important theoretical step forward (Amorim Neto and Tafner 2002; Pereira, Power and Rennó 2005; Amorim Neto 2006; Kim 2006; Alemán and Calvo 2010). Yet, despite this acknowledgment, the analysis of the strategic environment leading to that choice is largely taken for granted or left in the dark. If decree enactment entails a choice to bypass the legislature, even quiescent legislatures are a part of the strategic environment leading to the choice of decrees. Yet, of the works cited in this paragraph, only Kim (2006) approaches the problem from this perspective.

1.3.2 A Proposed Shift in Assumptions

The work presented in this book builds on prior contributions while proposing some important distinctions. The game-theoretic framework I present suggests that if legislatures were as helpless as some of the literature has portrayed them to be, we would never observe the enactment of statutes, which is not the case. If executives could always get their way, statutes would be unnecessary. Furthermore, by taking into account the "legislative" prerogatives in hands of the judiciary, we can further understand the scope of constraints on legislative choice. To overcome the possible limitations stemming from the three assumptions summarized in the previous subsection, this study emphasizes a different set of assumptions.

The first point I make is that executives are not the imperial actors they are construed to be. I assume all politicians[8] derive their policy preferences from external agents' preferences. In line with this assumption, external agents are the driving force behind the enactment of policies.[9] By using their influence (resources), they bring politicians together around policies, and in so doing they shift the balance in favor of one legislative instrument or the other. Politicians lend their support to the policies backed by external agents, who in turn provide the resources politicians need to advance their political careers.[10] Thus, when analyzing the choice

---

[8] This includes the executive, legislators, and supreme court justices.

[9] In Cox (2016), those demanding policies also play an important role in bringing about the institutional reforms he seeks to explain.

[10] In line with this assumption, in Chapter 2 I present a vote-buying game in which two agents (one favoring policy change, the other favoring the status quo) compete for politicians' support for their preferred policy goals. The framework builds on Groseclose and Snyder (1996) and Diermeier and Myerson (1999). The influence of external agents need not be measured in money; organized labor, for instance, may offer valuable organizational resources.

to enact policies, interpreting the behavior of politicians absent interest groups misconstrues the strategic environment.[11]

The second point I make is that legislatures are fundamental actors in the policymaking process, as are supreme courts. By explicitly taking into account the incentives of legislators and supreme court justices, and the role they play in enacting policies, we can account for variations in outcomes within a single country, i.e., why some policies come about through decrees and others through statutes.[12] Furthermore, we can make sense of the variation in the use of decrees and statutes across countries.

If interest groups could always enact their preferred policies by decree, they would, since it would save them resources. The reason they do not is that they simply cannot, because other actors have a stake in the process: legislators know that there are gains to be made from law enactment, and that they can claim their rights to those gains. In brief, whether a policy is enacted by decree or statute, legislators (and supreme court justices) are part of the agreement sustaining the piece of legislation. The enactment of decrees does not imply that the legislature has been excluded from the policymaking agreement.

Finally, the third point I make is that decrees cannot be analyzed in isolation from other legislative choices. The choice of decrees or statutes must be analyzed as the result of a single process, like heads or tails are alternative results of flipping a coin. Whenever a policy is to be enacted, actors know that it may be done through one of two paths; and whenever a decree is enacted, a decision has been made to avoid the standard congressional path, i.e., enactment by statute. Hence, the choice leading to the outcome matters, and we must understand the determinants, strategies, and preferences that play into that choice.

[11] I acknowledge that under certain circumstances, executives may act as agents of policy, promoting policies that maximize their utility and not external agents' utilities. In such circumstances, it is reasonable that they would use public resources to fund enactment. Yet, while this is the mainstream approach to executive leadership in the legislative process within Latin American politics, I stress that it is not always nor necessarily the case. Moreover, I emphasize that one must be extremely cautious when attributing agency to the executive, as the potential for error (i.e., not identifying external agents' interests) is broad. Under certain conditions, but by no means always, expropriations, taxes, or amnesties may be sought solely out of concern for political survival. The Kirchners, in Argentina provide an example of agency through their October 2008 decision to nationalize private pension funds (AFJP), which made a large amount of cash available to them at a critical moment of economic downturn.

[12] Cox's recent book emphasizes that avoiding unilateral executive legislation entails a chain of constraints on the executive, the aggregate strength of which is only as strong as its weakest link (Cox 2016).

1.4 CONFRONTING THE PUZZLE FROM A DIFFERENT STANDPOINT

In my characterization, developed at length in the following chapter, agents that are external to the government[13] vie to make contributions to politicians in order to get their support for the enactment of their preferred policies. In doing so, a decision is made with respect to the policymaking "path," that is, whether to pursue the desired policy through executive decree or congressional statute. Because legislators seek to maximize the contributions they extract from the policymaking process, they enact the policy supported by the highest contributor.[14] Apart from contributions, legislators also value their decision rights, that is, the prerogatives that enable them to decide over policy and tap into external agents' resources, and they are willing to enact or reverse policy to enforce those rights.[15]

Interest groups assess the situation, well aware of the alternative legislative scenarios that can unfold. They develop strategies to obtain their

---

[13] Agents may be interest groups, groups from civil society broadly defined, or electoral constituents. The key is that they have the capacity to influence policymaking by providing politicians with the types of resources that they need to further their political goals – either campaign contributions (that need not be in money), organizational capacities, etc.

[14] In this sense, politicians' preferences are derived from those of external agents. This distances my account from Tsebelis' (2002) approach to policymaking, which is particularly difficult to apply to contexts where parties are scarcely programmatic. While there is literature claiming that ideology runs strong in Latin American party systems (Wiesehomeier and Benoit 2009; Zucco and Power 2013), recent work also points to the effects of other forces affecting legislative behavior (Saiegh 2011; Zucco 2009; Zucco and Lauderdale 2011). In particular, Zucco and Lauderdale (2011) claim those forces at play are resources controlled by the president and channeled toward legislators. They argue these forces explain roll-call voting more than the ideological dimension, for instance. I argue that the claim that these resources come from the executive is a conjecture in Zucco and Lauderdale (2011), and just as validly one might conjecture that those resources stem from external agents (see Zucco 2013 on conditional cash transfers).

[15] This characterization ultimately takes a stance on the issue of the determinants of politicians' policy preferences. By stating that their policy preferences are derived from the preferences of external agents, I claim that politicians' *observed* preferences (which are usually taken to be their own, and somewhat engrained) are not intrinsic, but rather instrumentally derived (note the rich debates on parties and what can be induced from observed voting patterns: Cox and McCubbins 1993; Schickler and Rich 1997a and 1997b; Groseclose, Levitt, and Snyder 1999; Krehbiel 1992, 1998, 2000; McCarty, Poole, and Rosenthal 2001; Snyder and Groseclose 2001). I claim that politicians ultimately value holding and advancing their positions and policy is a means to that end. Whether we observe a consistent policy record or oscillation to and fro is beyond the point, as both observations may be aligned with the same underlying courting of external agents. Different polities, of course, deal in different ways with the connection between politicians and external agents, and whereas some polities have powerful institutions and organizations that channel the resources of the latter to the former, other polities offer little in that respect. Ultimately, this discussion is about, yet exceeds, parties.

preferred policies while minimizing expenditures, which are associated to the number of actors involved in deciding the policy. When they decide to promote a new policy, they take several factors into account: Who opposes the new policy? What resources will opponents bring to bear on the dispute? What paths are constitutionally open to this policy? What path is deemed most efficient? Ultimately, the path they choose is the one that minimizes expenditures.

Legislators, and politicians, in general, are interested in maintaining and advancing their careers, which implies maintaining or extending their positions and those of their allies. Lobbyists provide them with the means to these goals by compensating politicians' support in the law-making realm. Decision rights determine who can decide on questions of policy, and, as a consequence, they provide the key to valuable resources. Politicians rely on their rights to gain access to interest groups' resources, and depending on the resources at stake, they may be willing to defend their decision rights when these are violated. The conditions under which they will do so vary: I present them below when referring to institutional commitment and elaborate on them in Chapter 2.

This account places fundamental emphasis on decision rights *per se* and on their valuation. Agents seeking policies know that constitutional rules[16] establish the procedures for and the limits to policy enactment. They know that decision rights are constitutionally allocated and that they determine which actors can decide what and on what terms. Constitutions sometimes limit what can be enacted by decree by including emergency conditions, or by excluding certain subject matters from CDA (see Table 3.A.1 in the Appendix 3.A to Chapter 3 for four examples of these limitations imposed by constitutions). Lobbyists also know that congress and the supreme court can challenge decrees that exceed the executive's purview. They know that congressional statutes can overturn legislation enacted by decree; they know that congress can impeach the president, and that the courts can ultimately overturn legislative decisions. This suggests that constitutional rules are an important determinant of the choice of legislative instrument. I argue that additional factors affecting the choice are the valuation that interest groups assign to policies (which I have argued is the *sine qua non* of policymaking), and politicians' valuation of their decision rights (which I refer to as institutional commitment).

---

[16] I.e., rules that allocate decision rights throughout the policymaking process.

Decision rights determine the costs agents confront when pursuing policies. Chapter 2 operationalizes those rules as hurdle factors, following Diermeier and Myerson (1999). Hurdle factors provide synthetic information regarding the decision-making rules that are in place at a given time, with higher values representing higher levels of difficulty to reach decisions. They are determined exogenously by the constitutional rules that determine legislators' decision rights, and typically vary across actors (the executive, members of congress, supreme court justices), decisions (passage of a law, override of a veto, impeachment), and countries.

Institutional commitment represents the value that politicians assign to their prerogatives.[17] It brings into consideration the notion that politicians with decision rights over the policymaking process will not simply tolerate violations of those rights, as they are essential to their maximization of gains. If contraventions were tolerated without further ado, we would expect all policies to be enacted by executive decrees (at the lowest hurdle factor), and congress would consistently be excluded from agreements. This is clearly not the case. Due to institutional commitment, politicians enforce their decision rights. There is variation in the extent to which different congresses do so, and levels of institutional commitment determine this variation. Note that institutional commitment and hurdle factors are related concepts. During times of constitution writing, when politicians establish decision-making rules, they are ultimately deciding on hurdle factors.[18]

I have already posited that institutional commitment emerges in the context of repeated games: actors (legislators) know that they will be faced with the same decisions repeatedly over time, and they estimate what their gains will be in the long term (their expected gains). Institutional commitment is higher when the gains expected from the

---

[17] Interestingly, this holds close resemblance to Cox's (2016) notion of *constitutional commitment*. Cox claims "legal commitment to a particular sovereign promise is only as strong as the weakest link in a chain of legal constraints placed upon the executive." In this book, too, at its highest level, institutional commitment effectively restrains executive unilateral action. While Cox's focus is on sovereign promises, one could easily apply the notion to other policies.

[18] While the rules guiding constitutional reforms are typically the most restrictive, other decisions require less restrictive majorities, and often various rules exist. I follow Diermeier and Myerson (1999) in arguing that hurdle factors are endogenously determined to maximize legislators' gains from their decision rights (I develop the link between rules and hurdle factors in Chapter 3). Similarly, I argue that variation exists across categories of legislation (such as ordinary legislation or constitutional amendments, within which the same hurdle factors apply), and politicians do not value all pieces of legislation equally even within a single category.

possession of those rights are higher. Thus, institutional commitment is a function of the elements that can affect those gains in expectation: (a) the factors affecting politicians' time horizon, and (b) the factors affecting external contributions.[19] These factors vary across countries, but also – albeit differently – within countries.

While the factors affecting the time horizon of politicians rarely vary within each country, those affecting external contributions do vary, and I argue that they vary across policy areas. Therefore, given a certain level of institutional commitment in any given country, we expect legislators' willingness to defend their decision rights to vary with policy areas.[20] If the stakes are high on a given issue, politicians will value legislating on that issue more than legislating on issues for which the stakes are low. Like in the cross-country setting, this notion stems from the expected payoffs of legislating on different issues over time, and takes into account not only current but also future gains.

To understand better why institutional commitment varies with issues, note that different policy areas entail different prospects of gain extraction. In my characterization, if a policy is uncontested, or if the level of contestation is very low, then the gains to be extracted from legislating in that area are low, which implies that legislators' inter-temporal calculations will make them less willing to defend their decision rights in those cases. If, instead, the stakes around a given policy are high, because two very powerful (resourceful) groups are in confrontation on the issue, then the prospects for gains are high, and institutional commitment is heightened, i.e., legislators will want to enforce their decision rights. Thus, institutional commitment is determined exogenously by the profits to be derived through the use of decision rights, and it varies across countries and policy issues. I assume it is equal for all members of a given institutional body (i.e., all congress members, all supreme court justices), and that it varies across those bodies.

Certainly, one may wonder why politicians, depicted here as maximizing external contributions, and with no direct preferences over policy,

[19] When a given issue commands few resources, the expected payoffs from legislating on the issue over time are lower, causing commitment to decision rights to be lower. Likewise, longer time horizons cause commitment to be higher.

[20] Politicians' varying esteem for different policy issues is reflected in constitutions each time a constitution establishes specific legislative rules for particular policy areas. The constitutions of Brazil and Chile stand out in this regard within the region, but most constitutions around the globe establish legislative procedures that vary across policy issues (i.e., supermajorities to change specific policies, executive regulation of others, etc.).

would be committed to institutions. What at first glance may seem puzzling is actually not. Institutional commitment implies attachment to established decision rights that guarantee continued access to agents' contributions. Legislators who seek to maximize contributions from external agents are unlikely to remain quiet when these contributions are diverted to other actors in violation of established rules.[21]

Finally, some notes on the limits to CDA. I mentioned above that constitutions that provide executive decree authority usually establish the conditions under which presidents can enact decrees. Most commonly, they restrict enactment to situations of national emergency, and, additionally, some constitutions exclude certain subject matters from decree authority. Yet note that while these boundaries fare well in theory, their effects vary in practice. Presidents do issue decrees that are not in compliance with the established rules (and in that sense, are unconstitutional or illegal). I claim that the variation in this practice is a function of politicians' institutional commitment.

Most analyses of executive decree authority are silent on this point. It is not clear whether they assume that the restrictions are complied with and that when policies cannot be constitutionally enacted by decree they are simply enacted by statute, or whether they have just overlooked the rule. In contrast, I make a point of distinguishing between constitutionally valid decrees and decrees that are unconstitutional. The choice facing agents, then, can be either between congressional statutes and constitutionally valid decrees, or between statutes and unconstitutional decrees. These are two distinct options, with very different implications (Chapter 2).

To sum up, I have claimed above that the choice of legislative instrument is incited by external agents, and is a function of their valuation of the policy at stake, the allocation of decision rights (i.e., the hurdle factors related to each instrument), and politicians' institutional commitment. Formally, the choice is a function of four factors:

$$\text{Choice} = f(r, l, V, W) \tag{1.1}$$

where r is the hurdle factor given by the allocation of decision rights, l is the level of institutional commitment, and V and W are the two external

---

[21] Institutional commitment arises from the logic of the repeated version of the game presented in the next chapter.

agents' respective valuations of policies.[22] The empirical work focuses on formal rules r, and on levels of institutional commitment l.

1.5 A ROADMAP OF THIS BOOK

While taking important insights from most of the literature reviewed above, the theoretical foundations of this book are owed to Groseclose and Snyder (1996) and Diermeier and Myerson (1999). Chapter 2 presents a theory of policy choice that presumes applicability in a broad range of countries – variation in outcomes hinging fundamentally on levels of institutional commitment. I follow these authors to present a policy proposal game in which a key consideration is the hurdle factor imposed by institutions. Because I am interested in providing an explanation of applicability to contexts with variation in the extent to which rules are enforced (see Levitsky and Murillo 2005), I use the repeated game rationale to introduce the notion of institutional commitment, which is a self-interest understanding of politicians' willingness to defend their decision rights.

Chapter 2 seeks to provide an explanation to the puzzle that stems from the co-existence of a set of very similar institutional prerogatives with a set of considerably different outcomes. It does so by presenting a formal theory of policy adoption that has the choice of legislative instrument built in. Until now, outside of US politics, all analyses of the legislative process and of executive decrees have modelled these choices as pertaining to different spheres or arenas. My claim, instead, is that lawmaking must be analyzed as a process that can evolve through different pathways. Chapter 2 explains why the choice of pathways is far from trivial. The model enables us to explain not only under what conditions we can expect the choice of decrees, but also, just as importantly, when it is most likely that statutes will be the instrument of choice. Hence, Chapter 2 provides the foundations for broader claims made in the book regarding the enforcement of decision rights and effective checks and balances.

The main prediction stemming from the model is that the choice of legislative instrument is fundamentally a function of levels of institutional commitment. At low levels of institutional commitment, we expect

---

[22] It is worth highlighting that V and W also enter the equation indirectly through their long-term effect on l, which stems from the logic of repeated games, as I have explained in the previous paragraphs.

decrees to be the instrument of choice, and decrees are less likely as levels of institutional commitment rise. Above a certain critical level, statutes become the instruments of choice. Because institutional commitment varies across countries, but also within countries, these predictions can be tested at both levels of analysis. My approach to those tests is the topic of the following chapter.

In Chapter 3, I show how the theory presented in the previous chapter can be translated into empirical indicators and tested. This is the chapter of the book where I describe how I measure my key dependent variable and how I constructed several independent variables to capture expected effects. As such, Chapter 3 is a bridge between the theory presented in Chapter 2 and the remainder of the book. But I also use this chapter to fine tune some of the conceptual work not covered in Chapter 2. Most importantly, I bring in considerations from the repeated version of the lawmaking game, that is, when the game that I present in Chapter 3 as happening once, is repeated over time. The concept of institutional commitment is best explained in this chapter, and I present how I go about measuring it. Among other things, this chapter serves as a methodological roadmap to the following chapters.

Chapters 4, 5, and 6 are the empirical core of the book. Chapter 4 analyzes the choice of statutes versus decrees, or *medidas provisórias*, in Brazil. The enactment of a constitutional reform in 2001 that affected the allocation of legislative decision rights created an ideal situation to test the implications of my model under two different sets of institutions. The constitutional reform is convenient as we rarely have the opportunity to test the effects of institutions when analyzing single countries. The chapter on Brazil provides a test of the implications of my theory when holding the level of institutional commitment at the intermediate range, while also evaluating the theory against the alternatives. Chapter 5 carries out a parallel analysis for the case of Argentina. Here, too, a constitutional reform, carried out in 1994, benefits my research design. The chapter on Argentina provides a test of the implications of my theory at low levels of institutional commitment, while also evaluating the theory against the alternatives. The findings from these chapters provide support for the comparative implications of the theory and for my key explanatory variables in each country while presenting uneven evidence in support of the alternative explanations.

In Chapter 6, I put the theory to the test by conducting cross-country statistical analysis of the determinants of reliance on decrees in countries that have enabled CDA. The chapter tests the validity of the comparative-level claims made in this book by analyzing seven Latin American cases in which similar institutional settings provide quite different levels of reliance on decrees. The findings reveal that politicians' level of institutional commitment effectively explains *levels of reliance on decree authority*. The effects of the main explanatory contenders, partisan context and economic crises, undoubtedly important factors, are not as consistent and sometimes even difficult to interpret.

In Chapter 7 I take stock from the findings of this book, both theoretical and empirical, and draw conclusions with an emphasis on the differences in levels of institutional commitment across countries, and how these affect the outcomes in each. The conclusions speak to the issue of the structure of checks and balances, how these are affected by levels of institutional commitment, and what scenarios one may expect in terms of variations in current levels of institutional commitment.

2

Decrees versus Statutes

Choice of Legislative Paths in Separation of Power Systems

The government will announce the expropriation first; they will later analyze whether a statute or a decree is more convenient.

(Statement made by a top government official, referring to rumors that the government intended to expropriate Argentina's privatized flag carrier, Aerolíneas Argentinas)[1]

La Nación, Argentina, October 23, 2008

2.1 INTRODUCTION

Why do we sometimes see policies enacted by executive decree, and yet others see policies come about by congressional statute? The conditions under which decrees are enacted constitute a dilemma that has long interested students of institutions, especially in countries where the constitution explicitly establishes decree authority. By exploring the strategic calculations faced by actors who seek policy change, this chapter uncovers the conditions that favor the use of one instrument over the other. Formal rules written into constitutions prove to be consequential as do the resources in the hands of the actors who seek to promote or hinder policy change.

Wherever constitutions have granted decree authority to executives, decrees prove to be the easiest and least costly way to attain policy change. This alone can constitute a forceful incentive to avoid the statutory path to lawmaking. However, even where decrees are constitutionally valid,

---

[1] *"La expropiación se anunciará, como primera medida; después se verá qué conviene, si ley o decreto."*

we see the enactment of new policy by statute. Not only are we in need of an explanation of the determinants of executive decrees, but related to that, we must understand the conditions under which the statutes are preferred to decrees. Why would actors seeking policy change choose to bring it about using instruments that increase their costs? This chapter identifies the conditions under which decrees are the path of least resistance. I claim that the politicians' institutional commitment to their decision rights can reverse the convenience of decrees and make congressional statutes the preferred path. While delineating the arena in which different politicians are free to move, such enforcement stands at the core of checks and balances.

The model that this chapter puts forth suggests that where policies may be enacted by means of a constitutional executive decree, we should expect decrees to be the favored instrument of policy change, since it is the least costly for proponents. Only when policies cannot validly be enacted by decree, do other instruments enter consideration. I will show that statutes, which are the logical substitute, imply higher costs. To sidestep those costs, one option is to enact decrees that are not constitutionally valid, that is, decrees violate decision rights. That many unconstitutional decrees are enacted all the same is no secret among politicians as

"Decree-laws dominated the period prior to 1988 because the previous constitution enabled the executive to enact legislative decisions in some cases. Nowadays it is medidas provisórias,[2] you see? The situation is so serious that the constitutional prerequisites for medidas provisórias are not met in most cases. Most medidas provisórias are not constitutional."[3] (Deputado interviewed in Brasilia, November 24, 2005)

This chapter contends that the extent to which unconstitutional decrees are enacted is a function of politicians' (legislators and justices) willingness to enforce their decision rights, which I denote as "institutional commitment." The model finds that at higher levels of institutional commitment, the costs associated with the enactment of unconstitutional

---

[2] "*Medidas provisórias*" is the name given to executive decrees in Brazil. The expression can be translated as "provisional measure" or "provisional decrees."

[3] "*No período anterior a 88 dominavam os decretos-leis, porque na constituição anterior você tinha atos legislativos, baixados pelo Executivo em alguns casos. Atualmente são as medidas provisórias, claro? E é tão grave a situação que os pressupostos da constituição pra discussão de medidas provisórias não são satisfeitos na maior parte dos casos. A maior parte das medidas provisórias são inconstitucionais.*" The deputado's identity is kept anonymous, as agreed before the interview.

decrees rise. As long as the costs imposed by institutional commitment are lower than the costs associated with the enactment of statutes, lobbyists looking for policy change will seek the enactment of decrees. Statutes will only be enacted when doing so is less costly to lobbyists than the enactment of unconstitutional decrees.

The arguments presented in this chapter fall back on a concise set of assumptions, which I lay out carefully in Section 2.4. Succinctly presented, I assume the lawmaking process is externally driven: Absent external agents with an interest in policy change, we would not observe the enactment of new policies. Additionally, I argue that in separation-of-power systems we must analyze the interactions among all branches of government to understand the strategic calculations determining outcomes, since looking at decrees as solely led by the executive is misleading. Executives act in settings where they must take into account the preferences of other actors who are vested in their decisions. Moreover, the decision to enact decrees is not independent of the rules guiding the congressional statutory process, or even the rules guiding judicial review of those policies. Actors' decisions favoring one legislative instrument over another are determined by the rules that are in place, together with the resources that are available to them throughout the process.

An important goal of this chapter is to provide theoretical guidance as to why our observations (i.e., the profuse, yet not exclusive, use of executive decrees) do not match up with the widely held understanding of lawmaking in Latin America that characterizes legislatures as passive players in the process. Ultimately, the chapter provides the foundations of the book's approach to the issue of checks and balances and the bottom-up process that leads to their enforcement.

The chapter is organized as follows: Section 2.2 introduces the approach I take to the analysis of policy enactment, emphasizing key theoretical antecedents as well as differentiating this work from them. Section 2.3 makes the key assumptions explicit and presents the game, which models the choice of legislative instruments; this is the section that draws the main implications of the theory. Section 2.4 presents theoretical conclusions.

2.2 A THEORETICAL MODEL OF CHOICE OF LEGISLATIVE INSTRUMENTS

In this section, I briefly present the approach to lawmaking that this chapter takes. Before presenting the formal specifications of the model in the following section, I briefly sketch an outline of the model. First, the driving actors in my formulation are interest groups, which use their resources to enact their preferred policies. I argue that politicians do not have direct policy preferences; rather, they are willing to lend their support to those actors who can provide them with the resources that they need to attain what they value most: the advancement of their political career. In line with this assumption, I present a vote-buying game in which two agents (one favoring policy change, the other favoring the status quo) compete to get politicians to support their preferred policy goals. The framework builds upon Groseclose and Snyder (1996) and Diermeier and Myerson (1999),[4] though I depart from their setting in ways that I specify below.

Agents external to the government make contributions to politicians to get their support for the enactment of the policies they need. As stated in Chapter 1, what distinguishes agents from other actors in this game is that they are not politicians, yet they may be interest groups, groups from civil society – broadly defined – even electoral constituents. External agents influence policymaking by providing politicians with the resources they need to further their political careers. These resources can come in the form of campaign contributions, but they need not be made in money, or they can take the form of providing organizational capacities, among others.

As in Diermeier and Myerson (1999), legislators maximize those contributions and enact the policy supported by the highest bidder. I depart from Diermeier and Myerson's framework by asserting that legislators also value their decision rights, and they are willing to enact or reverse policy in defense of those rights. The approach pays considerable attention to the gains politicians extract from their legislative prerogatives. In my model, politicians value the resources that they can extract from lobbyists, but they do not have direct preferences over policy itself.

When policy change occurs, whether it is via the passage of a law by congress or by executive decree, it always comes about because someone promoted it. When no single actor is interested in carrying out a change in policy, the status quo endures. Interest groups assess the situation and the alternative legislative scenarios that could unfold; their strategies are developed to obtain their preferred policies given the existing constraints.

---

[4] Whereas Groseclose and Snyder (1996) are interested in showing that vote buyers minimize long-term costs by buying supermajorities instead of minimal winning majorities, that specific point is of secondary interest here. For comparative purposes, I build on the notion of hurdle factors presented by Diermeier and Myerson (1999) to help identify the costs imposed on decision-making in different countries.

When they decide to promote a new policy, they take several factors into account: Who opposes the new policy? What resources will opponents bring to bear on the dispute? What paths are constitutionally open to this policy? What path is most efficient?

Legislators, and politicians in general, are interested in maintaining and advancing their careers, which implies maintaining or extending their positions and those of their allies. Lobbyists provide them with the means to these goals because they are willing to compensate politicians for their support in lawmaking. In this way, decision rights provide the key to the lobbyists' valuable resources: Politicians use their rights to gain access to interest groups' resources, and depending on the extent of the resources that they can extract, they are willing to defend their decision rights when encroached upon. The conditions under which they will do so vary; I elaborate on them when I refer to institutional commitment in the next section.

Those seeking new policies know that constitutional rules establish the procedures and limits to policy enactment; i.e., they know that decision rights have been constitutionally allocated, determining which actors can decide what and on what terms. Among other things, the constitution has established limits to what can be legislated by executive decree. Lobbyists additionally know that congress and the supreme court can challenge executive decisions that exceed executive turf. They know that congressional statutes can overturn legislation enacted by decree; they know that congress can impeach the president and that the courts can overturn legislative decisions. This knowledge influences their decision to pursue the enactment of their preferred policy by either statute or decree. Deciding to pursue policy change through a certain path does not ensure success *per se*. If the status quo does not have sufficiently strong supporters, or when it has no support at all, the enactment of a new policy is unproblematic, and the proponent of a new policy can easily gain the legislators' support. Yet it seems reasonable that wherever agents defending the status quo are more influential (i.e., when they command more resources), it becomes more costly to change the status quo – sometimes inhibiting change altogether. The model that I present in Section 2.4 provides formal support for these claims.

Policies that do not have challengers are easiest (cheapest) to enact, and they will typically be enacted via decree, since the fact that a single legislator, the president, is involved in decree enactment makes decrees the simplest, fastest, and cheapest choice for lobbyists. However, if the enactment of a policy by decree violates congressional decision rights (i.e., if an *unconstitutional* decree is enacted), congress and the supreme court will be motivated to challenge the policy merely on institutional grounds (that is, in defense of their decision rights). This means that the actors interested in policy change make a consequential initial decision regarding how to pursue it. What instrument is most convenient? The initial decision then regards the legislative instrument itself. As evidenced in the previous section, the literature has paid insufficient attention to this specific decision and its implications for the type of policies enacted.

To mend the gap, this chapter analyzes the conditions under which external agents choose different legislative instruments as part of a vote-buying dilemma. In the following section, I present the game formally. Readers who are not trained to read formal models may skip the remainder of this chapter, as the intuition of the model has been introduced already, and its main conclusions are revisited in the chapters that follow. The model predicts the conditions under which we should expect the enactment of decrees versus statutes. The factors guiding these propositions are the constitutional rules of lawmaking, the politicians' valuation of those rules, and the agents' valuation of their preferred policies.

2.3 THE GAME

This section presents a strategic game. It introduces the players and assumptions first, and then it takes a roundabout approach to explain how the notions of constitutional rules, hurdle factors, and institutional commitment will be used. This sets the stage to present, toward the end of this section, the game dynamics and how policy change occurs.

2.3.1 Players and Assumptions

Following Diermeier and Myerson (1999), consider a situation in which two agents have preferences over policy change. Agent 1 is for policy x and Agent 0 is in favor of the status quo q. Agent 1 prefers policy x to q by W, while Agent 0 prefers the status quo by V. Agent's values W and V are defined as

$$W = U_1(x) - U_1(q)$$

and

$$V = U_0(q) - U_0(x)$$

Agent 1 wants the new policy to be enacted, and she knows that Agent 0 is willing to expend resources to prevent it.[5] To attain the policy change that she wants, Agent 1 is willing to spend up to W, distributing it among politicians to ensure their support. Her goal is to do so while minimizing her total expenditures, that is,

$$\min \sum w_i$$

where w_i is Agent 1's offer to politician i and $\sum w_i \leq W$. Agent 1's utility function is $W - \sum w_i$, and she seeks to maximize it. Agent 0's goal is identical, with contributions denoted, v in this case, and $\sum v_i \leq V$.

Both agents know each other's valuations W and V before the first move is made. I assume that the competing agents move sequentially and that Agent 1, the agent in favor of policy change, moves first. As Groseclose and Snyder (1996) point out, the assumption of sequential moves is analytically convenient,[6] but it is also in-line with actual coalition building, especially when the status quo is the favored policy (i.e., all policies must beat the status quo). Furthermore, if the legislators incur an opportunity cost by legislating (for example, they could be working on other pieces of legislation or campaigning), then the agent who wants the policy to change must compensate them to attend to her project while the agent defending the status quo is perfectly happy that they are devoted to another matter and can intervene later to stop them from supporting the change. From the conservative agent's perspective, it is optimal when legislators are busy doing something else, so it is effectively the agent who wants change who moves first.

In turn, politicians seek to maximize the resources they can extract from the legislative process, which are critically linked to the established allocation of decision rights. Similar to the setup in Groseclose and Snyder (1996), politicians have preferences over a political resource that they receive from the agents (which is quantifiable and, for simplicity, may be measured in money). They favor the highest bidder by supporting his or her preferred policy. In turn, if neither agent offers the legislators[7] anything, the legislators will do nothing (hence favoring the status quo),

---

[5] For presentational clarity, I describe Agent 1 and the president with feminine pronouns and Agent 0 and legislators with masculine pronouns.

[6] Note that the simultaneous version of the game presented here is a Colonel Blotto game (Gross and Wagner 1950).

[7] Sometimes I refer to all actors with prerogatives to initiate legislation as legislators; i.e., the executive and members of congress are considered legislators when performing that function.

and if both agents offer the same (positive) amount, the legislator will support the initiative before him. In brief, politicians will not enact policies that are not sponsored by anyone.

While this chapter argues that politicians will only enact policies when prompted by external agents, it also claims that politicians value their decision rights and will take action in defense of their prerogatives. Politicians value their decision rights precisely because they provide the key to the resources that they can extract from the legislative process. If the politicians' decision rights are violated, for example, by the enactment of an *unconstitutional* decree, they will react to enforce their rights. The extent to which they do so varies as a function of their level of institutional commitment. I specify politicians' valuation of institutional commitment below. I assume that levels of institutional commitment vary by country and explain this further below and in Chapter 3.

Politicians' payoffs y are a function of their decision rights, which are expressed in terms of hurdle factors r,[8] and of Agent 0's value V and Agent 1's value W, following Diermeier and Myerson (1999). Additionally, payoffs are a function of their "institutional commitment" l. I denote payoffs by $y(r, l, V, W)$. Hurdle factors provide synthetic information regarding the decision-making rules that are in place at a given time; they are determined exogenously by the constitutional rules that determine the legislators' decision rights.[9] Typically, they vary across actors (the executive, members of congress, supreme court justices), decisions (passage of a law, override of a veto, and impeachment, among others), and countries. Institutional commitment is also determined exogenously by the rules that affect the politicians' expectations regarding their tenure. Within each country, institutional commitment is equal for all of the members of a given institutional body (i.e., all congress members, all supreme court justices), but it varies across branches of government.

2.3.2 Constitutional Rules, Hurdle Factors, and Institutional Commitment

Before moving on, the notions of hurdle factors and of institutional commitment merit further explanation. I take the concept of hurdle factors

---

[8] Hurdle factors are a proxy for decision-making rules. I explain the concept immediately below.

[9] Constitutional rules are taken as given here. Although politicians have the prerogative to alter constitutional rules, I take the constitutional decisions (made in previous periods) as given. Where constitutional rules change, I consider the impact of the different settings. Diermeier and Myerson (1999) analyze how players may seek to alter some of these rules endogenously.

directly from Diermeier and Myerson (1999), where it is used to quantify the level of difficulty brought into the legislative process by the different actors with decision rights. Technically, the hurdle factor is the factor by which the agent seeking policy change must multiply her opponent's valuation of policy V in order to outbid him (Groseclose and Snyder 1996).[10] Recall that legislators will favor the policy supported by the highest bidder and that the agent seeking policy change, Agent 1, moves first. As the hurdle factor increases, so does the cost of enacting legislation. Where a single legislator is in charge of enacting laws (imagine a dictator), the hurdle factor is simply $r = 1$ and represents the one decision that needs to be secured to enact (or block) a policy. While r could never be lower than 1, systems with more complex allocations of decision rights, which incorporate more institutional actors to the process, present higher overall hurdle factors.

To illustrate how hurdle factors are calculated and implemented, and how different rules raise or lower the factor, consider the case of a large unicameral legislature with a supermajority requirement that a fraction Q needs to support a bill for it to pass, and $Q < 1$. In collective bodies where majority rules are in place, the hurdle factor is $r = 1/(1-Q)$, since any coalition with more than $1-Q$ can block a bill, and Agent 1 cannot guarantee passage of the bill unless she promises V to each $1-Q$ fraction of the chamber (note that V is exactly how much Agent 0 can offer, and he only needs support from a fraction $1-Q$ of the chamber to guarantee blockage). Say, for example, that the supermajority that is in place is such that $Q = 2/3$, then $r = 1/(1 - (2/3)) = 1/(1/3) = 3$. Any coalition with more than $1-Q = 1/3$ of the chamber can block the bill. Agent 1 must guarantee V to each $1/3$ (otherwise, there will always be at least $1/3$ of the chamber willing to receive V from Agent 0 to block). Therefore, the total promised to the whole assembly must be $V/(1-Q)$ and in the example $V/(1-Q) = 3V$.[11] In this sense, the hurdle factor is the factor by which Agent 1 must multiply Agent 0's resources to achieve a policy change. Different majority requirements either raise or lower the hurdle factor, and legislatures typically apply different rules to different decisions.

---

[10] Groseclose and Snyder (1996) show that in a setting governed by majority rule, Agent 1's valuation must meet the condition $W \geq 2n \ V/(n + 1)$, where n is the number of members in a legislature; for large n, 1's total payments are approximately $2V$. Diermeier and Myerson (1999) denote this the "hurdle" factor, and they specify $r = 2n/(n + 1)$ if n is odd, and $r = 2$ if n is even (and large). The idea extends to other majority requirements.

[11] Note that r changes with Q. For the case of $Q = 1$ (perfect unanimity) the hurdle factor goes to infinity as n goes to infinity. When individuals (and not collective bodies) are in charge of decisions, fractions are not at stake and r represents the single individual: $r = 1$.

Moreover, political systems can further organize themselves in ways that affect the hurdle factor by creating rules that complement the most basic decision-making rules (which are usually but not always established at the constitutional level). The case of a chamber that approves bills by majority rule but additionally requires that the chairman of a gate-keeping committee approves a bill before it can come to a vote on the floor represents a way to increase the hurdle factor. This is so because, regardless of the rule in place, the hurdle rises whenever a decision must pass through an additional instance of decision making. Another way to think of this is as adding a veto player to the process: Agent 1 must pay $2V$ to the chamber majority and $1V$ to the committee gatekeeper (the additional veto player), a total of $3V$; otherwise, Agent 0 can block the bill by giving V either to the committee chair or to any one-half of the chamber. A different rule, delegating the decision right entirely to a committee chair such that the floor approves anything that the chairman of that committee approves would have the opposite effect of lowering the hurdle to 1.

Summarizing, hurdle factors allow us to classify different legislative processes according to the number and size of blocking coalitions.[12] The value of r is central in determining the cost of lawmaking: As r increases, so does the cost of passing policy changes. In this chapter, I specify different hurdle factors, contributed by different actors: t (the executive), s (the senate when deciding by simple majority rule), h (the lower house when deciding by simple majority rule); s_o, s_e, h_o, h_e (those same actors when deciding overrides – subscript o – or impeachment – subscript e).[13] The model I present shows how variation in these factors across countries leads to different choice scenarios when deciding policy change.

Institutional commitment, in turn, brings into consideration the notion that encroachment of decision rights that are essential to a politician's maximization of gains will simply not be tolerated by the actors whose rights are violated. If they were, we would expect to see only executive

---

[12] This is somewhat related to Tsebelis' notion of veto players, despite the difference in approaches (spatial models versus strategic games). The emphasis here is placed on constitutional rules and politician's valuation of those rules, as will soon become apparent. Given the approach taken here, I wish to convey a finer understanding of the different ways in which veto players interact and the relative weight of each under varying scenarios. In particular, the approach taken here provides additional leverage for analyzing very similar institutional structures.

[13] Hurdle factors need not be different, although they typically are. In unicameral settings, I refer to the one chamber in existence as the house and denote hurdle factors correspondingly.

decrees (at the lowest hurdle factor for agents), and congress would be consistently excluded from deals.

Of course, one may wonder why the politicians depicted here as maximizing external contributions, and with no direct preferences over policy, would be committed to institutions; this notion may seem problematic at first glance. Institutional commitment implies attachment to established decision rights that guarantee continued access to agents' contributions. Legislators who seek to maximize the contributions that they receive from external agents are unlikely to stay put when these contributions are diverted to other actors in violation of established rules.[14]

Institutional commitment and hurdle factors are different yet related concepts. When writing constitutions, politicians assign decision rights by indicating who will decide different things, and by indicating how they will do so they establish hurdle factors.[15] Commitment to those rules, i.e., the decision rights that enable legislation, vary with issues. Variation in expected values of V and W regarding different issues interact with levels of institutional commitment: If the stakes are high on a given issue, politicians will value legislating on that issue more than legislating on issues where the stakes are low. This stems from the expected payoffs of legislating on different issues in a repeated game. Institutional commitment represents the varying willingness to enforce decision rights and is higher when the expected gains deriving from the possession of those rights are higher.[16]

We write institutional commitment l, and l varies across actors, such that l_A denotes the congress' level of institutional commitment and l_B the supreme court's. Note that $\sum^n_{i=1} a_i = l_A$, where n is the number of members of congress, and a_i is each member's valuation of her decision rights. Likewise, $\sum^m_{k=1} b_k = l_B$, where m is the number of supreme court members and b_k is each member's valuation of her decision rights.

---

[14] Institutional commitment arises in the repeated version of the game.

[15] While the rules guiding constitutional reforms are typically the most restrictive, other decisions require less restrictive majorities, and, often, various different rules exist. I follow Diermeier and Myerson in arguing that hurdle factors are determined to maximize the legislators' gains from their decision rights. Similarly, I argue that there is variation within categories of legislation (regarding which the same hurdle factors apply), and politicians do not value all pieces of legislation equally even within a single category (such as ordinary legislation or constitutional amendments, among others).

[16] When a given issue commands fewer resources, the expected payoffs from legislating on the issue over time are lower, causing commitment to decision rights to be lower. I do not present repeated games in this book.

2.3.3 Game Dynamics and Policy Change

Up to this point, I have presented a situation in which two agents compete for policy. Politicians act as a function of the contributions that they receive from external agents, and these contributions are, in turn, made possible by the agents' valuations V and W. The agent who can outbid the other gets his/her preferred policy outcome.

With the information provided thus far, I describe the equilibrium of the game in its most general form. It is crucial to determine whether the maximum expenditure that Agent 1 can make, rV (i.e., the hurdle factor multiplied by Agent 0's value of the status quo) and politicians' valuation of institutional commitment, l, are greater than or less than Agent 1's value W.

    (a) If $rV + l < W$, then Agent 1 offers $rV + l$, and Agent 0 offers nothing (because to block the proposal, he would have to spend more than what it is worth to him), and policy is changed in the direction favored by Agent 1.

    (b) If $rV + l > W$, then neither agent makes an offer, and the proposal does not pass; Agent 1 knows she cannot afford to contribute enough to change policy.

The game I present depicts the interactions that take place when agents set out to change policy. We often think of law-making in simplified ways, which we use as shortcuts to more complicated processes: We think of decree enactment in isolation, lawmaking as a process that involves the executive and congress alone, impeachment as having little to do with lawmaking, and judicial review as an *ex-post* procedure. Here I recognize that legislation takes place in the shadow of possible judicial review and even impeachment.

Before delving into the broader game and drawing out implications, it is convenient to take a stepwise approach in the analysis of some of its components. The game, which ultimately analyzes the determinants of the choice of one legislative instrument versus another, may be thought of as a set of several smaller games. Along the decree path there is a bid for a decree, a bid for impeachment in reaction to the decree (which is how the legislature can block a decree with insufficient support), and bids for judicial reversal if the impeachment is unsuccessful (in which case blockage occurs in the judiciary). Along the statutory path, there is a bid for a statute that may entail a bid for an override. Figure 2.1 presents this game in extensive form.[17]

---

[17] The smaller games are presented separately, for clarification purposes, in Appendix 2.A.

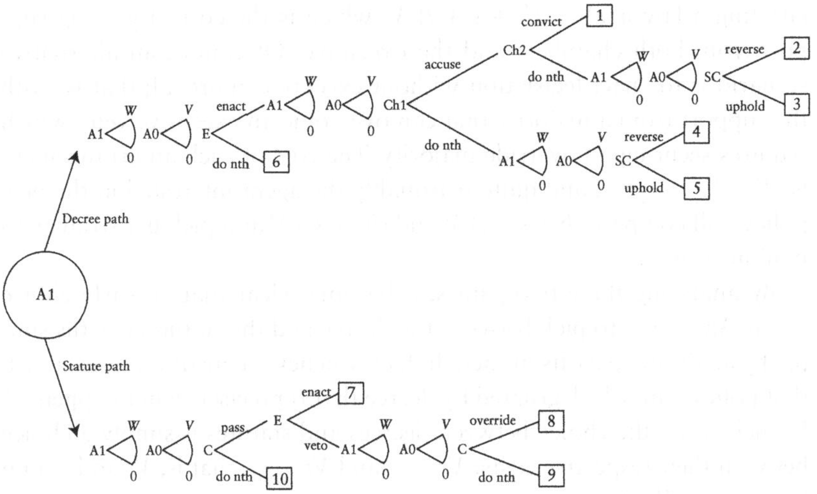

References: A1 = Agent 1, A0 = Agent 0, E = Executive, C = Congresss, Ch1 = Chamber 1, Ch2 = Chamber 2, SC = Supreme Court.

FIGURE 2.1. *The choice of legislative paths*

One way to think of policy change is to consider the interactions taking place when policies are enacted by executive decree. In this game, the two external agents compete to attain their preferred policy from the executive, who, in turn, will favor the highest bidder. The basic insight derived from the decree game is that the total cost borne by agents to enact a new policy is at its lowest when enacting legal decrees, since only support from the executive is needed. In terms of this game, the cost facing Agent 1 to enact policy x is $rV = tV = V$, and the enabling condition is $tV < W$. The decree game, included in Appendix 2.A, illustrates the simplest strategic calculations facing agents when aspiring to enact policy change via decree.

Certainly, this game simplifies the menu of options open to agents. Policy decisions may be made via congressional intervention in the process, so agents never face a single option; they choose between the different legislative instruments available to them. For this reason, it is important to analyze the congressional game, where the two agents typically compete for support from congress and the executive. The most basic insight derived from its consideration in isolation is that the cost of enacting policy is always greater than V, fundamentally because more than a single actor is involved in policymaking (note that $r = h + s + t$). Deciding by simple majority rule in bicameral settings, the usual cost of enacting a law is $rV = (h + s + t) V$, which is the cost of gaining support from both chambers and the executive. Of course, an alternative scenario is to enact legislation without executive approval; that is, with the support from a majority that can overcome an executive veto, which requires securing an override majority. The cost of such an arrangement is $rV = (h_o + s_o) V$, and quite reasonably the agent interested in the new policy will compare $(h + s + t) V$ and $(h_o + s_o) V$ and pick her strategy to minimize costs.

By analyzing these two games, it becomes clear that an early choice facing Agent 1 is to pick between the decree and the statutory paths simply by analyzing payoffs in each. In fact, whenever constitutions establish that policy x may be legislated by decree that is precisely what happens.[18] In such cases, the choice between decrees and statutes is simply a choice between their respective costs: Vr_{DECREE} and $Vr_{STATUTE}$, that is, Vt and V min $[(h + s + t), (h_o + s_o)]$.

Even intuitively, at this point, we can see that when given the choice, agents will always prefer to enact policies via decree due to cost minimization. If all matters could be legislated via executive decree, the equilibrium outcome would be that all policy change would be effectively enacted by decree. Yet congressional statutes are enacted on a regular basis. Constitutions limit the matters that may be enacted via decree, and the choice between instruments becomes problematic when the policy sought is a matter that the constitution explicitly excludes from decree domain. This gives way to more complex interactions: judicial review as well as impeachment merit consideration.[19] When a decree is unconstitutional, it may be reversed.

Consider the enactment of an unconstitutional decree. Legislators who value their decision rights may impeach the president if she encroaches upon those rights. Impeachment forces the executive out of office (I assume that illegal decisions made by the executive are overturned as part of the impeachment), reinstating the *status quo ante*. In this game, agents compete to attain their preferred policy, but besides outbidding each other they take into account the legislators' institutional commitment. Legislators value their decision rights at a_i, and likewise value agents' contributions (v_i and w_i). In this game (as well as in the judicial game), an action may come about in the absence of external contributions

---

[18] Constitutional inclusion guarantees that legislators or the judiciary will not block those executive decrees, as they comply with the constitution.

[19] Both games are presented and explained thoroughly in Appendix 2.A; only the basic insights are presented here.

as a function of institutional commitment. Agent o favors impeachment because it reinstates his preferred policy. Agent 1, who previously sought politicians' support to enact policy, in this scenario seeks to block their actions. If she does not block in at least one chamber, impeachment takes place and policy is reversed.[20]

Agent 1's contribution to legislators must exceed the total utility that legislators derive from defending their decision rights, which is composed of their valuation a_i plus Agent o's contribution.[21] Whereas the hurdle factor r affects the cost of getting politicians to act, the inverse of the hurdle factor, r^{-1}, is required to block actions.[22] In fact, as shown in Appendix 2.A, if Agent 1 can offer $\{[(V/n) + \varepsilon] + a_i\}$ to a coalition of $(r^{-1} n + 1)$ legislators in one chamber,[23] she can prevent impeachment and therefore maintain policy x. What is interesting in this setting is the difference in the politicians' motivations. Note that the legislators' valuations alone may be sufficient to render Agent 1 unable to block the impeachment (when the legislators' valuations are higher than what Agent 1 has to offer, W). Indeed, if $(r^{-1}) l_A > W$, there is nothing Agent 1 can do to stop impeachment.

Alternatively, a decree that has violated decision rights may be overturned by judicial review. Like legislators, supreme court justices derive utility from preserving constitutionally established decision rights (at b_k) and do not require external contributions to overturn decrees. As with impeachment, Agent 1 wishes to block the reversal of policy; if she can offer $(b_k + (V/m) + \varepsilon)$ to $((r^{-1}m) + 1)$ members of the supreme court, she can prevent the reversal of policy x.

Having analyzed some key interactions that take place whenever agents seek to change policy, I now turn to the broader game of choice of legislative instruments.

---

[20] In this game, as in the others, I assume that Agent 1 moves first. She does so, here, to stop an action (impeachment, which also reverses x) that will otherwise take place inevitably. If Agent o moved first, impeachment would not constitute a credible threat below a certain level of institutional commitment. By not moving first, Agent o allows the threat of impeachment to deter illegal decrees even at low levels of institutional commitment. The Appendix to this chapter provides a comparison of costs and payoffs in each case.

[21] Agent 1 must surpass that utility given that we've assumed when legislators are indifferent between two non-negative contributions they act, and here Agent 1 needs to block their action.

[22] Recall that a fraction Q is needed to secure action. To block action, $1-Q$ is needed – more precisely, $[(1-Q) + 1]$. Whereas we define the hurdle factor $r = 1/(1-Q)$, the inverse of the hurdle factor is $r^{-1} = (1-Q)$.

[23] Only one chamber is needed to block impeachment; which one is chosen depends on h_e and s_e as well as n, the number of members in each.

2.3.4 Choice of Legislative Instruments

The full model analyzes the determinants of policy change in settings where actors may pick among different legislative instruments. An agent's initial decision to pursue policy via executive decree or congressional statute gives way to diverse paths and reactions by the different actors with decision rights over policy. If a policy is changed via decree and congressional prerogatives have been violated, congress may intervene to impeach the president. In turn, the supreme court may intervene to reverse an unconstitutional decree. Figure 2.1 presents the game in extensive form. Terminal histories are numbered 1–10, with payoffs listed in Table 2.A.1 in Appendix 2.A of this chapter.

As noted above, hurdle factors vary across countries and time, and the outcomes of the game will depend critically on those values. In particular, the hurdle factors and the agents' valuations of policy, together with the politicians' institutional commitment, determine the choice of legislative paths. Agents wishing to enact their preferred policy will seek the path of least resistance: The one that gives them the desired policy while minimizing expenditures.

The game has several stages. At the first stage, Agent 1, who seeks to change policy, chooses the path of least resistance (decree or statutory). We can think of the events that unfold along each of the paths as bringing together the smaller games mentioned above (each time agents make bids, one of the smaller games begins). The game is solved by backward induction, which requires the identification of payoffs at all terminal histories.

Agent 1's initial choice is a function of the comparison between the hurdle factor associated with the enactment of a decree r_{DECREE} versus the hurdle factor associated with the enactment of a statute $r_{STATUTE}$, external agents' valuations V and W, and the levels of institutional commitment l. The constitutionality of decrees is fundamentally relevant to the outcome. Agent 1 knows whether enacting policy x by decree complies with the constitution or not. Her choice of one path or the other is affected by that information since it may alter the cost imposed by the decree route. Although one might think that policies that cannot be constitutionally enacted via decree have no solution but to go through the congressional route, the existence of decrees on matters that the constitution forbids that are legislated by decree provides evidence to the contrary.

Table 2.A.1 presents payoffs at all terminal histories under the different scenarios of constitutional and unconstitutional decrees. In the paragraphs that follow, I describe optimal strategies along each of the paths to give way to the description of the sub-game perfect equilibrium (SGPE) of the game. Let us now consider each actor's optimal strategies along the decree path.

Proposition 1: The enactment of a constitutionally valid decree is a SGPE.

If the enactment of a given policy by decree is constitutionally valid, that policy will be enacted via decree (at the lowest cost to Agent 1), and the other players will not intervene to contest the decree. As long as Agent 1 can outbid Agent 0, enacting a decree is a SGPE: It constitutes Agent 1's optimal strategy. It is also Agent 0's optimal strategy, whenever $V < W$, not to seek a reversal, which is a dominated strategy; since Agent 0 was unable to outbid Agent 1 at the decree game, he would not be able to outbid her at seeking reversal. The legislators' and the supreme court justices' optimal strategies are not to react to the policy – their decision rights are not violated – and Agent 0 cannot afford to outbid Agent 1. Thus the decrees are accepted.

Proposition 2: It is generally less costly to enact constitutionally valid decrees than statutes. Where constitutions authorize the executive to enact policies by decree, valid decrees will always be the preferred legislative instrument.

Guiding this proposition are hurdle factors. Where decrees are valid, agents' analyses of costs reduces to a comparison of hurdle factors, and decrees will always cost less as long as they are constitutional. Payoffs presented in Table 2.A.1 show that no player can be made better off by pursuing a different strategy: If the decree is constitutionally valid, the game ends either in terminal history 3 or 5 (depending on the number of members in each chamber, which determines which chamber is cheaper), with policy x enacted by decree.

The question then becomes this: Under what conditions will agents seek to enact illegal decrees? And, related to that, under what conditions might they prefer to enact statutes? Or, even statutes that delegate to the executive the authority to pass decrees on specific matters, making otherwise illegal decrees legal?

First, consider the enactment of an unconstitutional decree. As opposed to the case in which a decree does not encroach upon decision rights, an unconstitutional decree does. In the words of an Argentine legislator,

"The Supreme Court can always allege that a decree is not valid because it does not meet the urgency requirements; for this reason, it is always preferable for the president to have an explicit congressional delegation. Delegations enable the president to avoid legal actions against her, such as the Supreme Court declaring that absent the requisite of need and urgency, this or that decree is not constitutional."[24] (Diputado interviewed in Buenos Aires, August 18, 2005)

The supreme court's decision to uphold or reverse legislation, as well as the legislature's decision to impeach the executive, is central to the description of the equilibrium. Given payoffs at terminal histories 1–6, along this path, Agent 1 maximizes payoffs by enacting a decree and impeding impeachment and judicial reversal. Policy change through an illegal decree occurs if and only if

$$W > Vt + [(a_i + (V/n) + \in \varepsilon) \cdot ((\min (h_e^{-1}, se^{-1})) \, n + 1)] $$
$$+ [(b_k + (V/m) + \varepsilon) \cdot ((j^{-1} m) + 1)] \qquad (2.1)$$

That is, unconstitutional decrees occur if Agent 1 can afford to contribute to legislators and justices more than the utility they would derive from impeachment and judicial reversal, linked to their valuation of decision rights a_i and b_k, plus the contribution V that Agent 0 would make to further motivate their action. Hence, the cost to Agent 1 of an illegal decree is $Vt + \{[(a_i + (V/n) + \varepsilon) \cdot ((\min (h_e^{-1}, s_e^{-1})) \, n + 1)] + [(b_k + (V/m) + \varepsilon) \cdot ((j^{-1} m) + 1)]\}$. She compares this cost to that of a statute.

Proposition 3: The cost of unconstitutional decrees may be higher than that of legal decrees as a function of institutional commitment.

In particular, the cost of unconstitutional decrees is higher than that of legal decrees whenever the second and third terms of the right-hand side in equation (2.1) – that is, the utility legislators and justices would derive from impeachment and judicial reversal, linked to their valuation of decision rights a_i and b_k – are greater than zero. The cost of an unconstitutional decree will only be equal to that of a constitutionally valid decree if $a_i = b_k = 0$.

Yet analysis of the costs and payoffs originated by the enactment of decrees alone is insufficient to explain the choice in favor of decrees or statutes. We must consider the costs and payoffs along the statute path. Therefore, second, consider the enactment of the same policy by statute. When enacting a statute, Agent 1 can choose between (a) getting the bill passed with both congressional and executive approval, or (b) getting it

---

[24] "*La CSJN siempre puede alegar que el DNU no es válido porque no se presentan las condiciones de urgencia, y entonces es siempre necesario y preferible que el Ejecutivo cuente con una delegación explícita. Se delega para cubrirse frente a posibles acciones legales, que la Corte pudiera declarar que ausente la necesidad y urgencia, tal o cual DNU no es constitucional.*"

passed without the executive's approval by securing an overriding majority in congress. The decision to exclude the executive depends on a simple comparison: that of $V(t + s + h)$, the cost of getting the bill approved by congress and signed by the executive, and $V(h_o + s_o)$, the cost of an override majority. We know Agent 1's main concern is to achieve passage while minimizing expenditures. If $V(t + s + h) < V(s_o + h_o)$, and as long as she can afford it; i.e., if $W > V(t + s + h)$, Agent 1 will make an offer that secures support from congress and the executive, such that the game ends in terminal history 7. If, instead, override majorities are cheaper, that is, if $V(t + s + h) > V(s_o + h_o)$ (as in Peru and Brazil) and $W > V(s_o + h_o)$, then Agent 1's optimal strategy is to bring congress in and exclude the president, so Agent 1 will offer congress $V(s_o + h_o)$.

Proposition 4: Statutes may be enacted with or without executive approval. Constitutional rules determine the choice.[25]

Third, after having analyzed each path separately, Agent 1 is in a position to choose between them. Whereas the decree path imposes a cost of

$$Vt + \{[(a_i + (V/n) + \varepsilon) \cdot ((\min (he^{-1}, se^{-1}))n + 1)]$$
$$+ [(b_k + (V/m) + \varepsilon) \cdot ((j^{-1} m) + 1)]\} \qquad (2.2)$$

the cost of a statute is

$$\min [V(t + s + h), V(s_o + h_o)] \qquad (2.3)$$

Which path will Agent 1 choose? The choice is a function of variables that vary across cases: h, s, h^{-1}, s^{-1}, s_o, h_o, a_i, and b_k. While the values of hurdle factors are straightforward (derived directly from constitutional rules), a_i and b_k are not.[26] In the comparison above, hurdle factors indicate that absent institutional commitment, statutes would be costlier than unconstitutional decrees. When $a_i = b_k = 0$,

---

[25] These vary by country. To illustrate the point, consider the relatively easier override procedure in Brazil, which effectively lowers the overall hurdle by establishing that overrides be supported by a majority of the members of each chamber (identical requisite for a simple passage). All else being equal, statutes can be enacted without executive approval (i.e., executive veto) at a lower cost than if an executive approval is sought. In Peru, under the current constitution, which makes the override majority identical to the first passage majority, the situation is the same. The case of Chile, in turn, reveals that impeachment procedures are less restrictive than override procedures; as the model will show, this makes blocking impeachment more difficult, which works in defense of the status quo. Overall, variations in these rules have implications for the feasibility of the decree path as the model will illustrate.

[26] Levels of institutional commitment a_i and b_k are not directly observable. However, this book claims that they are associated with the legislators' and justices' security in their jobs. Levels of institutional commitment are expected to vary across countries.

$Vt + \{[(a_i + (V/n) + e) \cdot ((\min (b_e^{-1}, s_e^{-1})) n + 1)] + [(b_k + (V/m) + e) \cdot ((j^{-1} m) + 1)]\} < \min [V(t + s + h), V(s_o + h_o)]$ This equation shows that where institutional commitment is zero, Agent 1 prefers the decree solution. The cost of illegal decrees is increasing in a_i and b_k as well as in $r - 1$, n, and m. There exist critical values of a_i and b_k that allow us to establish indifference between the two paths, and, likewise, when statutes are preferred to decrees.[27] The intuition is that as institutional commitment increases (i.e., the cost of blocking the reversal of illegal decrees increases), congressional statutes are more likely.

Proposition 5: As institutional commitment increases, so does the cost of unconstitutional decrees.

This stems directly from equation (2.1) and is a statement about the cost of unconstitutional decrees, which are largely influenced by values of a_i and b_k.

Proposition 6: Above a critical value of institutional commitment, the cost of unconstitutional decrees is higher than that of statutes.

Values of institutional commitment a_i and b_k effectively determine the SGPE of the game. Below critical values of a_i and b_k, and sufficiently high levels of W, Agent 1 will always choose decrees (and the game ends in terminal history 3 or 5 depending on the number of members in each chamber), and above that value, she will choose statutes (and the game ends in terminal history 7).

The following predictions emerge:

(a) When decrees are legal, we expect them to be the legislative instrument of choice.
(b) The frequency of decrees is a function of institutional commitment.
   (b.1) At low levels of institutional commitment, we expect more unconstitutional decrees than otherwise.
   (b.2) When institutional commitment is lowest (i.e., 0), we should expect to see decrees, regardless of their constitutionality.
   (b.3) Critical values of l exist beyond which statutes are preferred to illegal decrees.

---

[27] By rearranging the components of the equation, the closest we come to establishing a value of a_i at which Agent 1 is indifferent between the two paths is, from
$Vt + \{[(a_i + (V/n) + \varepsilon) \cdot ((\min (b_e^{-1}, s_e^{-1})) n + 1)] + [(b_k + (V/m) + \varepsilon) \cdot ((j^{-1} m) + 1)]\} = \min [V(t + s + h), V(s_o + h_o)]$, we know that
$a_i = \{[[\min [V (t + s + h), V (s_o + h_o)]] - Vt - [(b_k + (V/m) + \varepsilon) \cdot ((j^{-1} m) + 1)]]/((\min (b_e^{-1}, s_e^{-1})) n + 1)\} - (V/n) - \varepsilon$.
When a_i is equal to the right-hand side of the equation, Agent 1 is indifferent between statutes and decrees; and, likewise, when a_i is greater than the right-hand side, statutes are preferred to decrees. A way to simplify the equation is when $b_k = 0$ and $a_i > 0$. In this special case, a_i can be derived once the hurdle factors are known.

(c) Statutes are the chosen legislative instruments if and only if (I.) enacting the policy by decree is unconstitutional, *and* (II.) the institutional commitment is high enough that unconstitutional decrees become costlier than statutes.

(d) Overrides only occur if the majority requirement for overrides is lower than or equal to the majority requirement for passage of bills.

(e) Impeachment never occurs.[28]

(f) Judicial review never occurs.

2.4 DECREES OR STATUTES?

The conditions under which each path is most convenient vary with (a) hurdle factors, and (b) institutional commitment, both of which vary across countries. Hurdle factors enable the identification of paths of least resistance to policy change: All else being equal, higher hurdle factors lead to higher levels of resistance to policy change.

I have claimed that the difficulties introduced in the legislative process by hurdle factors may be sidestepped via blunt violation of decision rights. For this reason, the politicians' commitment to enforce their decision rights (institutional commitment) ultimately determines which instrument is preferred. As institutional commitment varies, so does the cost of unconstitutional decrees, and therefore their likelihood.

The choice of instrument, as identified by the SGPE of the game, will vary with the validity of decrees. Recall that the possible scenarios for policy change are: (a) A policy meets constitutional requirements along both the decree and the statutory paths; (b) A policy makes for a constitutionally valid statute but not a constitutional decree.

The simplest case to consider arises when Agent 1's desired policy x meets constitutional requirements along both the decree and the statutory paths. The SGPE of this game indicates that decrees are always preferred. Agent 1's optimal strategy is to pursue the enactment of policy x by decree. Agent 1 pays the optimal amount (Vt), Agent 0 pays zero, the executive enacts the decree, and the game ends in terminal history 5 (legislators and supreme court justices do nothing). The condition for Agent 1's initial move is that $W > Vt$, and as long as that is true, we

---

[28] Incomplete information would affect this prediction. With some mutual uncertainty we might expect "mistakes" from time to time. The fact that impeachments are rare in the real world is consistent with the model. A similar logic applies to the next prediction, regarding judicial review.

should expect decrees; otherwise, the status quo remains and no bids take place. If, in practice, this scenario held always (that is, if nothing were excluded from CDA), then we would never see statutes enacted.

Matters become more interesting when a proposed policy x would meet constitutional requirements if enacted by statute, but not by decree. This case begs an explanation of the question: Why do we see statutes in a world in which decrees are a possibility? The key here is that the violation of congressional decision rights may incite reactions from other politicians, either in congress or the judiciary. Knowing this, Agent 1 must pay attention to the politicians' level of commitment to those rights. The SGPE of this game varies as a function of the legislators' and supreme court justices' institutional commitment, a_i and b_k, respectively. At sufficiently low levels of commitment, Agent 1 is still able to pursue the enactment by decree, as long as she can get the executive to enact it and avoid action on the part of congress and the supreme court (i.e., if Agent 1's valuation of policy x is greater than the sum of Agent 0's valuation of the status quo plus what Agent 1 would need to contribute to block coalitions in congress and the supreme court to prevent their reactions).[29] As long as the cost of executive support plus congressional and supreme court acquiescence is lower than the cost of a statute, decrees are preferred (and the game ends in terminal history 3 or 5). If that is the case, Agent 1 pursues a decree and pays the executive to enact, members of congress to withhold from impeaching the executive, and supreme court justices not to reverse the decree. Agent 0 does nothing.

The model suggests that without institutional commitment, as many presume is the case in Latin American countries and in new democracies in general, we would only observe the enactment of executive decrees.

2.5 FINAL REMARKS

This chapter has advanced a theory of policy change that is contingent on the choice of legislative instruments. In doing so, it has highlighted that institutional commitment has the force to limit presidential encroachment of decision rights. A polity's capacity to enforce checks and balances stems not from the rules that establish decision rights and guide the politicians' decision-making process, but from the politicians' willingness to enforce those rules. By narrowing in on the policymaking process, and

---

[29] Formally, $W > Vt + [(a_i + (V/n) + \varepsilon) \cdot ((\min (h_e^{-1}, s_e^{-1})) n + 1)] + [(b_k + (V/n) + \varepsilon) \cdot ((j^{-1} n) + 1)]$.

the inseparable question regarding the choice of legislative instrument, I shed light on the mechanism at play.

Within this theory, the forces that shape the policy process are external agents, who make their resources available to those politicians who provide support to their preferred policies. Legislators and politicians, who depend on resources either to stay in power themselves or to keep their political allies in power, value the decision rights that provide access to the most wanted resources.

The choice of decrees versus statutes hinges on the constitutional rules in place in a given country and the institutional actors' commitment to those rules. Where constitutional decree authority has been granted to executives, we should expect policy changes to be adopted exclusively by decree whenever possible, given its comparatively lower cost. In this light, the rise in decrees over the past decades in Latin America is hardly surprising. Since constitutions limit what can be adopted via decree, we might expect some regard for the established boundaries, and therefore a more cautious approach toward the use of decree authority. In contexts where institutional boundaries are perpetually disregarded, however, such expectations may not be reasonable. The only factor that can bring actors to comply with constitutionally imposed limits is the existence of sufficiently high levels of commitment to the established decision rights by actors within the system itself.

Only when decrees exceed the constitutional boundaries and levels of institutional commitment are above a critical level will the agents seeking new policies prefer to promote change via statutes. Under those circumstances – and those alone – will the agent seeking policy change either choose to have a policy enacted via a statute or not have it enacted at all. In all other cases (i.e., below that critical level), agents prefer to pursue policy change by decree, since the cost is lower. This implies that where decrees are used least relative to statutes, higher levels of institutional commitment are presumably present; whereas, if decrees are used with frequency, lower levels of institutional commitment may operate with all else being equal. Of course, the scope of legal executive decrees, which varies across countries (as shown in Table 3.A.1, included in Appendix 3.A in Chapter 3), should be taken into account when ascertaining this relationship and when testing.

The utility of the predictions advanced is twofold. It is *theoretical*, as it identifies components of the policy enactment process that are critical to our understanding of the determinants of policy stasis and change as well as the causes underlying the use of decrees and statutes. It is also *empirical* in that it enables the testing of the predictions against country-specific evidence and enables cross-country comparisons. Chapters 4–6 carry out the task of evaluating the predictions against data on Brazil and Argentina (Chapters 4 and 5), and against cross-national data (Chapter 6).

Additionally, one of the contributions of the theoretical approach taken in this chapter is the role assigned to external agents. As some readers may question the stance assigned to external agents, it is worth emphasizing that the book avoids taking a normative position with respect to actors' motivations and influence. This is especially the case regarding the role that external agents play in determining policy preferences. Instead, it positively assumes that external agents have the resources to shape politicians' actions. There is abundant evidence that politicians adjust their policy preferences in response to voters' and organized interest groups' preferences (Mayhew 1974; Arnold 1991; Clark 2010, among others). In this sense, if the external agents' preferences are common business in democratic politics, acknowledging the influence and its consequences should aid our understanding, and ultimately guide the design of mechanisms to adequately deal with any negative consequences that may arise.

Finally, the chapter directs our attention to constitutional design; that is, the specific allocations of decision-making rules that determine hurdle factors. Undoubtedly, the establishment of constitutional decree authority has led to the increased use of executive decrees across the Southern Cone, and as I have pointed out, this should hardly surprise us.

2.A APPENDIX: STRATEGIC GAMES AND PROOFS

2.A.1 Why Agent 1 Always Moves First

In this section, I provide the rationale behind the assumption that Agent 1 always moves first. If the reader has no quibbles with the assumption, the section may be skipped.

Suppose we are on the decree path – Agent 1 (A1) outbid Agent 0 (A0) in the first stage and the executive enacted a decree. Naturally, A0 would want congress to impeach the president and reverse the policy change. Can he do this? He has two ways of achieving this goal. One requires A0 to act first and support the legislators' willingness to impeach the executive for having encroached upon their decision rights. The other implies that A0 wait for A1 to react to the legislators' willingness to impeach.

I will consider the former of the two alternatives first. We know legislators value their decision rights at a_j, and they are willing to defend these rights; Ao is willing to contribute his valuation V to the cause. A1, in turn, is willing to contribute her valuation W to blocking impeachment efforts; she can contribute W to a blocking coalition. Given the majority requirement in place for the impeachment of the executive, the hurdle factor for impeachment is $r = s_e + h_e$. To block impeachment, the hurdle is s_e^{-1} or h_e^{-1}.

When moving first, Ao will have to outbid A1; to do so, Ao's resources, pooled together with the legislators' valuation, must exceed A1's resources. It is important to note that Ao needs to make his contribution not to a fraction of the legislature but to all legislators; although impeachment may require only 1/2 or 2/3 majority; if Ao is to ensure that the remaining fraction will not be sought by A1 to block, he will have to contribute to all legislators equally. Whereas A1 can contribute W to the blocking fraction of one chamber (r^{-1}, usually 1/3), Ao must contribute an equivalent amount to each fraction of each chamber to secure his desired result (i.e., rW).

Yet I have already mentioned that legislators derive utility from impeachment regardless of contributions. This affects both what Ao and A1 need to contribute to outbid their opponents. In particular, Ao may sum his resources to the legislators' valuations to outbid A1 and attain impeachment.

Ao moves first knowing A1's valuation $W > V$. What Ao needs to know is whether $\Sigma(a_i) + V$ is enough to outbid A1. How much is A1 willing to contribute to each legislator? A1 can contribute W, but her goal is to block impeachment, for which she needs to gain support from only a fraction of one chamber, which means that A1 can concentrate her contributions on this set of legislators. If she can contribute to this fraction of legislators more than the payoff, they would receive from the added utility of their valuation of decision rights plus Ao's contribution, the impeachment process will not succeed. If A1 contributes W to a fraction of legislators W (n/r), in order to outbid A1, Ao would have to make sure that all legislators receive an equivalent amount, that is, that $(\Sigma a_i + V) > rW$.

If $(\Sigma a_i + V) > rW$ is true, Ao moves first. How much would Ao offer? The most he can offer is V, but given that he wishes to minimize contributions, as long as $V > rW - \Sigma a_i$, Ao can offer exactly $rW - \Sigma a_i$ to all legislators,[30] and A1, knowing that she cannot outbid Ao, will offer nothing. Knowing that A1 will offer zero, Ao also offers zero, and impeachment takes place.

---

[30] Recall that I have assumed throughout that when legislators (politicians) are indifferent, they act.

This is optimal for Ao, but it is contingent on $(\Sigma a_i + V) > rW$, which does not always hold. Let's analyze what happens when $(\Sigma a_i + V) < rW$.

If $(\Sigma a_i + V) < rW$, Ao knows he cannot outbid A1, so he offers zero. A1 offers $(a_i + \varepsilon)$ to a blocking coalition $[(1/r + 1)\, n]$ and avoids impeachment. Knowing this and both agents' valuations, if $V < (rW - \Sigma a_i)$ such that Ao cannot outbid A1, we should not expect Ao to move first. Instead, it makes sense for Ao to let legislators seek impeachment motivated solely by their valuation of decision rights. This, in turn, will motivate A1 to block them. If A1 moves first to block impeachment, Ao can offer V/n to each legislator, and, by doing so, he increases the difficulty that A1 confronts to $[(a_i + V/n + \varepsilon) \cdot (1/r + 1)\, n]$.

Under these circumstances, would A1 move first? A1 has no choice but to try to prevent the impeachment process that will otherwise take place, so she is forced to move. Her offer, then, is determined by the fact that Ao can make an offer of V/n to legislators, even, if in equilibrium, she makes no offers.

2.A.2 Four Games

2.A.2.1 *The Decree Game*

If Agent 1 wishes to enact policy change via executive decree, she needs support from a single "legislator," i.e., the president. Figure 2.A.1 presents the structure of this game in its simplest form. The hurdle imposed by the executive is simply $t = 1$. As posited above, agents 1 and 0 compete to obtain their preferred policy outcome (x and q, respectively), and the executive can choose between enacting the decree or doing nothing, in which case the *status quo* stands.

Agent 1 is willing to spend up to W to get the executive to enact the decree. Agent 0 is willing to spend up to V to stop policy change from coming about. The game is solved by backward induction: Agent 0 prefers u(q) to u(x). He can offer as much as V to the executive to get q. Agent 0 knows Agent 1's valuation W.

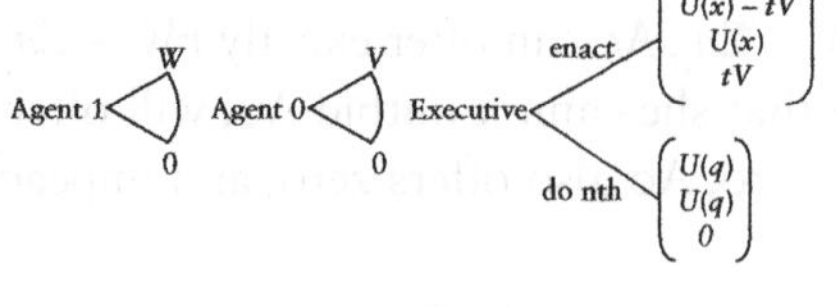

FIGURE 2.A.1. *The decree game*
Note: Hurdle factor $r = t = 1$.

Each terminal history presents payoffs in the order in which the players intervened: Agent 1's payoff first, Agent 0's payoff second, and the executive's payoff third.

As described above, it is crucial to determine whether the expenditure by Agent 1 rV is greater than or less than Agent 1's value W. In this case, $rV = tV$.

(a) If $tV < W$, Agent 1 offers tV, Agent 0 offers nothing, and the decree is enacted.

(b) If $tV > W$, then neither agent makes an offer, and the decree is not enacted.

The game shows that the total cost borne by Agent 1 to enact policy x is $tV = V$, and the enabling condition is $tV < W$. The only constraint to decree enactment is budgetary. The setting illustrates the simplest strategic calculations facing agents when aspiring to enact policy change via decree. In the following section, I argue that more complex institutional settings present more demanding scenarios, since policy change may be reversed. Institutional commitment does not play a role in the decree game when considered in isolation.

2.A.2.2 *The Congressional Game*

An alternative way to attain policy change is via statutes, in which case the game is slightly more complex. In this setting, the enactment of policy requires involvement by more than a single legislator. To pass a statute, it is also necessary to get a collective actor on board, i.e., congress. In most separation of power systems, the executive is a vital component of statute enactment: presidents are required to sign bills when they approve or to veto when they do not.[31] Figure 2.A.2 presents the structure of the congressional game with an override.

---

[31] In several Latin American countries, presidents have prerogatives beyond the typical block veto with which we are most familiar. Tsebelis and Alemán (2005) present a detailed analysis of the types of vetoes in place in eighteen Latin American countries and their implications for public policy. In Argentina and Brazil, the president can veto parts of bills and pass the remaining parts, the fallback option being the non-vetoed parts of the new policy in both countries (if congress does not reach an override majority). In Chile and Peru, the president can also make amendatory observations, and while the fallback option if an override does not occur in Chile is the new – observed – policy, in Peru it is the status quo ante (Tsebelis and Alemán 2005, Table 1). The variations certainly have implications for the overall game of policy enactment that are interesting to explore. Palanza and Sin explored the case of Argentina (2013, 2014); Palanza, Reynolds, and Sin looked into the case of Brazil ("Veto Bargaining in Brazil," presented at the 2016 meeting of the GEL/ALACIP); and Palanza (2020) looked into the Chilean case. Here, however, I abstract from these specificities and analyze the game in its simplest and more general form.

$$\begin{bmatrix} U(x) - V[t+s+h] \\ U(x) \\ hV \\ sV \\ tV \\ 0 \end{bmatrix} \qquad \begin{bmatrix} U(x) - V[s_o + h_o] \\ U(x) \\ h_o V \\ s_o V \\ 0 \end{bmatrix}$$

enact — Executive — override — Ch2 — override

pass ⟨ veto

Ch2 ⟨ A1 ⟨ A0 ⟨ Ch1 ⟨ do nth

W   V   override

pass ⟨ Ch1 ⟨ do nth

A1 ⟨ A0 ⟨ do nth

$$\begin{bmatrix} U(q) \\ U(q) \\ 0 \\ 0 \\ 0 \\ 0 \end{bmatrix} \quad \begin{bmatrix} U(q) \\ U(q) \\ 0 \\ 0 \\ 0 \\ 0 \end{bmatrix} \qquad \begin{bmatrix} U(q) \\ U(q) \\ 0 \\ 0 \\ 0 \end{bmatrix} \quad \begin{bmatrix} U(q) \\ U(q) \\ 0 \\ 0 \\ 0 \end{bmatrix}$$

FIGURE 2.A.2. *Congressional decision-making*

Note: Hurdle factor of ordinary passage $r = t + s + h$; hurdle of override $r_o = s_o + h_o$.

The participation of more institutional actors (the two chambers of congress and the executive)[32] increases the cost of enacting policy, since the agents will need to bring in all the actors with decision rights. The executive imposes a hurdle given its veto prerogative, $t = 1$. Additionally, agents need support from members of congress – of both the upper and lower chamber in bicameral settings. As explained above, the cost imposed by each chamber depends on the rules guiding decision-making in each; where a simple majority is required to pass laws, large chambers impose a cost of 2, with payoffs distributed equally amongst the legislators involved in the passage of the bill.[33] I denote the lower chamber's hurdle factor h and the upper chamber's hurdle factor s. Most commonly, legislative chambers pass ordinary bills by majority rule.[34] In that case, $h = s = 2$ in this game. The overall hurdle factor of a simple passage is $r = h + s + t$.

However, we know that vetoes sometimes occur, and we know that executive vetoes can be overridden by congress. Whenever congress overrides vetoes, statutes are attained without executive agreement. Consider a scenario in which Agent 0, by some unknown craft, co-opts the executive to veto the bill; in that case, Agent 1 will need to secure support from an

[32] Where only one chamber exists, such as in Peru under the 1993 Constitution, the game simplifies to a single chamber; the hurdle diminishes in that case, but our overall understanding of the game is the same.

[33] From Groseclose and Snyder (1996) we know that an optimal solution exists in which each legislator gets the same amount v (since by convexity a symmetric linear problem like this one must have a symmetric solution). To keep Agent 0 from blocking passage of the bill, Agent 1 must pay $\sum_{i \in N} v_i \geq V$ to any coalition of $(n + 1)/2$ legislators if n is odd, or to $n/2$ legislators if n is even. Hence, when n is odd, we have $v = 2V/(n+1)$ and $r = nv/V = (n/V) \cdot (2V/(n + 1)) = 2n/(n + 1)$. When n is even, $v = 2/Vn$ and $r = nv/V = 2$.

[34] Certainly, qualified majorities are required for specific bills, and this varies by country.

override majority in congress if policy x is to be enacted.[35] In some cases, obtaining an override majority in both chambers may impose a higher hurdle than getting the executive and a simple majority in each chamber to sign off the bill.[36] Since override procedures sometimes impose different majority requirements, I denote the override hurdle $r_o = h_o + s_o$.

Terminal histories show players' payoffs in the order in which players move: Agent 1 first (and then sixth), Agent o second (and then seventh), Chamber 1 third (and eighth), Chamber 2 fourth (and last).

In this case, Agent 1 can choose between making contributions to both congress and the executive or to an override majority alone. To describe the equilibrium of this game, we must determine whether Agent 1's valuation W exceeds Agent o's multiplied by the hurdle factor.

(a) If min $[(t + s + h) V, (s_o + h_o) V] < W$, Agent 1 offers min $[\cdot]$, Agent o offers nothing, and policy is changed.

(b) If min $[(t + s + h) V, (s_o + h_o) V] > W$, neither agent makes an offer, and the bill does not pass; Agent 1 knows she cannot afford to pay enough to change policy.

An interesting point is that whenever the cost of an override is lower than $h + s + t$, Agent 1 will prefer to leave the executive out; otherwise, she will expend $(h + s + t) V$ to avoid the veto. Whenever $(t + h + s) < (h_o + s_o)$, Agent 1 will prefer that the statute be passed with executive approval.[37]

2.A.2.3 The Impeachment Game
Consider the situation in which a decree has been enacted as a result of Agent 1's actions. Agent o's ideal policy, the *status quo ante* that I denote as q, has been overruled. Agent o can acquiesce, or he can try to overturn the new policy by using the constitutional mechanisms at hand. Several things can be done to overturn a policy decision: proposing a new bill that reestablishes the *status quo ante*, resorting to judicial review (which overturns the policy decision), and resorting to the impeachment of the executive who was responsible for the policy decision.

---

[35] I will ignore partial vetoes and amendatory observations for now. Although these variants on the veto introduce significant differences in the strategic calculations facing actors (Tsebelis and Alemán 2005), here I look at the general setting to understand the nature of the game taking place.

[36] That is precisely the case in Argentina and Chile, although not in Brazil, of the cases that I analyze in more depth.

[37] That is the case in Argentina and Chile; Brazil and Peru impose lower hurdles on the override, such that the condition does not hold (a testable implication is that in these cases we should expect more overrides).

In the analytical framework proposed here, an agent who has failed to block change is in a disadvantageous situation, since he was already unable to outbid Agent 1, and the same constraints affect the possibility of successfully proposing new courses of action. An agent who failed to defend the status quo in a decree game will certainly not be able to attain an impeachment process, since the condition to block a decree, $V > rW = V > tW$, is less restrictive than any condition involving the hurdle of impeachment. If external contributions alone led the policymaking process, this would very well become a static situation, and one where any policy could be enacted by decree.

However, external contributions, as I have argued, are not the single determinant of policy enactment. Politicians value their decision rights, and it is in their best interest to carry out an impeachment. Agent 0, who benefits from the reversal of policy x, is willing to contribute V to this endeavor.

In general, impeachment processes require that a majority in the lower chamber accuse and a majority of the Senate convict for removal to take place. Let s_e denote the hurdle imposed by the senate, and h_e denote the one imposed by the lower chamber, so any agent seeking impeachment would confront a hurdle $r_e = (s_e + h_e)$. Countries vary in their constitutional requirements on impeachments, and some countries impose more demanding hurdles than others: The impeachment of the president in Argentina requires a 2/3 majority in each of the chambers, while the less demanding Chilean requisite is a simple majority in the lower chamber and 2/3 in the Senate. Clearly, more restrictive hurdle factors make blocking impeachment easier.

Admittedly, impeachments are rare events, and for good reasons, which this game lays out. Nevertheless, just as with other prerogatives that are not exercised, their mere existence conditions behavior through anticipation. Legislators have the right to remove presidents from office. The question is: Under what conditions will they be more or less inclined to do so?

The extent to which encroachment harms legislators provides a response. When the decision rights of members of congress are infringed upon, legislators fail to collect contributions that they would receive otherwise. Within rational choice analyses, this alone would move them to oppose encroachment and enforce their rights. Of course, one may argue that other factors are at stake and that ideological consideration may produce an attachment to certain rules. The reasons underlying a commitment to institutional procedures are discussed in the following chapter.

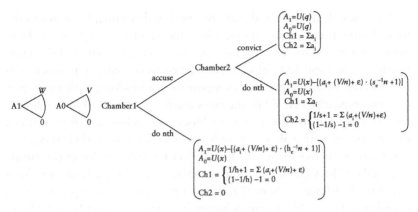

FIGURE 2.A.3. *Impeachment*

I refer to the legislators' valuation of their institutional prerogatives as their level of institutional commitment. The legislators' decision to pursue impeachment is critically dependent on their level of institutional commitment, $l = l_A$, but also on r, V, and W.

Each legislator i values his/her decision rights – call this institutional commitment – at $a_i \geq 0$, where $\Sigma a_i = l_A$, and a_i is the same across legislators. All else being equal, legislators will react to policies of which the adoption implies a violation of their decision rights, and they will do so as a result of their institutional commitment, i.e., the level of a_i.

One way to react is by impeaching the one actor who has benefited from the encroachment of their decision rights, the executive. I assume that following impeachment of the executive, an immediate reversal of the policy at stake occurs.[38] This makes impeachment particularly interesting for the agent who is in favor of the *status quo ante* and constitutes a threat to Agent 1. Following the logic in all the previous games, agents compete to block or favor the impeachment process, thereby affecting its feasibility.

Under these conditions, Agent 1 will move first to block an impeachment process that will, otherwise, take place (i.e., all else being equal, legislators will impeach the president in defense of their decision rights). Agent 0 moves second. Figure 2.A.3 presents the extensive form of the impeachment game. As before, actors have complete and perfect information.

---

[38] The assumption is in line with what we usually observe following the rare instances of impeachment of the executive.

The roles of Agents 1 and 0 are reversed in this game. Contrary to the logic driving the previous games, where the agent moving first sought to achieve the necessary majority for a decision to materialize, and the agent moving second sought to block, here the first mover intends to block congressional action. Agent 1 needs support from a blocking coalition to prevent the impeachment. While the rules guiding decisions of impeachment establish the hurdle factor at r, to block impeachment, Agent 1 needs the inverse of r, that is, r^{-1} of only one chamber, to outbid Agent 0.[39] The more restrictive the impeachment decision rule, the lower the hurdle imposed on blockage: If a 2/3 rule is in place, Agent 1 needs support from 1/3 of the legislators.[40] Note that Agent 1 need not attain support in both chambers; she can block impeachment by getting support from a blocking coalition in a single chamber, and she will pick the chamber so as to minimize expenditures, such that $r^{-1} = \min (h_e^{-1}, s_e^{-1})$.

Another condition that is different in this game is that Agent 1's contribution to each legislator must *exceed* his or her expected utility from impeachment (which is equal to the sum of the legislators' valuation a_i plus Agent 0's contribution).[41] Note that the legislators' valuations alone may be sufficient to render Agent 1 unable to block impeachment when the legislators' valuations are higher than what Agent 1 has to offer, W.

Indeed, if $(r^{-1} \cdot \Sigma a_i) > W$, Agent 1 can do nothing to stop impeachment. Only if $(r^{-1} \cdot \Sigma a_i) < W$, Agent 1 stands a chance. Agent 1 must make a contribution to a fraction r^{-1} of the legislators in one of the chambers such that it exceeds the sum of (a) their institutional commitment a_i and (b) Agent 0's contribution to each legislator V/n.

The onus of pushing the impeachment forward is not on Agent 0 but on legislators. The best Agent 0 can do to promote impeachment is to offer V (distributed symmetrically among the n legislators). If Agent 1 can offer $\{[(V/n) + \varepsilon] + a_i\}$ to a coalition of $(r^{-1}n + 1)$ legislators in one chamber, she can prevent impeachment.

Before I describe the equilibrium, note that Agent 1's choice of chamber is not trivial. In this game, the size of chambers matters in conjunction with the hurdle factor. Since Agent 1 only needs to pay off a subset

---

[39] Note that while $r = [1/(1 - Q)]$, $r^{-1} = (1 - Q)$, which is the fraction needed to prevent impeachment – more precisely, to prevent impeachment we need exactly $(n \, r^{-1}) + 1$.

[40] More precisely, $[n(1/3) + 1]$, since $n(2/3)$ is sufficient to act, and Agent 1 seeks to block action.

[41] This is so because I have assumed above that when legislators are indifferent between two non-negative contributions, they act. In this setting, Agent 1 needs to block the legislators' action.

of one of the chambers to block impeachment, she will naturally choose the chamber where the payments are lowest. Two factors determine these payments: the size of the chamber and the hurdle factor (which may vary across chambers). Agent 1 prefers the smallest chamber and the highest hurdle factor (or smallest r^{-1}). Ultimately, the joint effect of both variables will incline Agent 1 to make payments in one chamber or the other. This is captured in the expression $\{[\min (h_e^{-1}, s_e^{-1})]\, n + 1\}$.

To describe the equilibrium of this game, we must determine whether Agent 1's valuation W is sufficient to make the required contributions:

(a) If $([a_i + (V/n) + \varepsilon] \cdot \{[\min (h_e^{-1}, s_e^{-1})]\, n + 1\}) < W$, then Agent 1 offers precisely that amount, Agent o offers nothing, and the impeachment is blocked.

(b) If $([a_i + (V/n) + \varepsilon] \cdot \{[\min (h_e^{-1}, s_e^{-1})]\, n + 1\}) > W$, neither agent makes a contribution and the impeachment takes place.[42]

If Agent 1 has the resources to make the required contributions to legislators, impeachment is blocked. However, an additional issue must be taken into account, since it is not evident *where* – in which of the two chambers – it is blocked. To determine this, we need more information about the hurdle factors s_e and h_e. If $h_e \geq s_e$, the Nash equilibrium is that impeachment is blocked in the lower chamber (typically the accusation stage). If $h_e < s_e$, the impeachment is blocked in the Senate (after accusation but before conviction).

The logic laid out in this game of impeachment will become useful when drawing broader conclusions about the costs of changing policy and the relative costs of different legislative paths. I next turn to yet another game of relevance – judicial review.

2.A.2.4 The Judicial Review Game

Another way to reverse policy decisions is via judicial review. Consider once more the situation in which an executive decree has been enacted as a result of Agent 1's actions. Agent o may resort to the courts for reversal.

Although Agent o confronts the same resource problem as before, this problem does not inhibit review if justices have institutional commitment. If the supreme court derives utility from preserving constitutionally established decision rights, judicial review may take place regardless of Agent o's resources. I argue that just like congress members, supreme court justices have some level of institutional commitment, I_B. Each

---

[42] That is, if $a_i > [\, W/\{[\min (h_e^{-1}, s_e^{-1})]\, n + 1\}] - \varepsilon - V/n$.

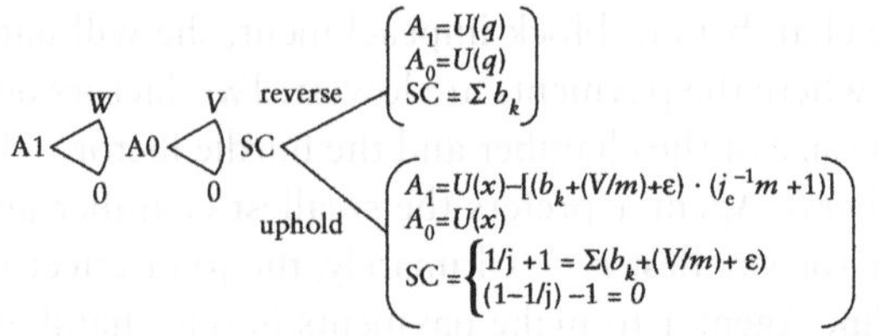

$$A_1 = U(q)$$
$$A_0 = U(q)$$
$$SC = \Sigma\, b_k$$

$$A_1 = U(x) - [(b_k + (V/m) + \varepsilon) \cdot (j_c^{-1}m + 1)]$$
$$A_0 = U(x)$$
$$SC = \begin{cases} 1/j + 1 = \Sigma(b_k + (V/m) + \varepsilon) \\ (1 - 1/j) - 1 = 0 \end{cases}$$

FIGURE 2.A.4. *Judicial review*

supreme court justice k values constitutionally established decision rights at $b_k \geq 0$, where $\Sigma^m_{k=1} b_k = I_B$, and b_k is the same across justices. They will act to reverse policies that violate decision rights as a result of their level of institutional commitment, i.e., the level of b. As with the legislators, the justices' valuation of institutional prerogatives varies across issues.[43]

When decision rights are encroached upon, the supreme court derives utility from challenging the authority that is responsible for the infringement. For example, if the executive issues a decree that violates congressional decision rights, the supreme court may decide to intervene. The supreme court's decision critically depends on the value of its institutional commitment I_B but also on r, V, and W.

Given supreme court justices' institutional commitment, the supreme court may take action to reverse a policy that violates decision rights regardless of the level of V. Figure 2.A.4 presents the extensive form of the game of judicial review.

As in the other cases above, Agent 1 moves first, but here, as in the impeachment game, she does so to prevent a reversal of x that will otherwise occur because, all else being equal, the supreme court will reverse an unconstitutional decree. If Agent 1 does not intervene, the supreme court will reverse policy x, so Agent 1 must block the decision. Agent 0 prefers the supreme court to carry out the reversal. The logic of this game is similar to that of the impeachment game in two respects: (a) Agent 1 intervenes to block a decision, and (b) Agent 1 faces an additional cost imposed by institutional commitment.

[43] Whereas legislators' level of institutional commitment may be easily linked to the defense of the gains that they extract from their decision rights, the same argument is made with respect to justices. Supreme court justices derive utility from their decision rights, as do all other actors, and they wish to continue to extract gains over time. Supreme court justices who continuously pass on the opportunity to exercise their rights and impose limits on the decisions of other actors may lose legitimacy and, with time, their rights altogether. Since they value these rights, they will exercise them if sufficiently blatant violations take place.

The hurdle factor of supreme court decisions is j. When seeking to block a decision the hurdle is $r^{-1} = j^{-1}$. Additionally, the supreme court may act to declare a policy unconstitutional without external intervention given its valuation of decision rights l_B. When Agent o's preferences and the supreme court's preferences are aligned, the difficulty Agent 1 faces increases. To get the supreme court to uphold a policy decision, Agent 1 faces competition with Agent o (who wants the supreme court to reverse the policy), and Agent 1 has to overcome the utility supreme court justices derive from ruling against unconstitutional decrees.

To describe the equilibrium of this game, we determine whether Agent 1's valuation W exceeds the sum of justices' institutional commitment and Agent o's valuation V multiplied by r^{-1}.

(a) If $[(b_k + (V/m) + \varepsilon) \cdot ((j - 1m) + 1)] < W$, then Agent 1 offers $[(b_k + (V/m) + \varepsilon) \cdot ((j-1m) + 1)]$, Agent o offers nothing, and the policy is upheld.

(b) If $[(b_k + (V/m) + \varepsilon) \cdot ((j - 1m) + 1)] > W$, neither agent contributes and the policy is reversed.

2.A.3 Proofs

We define the SGPE of an extensive game with perfect information by means of optimal strategy profiles: The strategy profile s^* in an extensive game with perfect information is a sub-game perfect equilibrium if, for every player i and every history h after which it is player i's turn to move, $u_i(O_h(s^*)) \geq u_i(O_h(r_i, s^*_{-i}))$ for every strategy r_i of player i, where u_i is a payoff function that represents player i's preferences and O_h is the terminal history consisting of h followed by the sequence of actions generated by s after h (Osborne 2004: 166).

In a finite horizon game, as the one in Figure 2.A.5 below, the SGPE may be found more directly by using an extension of the procedure of backward induction. Note that the boxed numbers denote terminal histories; whereas, circled letters denote nonterminal histories.

2.A.4 Decree Path

The decree path ends with judicial review (nonterminal history X). There are two sub-games of length 1 (from top to bottom): $S^*_1(1) = \{\text{uphold}\}$, $S^*_2(1) = \{\text{uphold}\}$. Recall that each supreme court justice k values constitutionally established decision rights at $b_k \geq 0$. Agent o's optimal offer

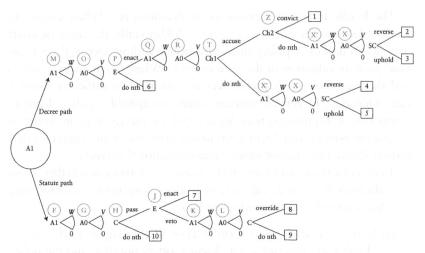

References: A1 = Agent 1, A0 = Agent 0, E = Executive, C = Congress, Ch1 = Chamber 1, Ch2 = Chamber 2, SC = Supreme Court. Circled letters identify non terminal histories; squared numbers represent terminal histories.

FIGURE 2.A.5. *Choice of legislative paths – terminal and non-terminal histories*

at nonterminal history X depends on the supreme court's level of institutional commitment b_k. Assuming it is 0, which would lead the supreme court to uphold the decree (by doing nothing), Agent 0's optimal offer at nonterminal history X is V, as the supreme court will reverse policy *x*, given this payment. Thus, the set $S^*(2)$ of strategy profiles consists of (V; reverse). This is the threshold Agent 1 must overcome. Given the set $S^*(2)$, Agent 1's offer of $[(b_k + (V/m) + \varepsilon) (j^{-1} m + 1)]$ is optimal at nonterminal history X'. The set $S^*(3) = \{[(b_k + (V/m) + \varepsilon) (j^{-1} m + 1)]$; 0; uphold\}. This set of strategy profiles is the SGPE of the judicial review sub-game.

The broader sub-game that follows incorporates impeachment (see Figure 2.A.7 below). Given the set $S^*(3)$, if the legislators' level of institutional commitment is 0, then Chamber 2's optimal action at nonterminal history Z is to do nothing. The set $S^*(4) = \{$do nothing; $[(b_k + (V/n) + \varepsilon) (j^{-1}n + 1)]$; 0; uphold\}. Before we can pay attention to Chamber 1's actions, we must analyze the sets of strategies that Chamber 1 confronts at nonterminal history T. The sub-game in which Chamber 1's move is first incorporates another sub-game that is equivalent to the judicial review sub-game described above. So, Chamber 1 faces two sets of strategies: $S^*(4) = \{$do nothing, $[(b_k + (V/n) + \varepsilon) (j^{-1}n + 1)]$; 0; uphold\} and $S^*(5) = \{[(b_k + (V/n) + \varepsilon) (j^{-1}n + 1)]$; 0; uphold\}. Note that $S^*(5) = S^*(3)$. In both

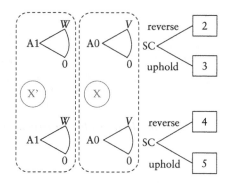

FIGURE 2.A.6. *Along the decree path, non-terminal histories X and X':
judicial review*

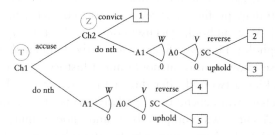

FIGURE 2.A.7. *Along the decree path, non-terminal histories Z and T:
impeachment and judicial review*

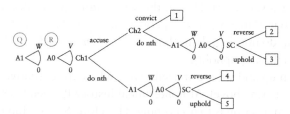

FIGURE 2.A.8. *Along the decree path, non-terminal histories R and Q:
impeachment – judicial review*

cases, the outcome is policy x, and in both, Chamber 1 receives no pay-off. Therefore, Chamber 1's optimal action at nonterminal history T is to do nothing. The set $S_1^*(6) = \{$do nothing; do nothing; $[(b_k + (V/n) + \varepsilon)(j^{-1}n + 1)]$; o; uphold$\}$ and $S_2^*(6) = \{$do nothing; $[(b_k + (V/n) + \varepsilon)(j^{-1}n + 1)]$; o; uphold$\}$.

The next step up along the decision tree leaves us at nonterminal history R (see Figure 2.A.8 above). Agent o's optimal action at nonterminal

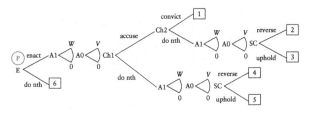

FIGURE 2.A.9. *Along the decree path, non-terminal history P*

history R is to make a twofold offer of V to Chambers 1 and 2 so that legislators will accuse and convict in the impeachment, which sustains policy
q (and ends the game at terminal history 1). At this nonterminal history,
the set of strategy profiles is $S^*(7) = \{$accuse; convict; $[(b_k + (V/n) + \varepsilon)$
$(j^{-1} n + 1)]$; V, o; uphold$\}$, $\{$accuse; convict; $[(b_k + (V/n) + \varepsilon) (j^{-1}n +$
$1)]$; V, o; uphold$\}$. However, $S^*(7)$ is a strictly dominated strategy. This
is so because knowing this, at nonterminal history Q, Agent 1's action
involves making a twofold offer directed to each of the chambers. Her
optimal strategy will depend on the relative costs of Chambers 1 and 2.
Ultimately, Agent 1 will compare both and choose $\min[(a_i^b + (V/n) +$
$\varepsilon),(b_k + (V/n) + \varepsilon)]$, determining whether the sub-game ends in terminal
history 3 or 5. It is her optimal action to offer o to Chamber 1 and $[(a_i^s +$
$(V/n) + \varepsilon)]$ to Chamber 2, or $[(a_i^b + (V/n) + \varepsilon)]$ to Chamber 1 and o to
Chamber 2 given $S^*(7)$. Hence, the set of strategy profiles $S^*(8) = \{$do
nothing; do nothing; o & $[(a_i^s + (V/n) + \varepsilon], [(b_k + (V/n) + \varepsilon) (j^{-1}n + 1)]$; o,
o; uphold$\}$, $\{$do nothing; do nothing; $[(a_i^b + (V/n) + \varepsilon)]$ & o, $[(b_k + (V/n) +$
$\varepsilon) (j^{-1}n + 1)]$; o, o; uphold$\}$.

One step up and we are at a sub-game where the executive moves first
(see Figure 2.A.9 above). At nonterminal history P, given $S^*(8)$, the executive's optimal action is to do nothing. Therefore, $S^*(9) = \{$do nothing; do
nothing; do nothing; o & $[(a_i^s + (V/n) + \varepsilon], [(b_k + (V/n) + \varepsilon) (j^{-1}n + 1)]$;
o, o; uphold$\}$, $\{$do nothing; do nothing; do nothing; $[(a_i^b + (V/n) + \varepsilon)]$ &
o, $[(b_k + (V/n) + \varepsilon) (j^{-1}n + 1)]$; o, o; uphold$\}$.

Given $S^*(9)$, at nonterminal history O, Agent o's optimal action is to
offer o, and at nonterminal history M, Agent 1's optimal action is to offer
Vt. This gives way to $S^*(10)= \{$do nothing; do nothing; do nothing; o &
$[(a_i^s + (V/n) + \varepsilon)], [(b_k + (V/n) + \varepsilon) (j^{-1}n + 1)]$; o,o,o; uphold$\}$, $\{$do nothing;
do nothing; do nothing; $[(a_i^b + (V/n) + \varepsilon)]$ & o, $[(bk + (V/n) + \varepsilon) (j^{-1}n + 1)]$;
o,o,o; uphold$\}$ and $S^*(11) = \{$enact; do nothing; do nothing; Vt, o &
$[(a_i^s + (V/n) + \varepsilon)], [(b_k + (V/n) + \varepsilon) (j^{-1}n + 1)]$; o,o,o; uphold$\}$, $\{$enact; do

FIGURE 2.A.10. *Along the statutory path, congressional decision to override or do nothing*

nothing; do nothing; $Vt, [(a_i^h + (V/n) + \varepsilon)] \& 0, [(b_k + (V/n) + \varepsilon) (j^{-1}n + 1)]$; $0,0,0$; uphold}. The set of strategy profiles $S^*(11)$ is the SGPE of the decree path.

To describe the SGPE of the sub-game subsuming the entire game shown in an extensive form in Figures 2.1 and 2.A.5, I first analyze the statutory path.

2.A.5 Statutory Path

This path ends with a game of congressional override. Using backward induction to describe the SGPE, we first look at the last sub-game and analyze optimal strategies.

There is only one sub-game of length 1 (Figure 2.A.11), and the set of strategies there is: $S^*(12) = $ {do nothing}. At nonterminal history L, Agent 0's optimal offer is zero (0). Thus, the set $S^*(13)$ of strategy profiles consists of {0; do nothing}.

Given the set $S^*(13)$, at nonterminal history K (see Figure 2.A.11 below), Agent 1's offer of $[(s_0 + h_0) V]$ is optimal; it has the capacity to attain an override that will secure policy x. Hence the set $S^*(14) = \{[(s_0 + h_0) V]$; 0; override}. This set of strategy profiles is the SGPE of the override sub-game.

The next sub-game incorporates the executive (see Figure 2.A.12 below). At nonterminal history J, the executive's optimal action is to enact (note that by doing nothing, policy is enacted by default). $S^*(15) = $ {enact; $[(s_0 + h_0) V]$; 0; override}. One step up and at nonterminal history H, congress' optimal action is to do nothing; $S^*(16) = $ {enact; $[(s_0 + h_0) V]$; 0; do nothing, override}. At nonterminal history G, Agent 0's optimal action is to offer 0, such that $S^*(17) = $ {enact; $[(s_0 + h_0)V]$; 0,0; do nothing, override}. At nonterminal history F, Agent 1's optimal action is to offer congress $(s + h) V$, such that congress will pass policy x, such that $S^*(18) = $ {enact; $[(s + h)V]$, $[(s_0 + h_0)V]$; 0,0; pass, override}.

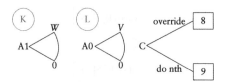

FIGURE 2.A.11. *Along the statutory path, non-terminal histories K and L: veto override*

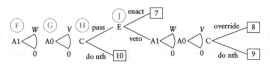

FIGURE 2.A.12. *Along the statutory path, nonterminal histories J, H, G, and F*

We finally arrive at the first step of the game, where the sub-game is equivalent to the game in Figure 2.1. Given the sets of strategy profiles $S^*(11) = \{$enact; do nothing; do nothing; Vt, o & $[(a_i^s + (V/n) + \varepsilon)]$, $[(b_k + (V/n) + \varepsilon) (j^{-1}n + 1)]$; o,o,o; uphold$\}$, $\{$enact; do nothing; do nothing; Vt, $[(a_i^h + (V/n) + \varepsilon)]$ & o, $[(b_k + (V/n) + \varepsilon) (j^{-1}n + 1)]$; o,o,o; uphold$\}$ and $S^*(18) = \{$enact; $[(s + h) V]$, $[(s_o + h_o) V]$; o,o; pass, override$\}$, Agent 1's optimal action at nonterminal history $\emptyset$ is to take the decree path. Hence $S_1^*(19) = \{$enact; do nothing; do nothing; Vt, o & $[(a_i^s + (V/n) + \varepsilon)]$, $[(b_k + (V/n) + \varepsilon) (j^{-1}n + 1)]$; o,o,o; uphold$\}$, $\{$enact; do nothing; do nothing; Vt, $[(a_i^h + (V/n) + \varepsilon)]$ & o, $[(b_k + (V/n) + \varepsilon) (j^{-1}n + 1)]$; o,o,o; uphold$\}$ and $S_2^*(19) = \{$enact; $[(s + h) V]$, $[(s_o + h_o) V]$; o,o; pass, override$\}$ is the set of strategy profiles that is the SGPE of the game.

TABLE 2.A.1. *Payoffs at terminal histories in Figure 2.1*

Terminal history	Legal decree	Illegal decree	Statute
1	A1: $[U(q) - Vt]$ Ao: $[U(q)]$ C: Ch1: $[0]$ Ch2: $[0]$ E: $[Vt + U$ (removal)$]$ SC: $[0]$	A1: $[U(q) - Vt]$ Ao: $[U(q)]$ C: Ch1: $\left[\sum_{i=1}^{n} a_i^b\right]$ Ch2: $\left[\sum_{i=1}^{n} a_i^s\right]$ E: $[Vt + U$ (removal)$]$ SC: $[0]$	n/a
2	A1: $[U(q) - Vt]$ Ao: $[U(q)]$ C: Ch1: $[0]$ Ch2: $[0]$ E: $[Vt]$ SC: $[0]$	A1: $[U(q) - Vt - [(a_i + (V/n) + \varepsilon)$ $(r^{-1}n + 1)]]$ Ao: $[U(q)]$ C: Ch1: $\left[\sum_{i=1}^{n} a_i^b\right]$ $((1/s) + 1)$ of Ch2: $\left[\sum_{s=1}^{n} a_i^s\right]$ $(1 - ((1/s) + 1)$ of Ch2: $[0]$ E: $[Vt]$ SC: $\left[\sum_{k=1}^{i} b_k\right]$	n/a
3	A1: $[U(x) - Vt]$ Ao: $[U(x)]$ C: Ch1: $[0]$ Ch2: $[0]$ E: $[Vt]$ SC: $[0]$	A1: $[U(x) - Vt - [(a_i^s + (V/n) + \varepsilon)$ $(r^{-1}n + 1)]_s] - [(b_k + (V/n + \varepsilon)$ $(j^{-1}n + 1))]$ Ao: $[U(x)]$ C: Ch1: $\left[\sum_{h=1}^{n} a_i^b\right]$ $((1/s) + 1)$ of Ch2: $[(a_i^s + (V/n) + \varepsilon)]$ $(1 - ((1/s) + 1)$ of Ch2: $[0]$ E: $[Vt]$ SC: $((1/j) + 1$: $[(b_k + (V/n) + \varepsilon)]$ $(1-((1/j) + 1))$: $[0]$	n/a
4	A1: $[U(q) - Vt]$ Ao: $[U(q)]$ C: Ch1: $[0]$ Ch2: $[0]$ E: $[Vt]$ SC: $[0]$	A1: $[U(q) - Vt]$ Ao: $[U(q)]$ C: $((1/h) + 1)$ of Ch1: $[(a_i^b +$ $(V/n) + \varepsilon)]$ $(1 - ((1/h) + 1)$ of Ch1: $[0]$ Ch2: $[0]$ E: $[Vt]$ SC: $\left[\sum_{k=1}^{j} b_k\right]$	n/a

(continued)

TABLE 2.A.I. *(continued)*

Terminal history	Legal decree	Illegal decree	Statute

5	A1: $[U(x) - Vt]$
	Ao: $[U(x)]$
	C: Ch1: $[o]$
	  Ch2: $[o]$
	E: $[Vt]$
	SC: $[o]$
		A1: $[U(x) - Vt - [(a_i^h + (V/n) + \varepsilon)$
		  $(r^{-1}n + 1)]_h] - [(b_k +$
		  $(V/n + \varepsilon)(j^{-1}n + 1))]$
		Ao: $[U(x)]$
		C: $((1/h) + 1)$ of Ch1:$[(a_i^h + (V/n) + \varepsilon)]$
		  $(1 - ((1/h) + 1)$ of Ch1: $[o]$
		  Ch2: $[o]$
		E: $[Vt]$
		SC: $((1/j) + 1$: $[(b_k + (V/n) + \varepsilon)]$
		  $(1 - ((1/j) + 1))$: $[o]$
			n/a

6	A1: $[U(q)]$
	Ao: $[U(q)]$
	C: Ch1: $[o]$
	  Ch2: $[o]$
	E: $[o]$
	SC: $[o]$
		A1: $[U(q)]$
		Ao: $[U(q)]$
		C: Ch1: $[o]$
		  Ch2: $[o]$
		E: $[o]$
		SC: $[o]$
			n/a

7	n/a	n/a	A1: $[x - (s + h)V - Vt]$ Ao: $[o]$ C: Ch1: $[Vh]$ Ch2: $[Vs]$ E: $[Vt]$ SC: $[o]$
8	n/a	n/a	A1: $[x - (s_o + h_o)V]$ Ao: $[x]$ C: Ch1: $[h_o V]$ Ch2: $[s_o V]$ E: $[o]$ SC: $[o]$
9	n/a	n/a	A1: $[q]$ Ao: $[q]$ C: Ch1: $[o]$ Ch2: $[o]$ E: $[o]$ SC: $[o]$
10	n/a	n/a	A1: $[x - (s + h)V - Vt]$ Ao: $[o]$ C: Ch1: $[Vh]$ Ch2: $[Vs]$ E: $[Vt]$ SC: $[o]$

3

Institutions and Institutional Commitment

The preceding chapter emphasizes the role of institutions and institutional commitment in explaining the choice of legislative instruments and policy. This chapter seeks to build a bridge to connect these concepts to the empirical work undertaken in the chapters that follow. While the role of institutions in affecting behavior and determining outcomes is fairly well established, the predominance of institutions has repeatedly raised skepticism among scholars of developing democracies. The reasons for this distrust are related to what Levitsky and Murillo (2005) term "institutional weakness," which they explain to be the result of diminished levels of stability and enforcement of institutions. They highlight an important condition regarding institutions, which is the extent to which their effects can be taken for granted.

Whereas in advanced democracies the rule of law is reasonably effective and established rules are most frequently observed, the same is not true in other environments. That rules are often questioned, circumvented, or utterly violated in polities undergoing severe regime transitions or civil war is a generally accepted claim. Yet it has not always been obvious that the same may be true for relatively stable political regimes that have been in place for a few decades. Nor has it been obvious that within those countries, different sets of institutions may vary in their characteristics (i.e., sets of rules structuring different aspects of a polity, such as the rules conforming the electoral system, which include not only the structure of the ballot, but also and importantly, nomination rules, whether primaries exist, and if so how they are carried out). The work of Levitsky and Murillo (2005) places the variation of institutions along this dimension on center stage.

A problem with claiming institutional weakness, however, is that one can easily fall into the temptation of assuming institutional effects away, a mistake of terrible theoretical consequence. It is often the case, within a given country, that while some institutions may be weak, others are strong; so strong, that they may be to blame for the lack of enforcement of the former (weak) institutions. What underlies institutional weakness is the lack of enforcement of those institutions.

The notion of *institutional commitment* brings these considerations to the fore. Yet, countering what Levitsky and Murillo propose, I claim that variation along stability and enforcement are not precise explanators of institutional weakness, at least not in the way they claim. For example, the weakness of the rules guiding the legislative process is to a large extent upheld by the reasonably stable and well-enforced rules that govern legislators' careers. The law-making rules themselves have also been fairly stable (at least as stable as most other rules in a newly established democracy). As for enforcement, the notion deserves further consideration. Of the two dimensions, enforcement seems to carry more explanatory weight since it is at the heart of compliance. But to say that a rule is not enforced leaves a great deal unsaid. Enforcement (and lack thereof) says little about the ultimate causes of strength or weakness. We can easily declare poor enforcement of a rule when the expected effects of that rule are not met, but this does not teach us much about the cause of its weakness or the locus of enforcement failure. In fact, following the literature on self-enforcing institutions (i.e., where no one has incentives to depart from the agreed-upon arrangement), one may argue that legislative rules are strong in this sense, as the outcomes, given the incentives that are in place, are quite stable (Weingast 2005).[1]

Despite this, a common misunderstanding is to identify the legislative process itself as being weak. I argue that the legislative rules themselves are not weak and devote the chapters that follow to try to show it. Weakness, or, more precisely, variations along a strength continuum, provides a poor characterization of institutional qualities. Where does the weakness of these rules rest? Are all the rules guiding the legislative process weak, or are some weaker than others? These questions urge us to probe further.

---

[1] The reference is to Barry Weingast's 2005 unpublished paper "Self-Enforcing Constitutions: With an Application to Democratic Stability In America's First Century," available on the author's website.

To move away from the notion of institutional weakness, I suggest avoiding characterizations of institutions themselves, and instead identify levels of *institutional commitment*, i.e., levels of willingness to enforce institutions (rules). The notion of institutional commitment identifies the actors responsible for enforcement, and provides a rationale for the variation along this dimension.[2] Actors (legislators, justices) endowed with decision rights over a process vary in the extent to which they are willing to defend their rights. The causes of that variation lay elsewhere, and are in many ways related to these actors' job security, which affects their time horizons and, consequently, their incentives to protect their decision rights.

The approach taken in this book seeks to further our understanding of the law-making process by focusing on the institutions that structure it, and by showing why there is variation in the extent to which those institutions affect outcomes. It is an effort to go beyond pointing out the culprits for legislative dislocation (be they instability, reelection rules, party rules, or others), and to make explicit not only the incentive structure, but also the specific way in which it affects the legislature.

3.1 ON RULES, HURDLE FACTORS, AND INSTITUTIONAL COMMITMENT

In Chapter 2, I described the choice of legislative instrument as a function of the allocation of decision rights (i.e., the rules), politicians' valuation of their rights, and external agents' valuation of policy. With my focus on the allocation of decision rights, I emphasize that a number of actors have prerogatives in the process. Furthermore, I stress that the way these actors (the executive, legislators, and supreme court [SC] justices) intervene in the legislative process is subject to variation across countries since different checks are put in place in each. Variations in override requirements or the veto prerogative alter the costs of the game substantially and merit consideration (Indridason 2011; Palanza and Sin 2014). In light of this complexity, to think merely about the strategic calculations of the executive, as most of the literature has done, seems to be an oversimplification.

---

[2] In contrast to Cox's (2016) notion of constitutional commitment, which is an attribute of policies, this book conceives institutional commitment as an attribute that politicians assign to decision rights. The notion seeks to explain why there may be variations in the enforcement of decision rights and, as in Cox's work, failure to prevent unilateral action by the executive as a result.

3.1.1 Hurdle Factors

The complexity of those rules is brought into consideration in Chapter 2 in a relatively simple way through the concept of hurdle factors, following Groseclose and Snyder (1996) and Diermeier and Myerson (1999). I use the concept as Diermeier and Myerson do, to quantify the level of difficulty brought into the legislative process by the different actors with decision rights. Hurdle factors increase with the number of actors participating in the process: If a single actor has the right to decide, say only the executive when enacting decrees, the hurdle factor is lower than if also a second actor, say a legislature, participates in the decision. Furthermore, if the legislature is bicameral, the hurdle factor will be higher still, reflecting the difficulty that a second chamber adds to the process. As the hurdle factor increases, so does the cost of enacting legislation. Different majority requirements either raise or lower the hurdle factor, and legislatures typically use different rules for different decisions. For example, if a legislature decides ordinary legislation by simple majority, the hurdle factor is lower than if a qualified majority of two thirds is required to pass that legislation. Systems with more complex allocations of decision rights, which incorporate more institutional actors to the process, present higher overall hurdle factors.[3] My theory suggests that the variation in these factors across countries leads to different choice scenarios when deciding policy change. This chapter describes how institutions enter my empirical analysis.

The fundamental point regarding hurdle factors in this chapter is that the rules that guide the legislative process contribute to the overall complexity and cost of enacting legislation, with some rules decreasing and others increasing these factors, as explained above. Assessment of the hurdle factors in the seven countries analyzed in Chapter 6 reveals that they are identical for six of those countries (Argentina, Brazil, Colombia, Ecuador, Nicaragua, and Peru). The exception is Chile, with a slightly lower hurdle factor. Decree authority seems to reduce those costs to the lowest possible, yet checks (i.e., rules placed along the process to guarantee other branches' decision rights) have the capacity to neutralize those

---

[3] As noted in the previous chapter, this notion bears similarity with Tsebelis' notion of veto players. The key difference is that in this book the true weight of hurdle factors is determined by politicians' valuation of the rules, i.e., their willingness to enforce them.

effects completely. The extent to which the checks are effective, however, varies considerably.[4]

3.1.2 Institutional Commitment

I have argued that the effectiveness of checks on the executive varies with levels of institutional commitment. I define institutional commitment as politicians' (legislators and supreme court justices) valuation of their decision rights, which determines their willingness to defend these prerogatives from violations by the executive. The more they value their decision rights, the more likely they are to defend those rights; conversely, where their valuation is low, the likelihood of enforcement declines.

The notion of institutional commitment rests on the assumption that politicians seek to maximize their gains while in office. For decision makers, this implies maximizing what they can gain through their decision rights. However, these benefits are subject to constraints: What or how much is at stake? How long will they be in possession of their prerogatives? What alternative courses of action are available? How are other actors expected to act? How do gains from the alternative courses of action compare? The responses to these questions vary with different institutional environments, that is, across different countries.

An important variable affecting their calculations is time.[5] The gains that legislators or justices can extract from their decision rights are different if they plan to be in possession of their decision rights for three years, as in Mexico, or to hold on to them for sixteen or more, as in Chile. Not only are they different because they will perceive the gains from being in office for a shorter period of time, they are different fundamentally because the nature of the game these individuals are playing is different.

---

[4] This resembles the point made by Cox (2016) about the effects of exporting British parliamentarism, which often do not lead to the same effects as those of the Glorious Revolution in England. Cox emphasizes that the overall constraint on the executive is determined by the weakest link, and countries that adopt many but not all the constraints of the English system that he analyzes may achieve a much lower level of executive constraint. The underlying causes in Cox and here, however, are different. Whereas Cox suggests that mere adoption of institutions determines constraints, I emphasize that only the commitment to enforce those institutions will impose true constraints.

[5] Remington (2014), when analyzing the use of decrees in Russia, gives a prominent explanatory value to time, arguing that political conditions affecting the legislative process vary with time: importantly, the timing of elections and the timing of the legislative process. Here, instead, time plays a role through its impact on politicians' expectations, which vary with their different temporal horizons.

The legislator who will likely be out of his legislative job in the next term (as is the case for most *diputados* in Argentina) is interested not only in maximizing what he can extract from his current decision rights, but, just as importantly, he is interested in maximizing his chances of getting the next job to which he aspires. A Lower House representative of the Argentine Congress reflects upon some drawbacks of legislators' short tenures in congress in a way that one can easily infer the incentive structure underlying what she describes:

"Lower House seats are but exchange tokens. Congress is not the place where one can make policy. Rotation is very high and when a national legislator leaves, because he hasn't been reelected, everything this legislator did during his tenure is lost, no memory of his work in Congress remains, and if he made progress in an area, this too is lost".[6] [Diputada interviewed in Buenos Aires, August 11, 2005]

Consider a legislator that sees no pre-established limitations on his reelection, and believes he can remain in his position for several terms. Next, consider another legislator who is quite convinced that she has extremely slim chances of staying in the legislature once her current term is up. Now imagine a decree has been enacted in violation of legislators' decision rights. While the first legislator will assess the immediate loss (resulting from deviation of external agents' contributions, visibility before his constituency, etc.), he will also evaluate the long-term consequences of allowing an encroachment on his rights and the losses that would accumulate over time. The second legislator, on the other hand, will focus on the short-term scenario, and as she does not expect to hold these decision rights in the future, she perceives no such thing as the accumulation of losses. These expected gains carry the seed of the first legislator's defense of his decision rights, as well as the second legislator's concession. In terms of institutional commitment, the first legislator has higher levels than the second.

That these considerations are, in fact, on legislators' minds is illustrated by the words of a Brazilian Lower House representative, which I transcribe immediately below. Brazilian legislators have intermediate

---

[6] "*Las diputaciones nacionales no son más que moneda de cambio. No es posible hacer política de Estado desde el Congreso. La rotación es altísima y cuando un legislador nacional se va, porque no renueva su banca, todo lo que este diputado hizo se pierde, no queda memoria de su trabajo, y si avanzó en un área, eso se pierde.*"

reelection rates, considerably lower than those of the United States, but higher than most other Latin American countries.

"So then, everything is improvised, everything is "jeitinho" (accomplished by circumventing the rules or social conventions), nothing is ever planned, one always responds to the moment, because I will not be here long. This gave way to a culture, which reflects upon the State. Each legislator, he is thinking about today. He is not thinking about tomorrow"[7] [Deputado interviewed in Brasilia, November 24, 2005]

The discussion on the determinants of institutional commitment is closely linked to a literature that discusses legislators' career motivations, briefly mentioned in Chapter 1. There, I said that this book assumes that the reelection motivation guiding analyses of US politics is not present across Latin American countries. While the electoral connection in the United States (Mayhew 1974) speaks of legislators' static ambition, other polities may confront incentives such that legislators' ambition is progressive (Schlesinger 1966; Rohde 1979; Samuels 2002), which goes hand in hand with political careers that have the legislature merely as a stepping stone in a succession of political positions.[8] This book claims that progressive ambition, i.e., an incentive structure that leads politicians not to see the legislature as a good place from which to work in politics, is associated to lower levels of institutional commitment. Progressive ambition leads to shorter tenures in congress and lower levels of institutional commitment by legislators. Static ambition is associated to higher reelection rates, and is, in turn, associated with higher levels of institutional commitment, as I have suggested above.

So variations in politicians' expectations regarding their tenure in office lead to different expectations regarding the benefits that will come from their actions in office. Institutional commitment introduces the idea that encroachment of decision rights that are essential to politicians' maximization of gains will be accepted only under certain circumstances, and they will not be tolerated otherwise. It is this variable that explains different outcomes in the presence of identical allocation of decision rights.

---

[7] "Então tudo é improvisado, tudo é o "jeitinho", nada é planejado, eu respondo sempre ao momento, porque eu não vou ficar mais aqui. Isso formou uma cultura, que reflete no Estado. O Parlamentar, ele está pensando no hoje. Ele não está pensando no amanhã." The deputado's identity is kept anonymous, as agreed before the interview.

[8] Work by Polsby (1968) also suggests that US legislators began to build careers in Congress only when Congress became an interesting enough place in the political scenario.

The description above suggests that the motivation behind levels of institutional commitment is far from principled. This book proposes that the defense of decision rights can stem from a self-interested calculation of gains.[9] Institutional commitment implies attachment to established decision rights that guarantee continued access to external resources. Legislators who seek to maximize the contributions that they receive from external agents (such as campaign contributions, organizational resources, votes, or bribes) are unlikely to abide when these contributions are diverted to other actors in violation of established rules.

3.1.3 Variation in Levels of Institutional Commitment

I have claimed that levels of institutional commitment vary across countries, and also within countries across issues. The variation across countries is a function of the different factors that affect legislators' and supreme court justices' expectations regarding how long they will remain in their positions, as explained in the previous section. Important in this regard are certain institutions, such as electoral rules and candidate selection procedures (which may be rules of the electoral system or rules established by parties), but also non-institutional traits such as historic levels of regime stability, among others. Variations of institutional commitment across countries enter my analysis at the comparative level, but they also form the basis for single-country analyses. This is so because I expect the overall level of institutional commitment of legislators and justices to determine the extent to which these actors will guard their decision rights in certain realms. This dimension of institutional commitment enables the predictions that at high levels of institutional commitment we expect never to see the enactment of decrees, and that at extremely low levels of institutional commitment (near or at zero) we expect never to see the enactment of statutes. However, most cases in Latin America fall somewhere in between, such that what we observe is a mix of decrees and statutes. Figure 3.1 presents this variation graphically.

Figure 3.1 presents the actual variation of reliance on decrees[10] in the seven countries for which data is available.[11] It suggests that beyond

---

[9] Yet note that self-interest and career concerns need not be contrary to constituents' preferences (Mayhew 1974; Arnold 1990).

[10] The level of reliance is measured as a ratio that is equal to zero when no decrees are enacted, and approaches one as the proportion of decrees increases.

[11] Nicaragua is excluded from the statistical analysis conducted later because of missing data for most independent variables.

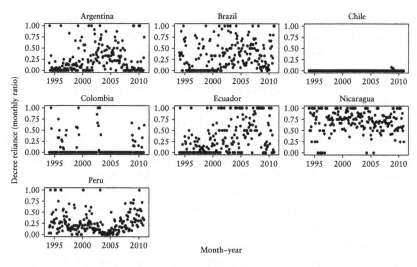

FIGURE 3.1. *Reliance on decrees, by month*
Source: Elaborated from multiple sources (See Appendix 3.A for details).

cross-country variation, an additional source of variation in the choice of decrees versus statutes emerges within each country. Within countries, the question of relevance becomes: under what conditions are statutes chosen over decrees? The response stems from the same factors used at the comparative level, and it is again a function of institutions, institutional commitment, and external agents' valuation of policy.

I claim that in the wide range of cases where we observe law making take place through a mix of decrees and statutes (countries that fall at intermediate levels of institutional commitment), politicians are more likely to defend their decision rights as expected gains rise. If what is at stake is negligible, legislators are better off going about other business, and they will not invest to enforce their decision rights against encroachment. This implies that given a certain level of institutional commitment in any given country, we expect legislators' willingness to defend their decision rights to vary with policy areas. If the stakes are high on a given issue, politicians will value legislating on that issue more than legislating on issues in which the stakes are low.

Evidence suggests that some key policies ignite high levels of dispute between the executive and the legislature, and often these are not policies about which interest groups are indifferent (as with bills establishing monuments or generating holidays). Mariana Llanos (1998) presents evidence that the executive met serious obstacles in the legislature during the privatization process that took place in Argentina during the 90s. Likewise, Etchemendy and Palermo (1998) show that labor reforms were trumped in Congress given the influence of labor unions in Argentina.[12]

As in the cross-country setting, the notion that institutional commitment varies across issues stems from the expected payoffs of legislating on different issues over time, and taking into account not only current but also future gains. To understand better why institutional commitment varies with issues, note that different policy areas entail different prospects of gain extraction. In my characterization, if a policy is uncontested, or if the level of contestation is very low, then the gains to be extracted from legislating in that area are low, which implies that legislators' willingness to defend their decision rights in those cases is low as well. If instead, the stakes around a given policy are high, because two very powerful (resourceful) groups are confronted on the issue, then the prospects for gains are high and institutional commitment is heightened, i.e., legislators will defend from encroachment.

Consequently, my argument emphasizes that different policy issues command different resources directly as a function of the confrontation between external agents competing for their preferred policy to prevail. This implies that we can reasonably expect high-stakes policy areas to be correlated with high levels of institutional commitment, and low-stakes policy areas to be correlated with low levels of commitment. The section that follows describes how these two dimensions of analysis are operationalized and integrated to the analysis.

3.2 EMPIRICAL IMPLICATIONS

This section seeks to make explicit the series of decisions and assumptions I make when bringing the theoretical model presented in Chapter 2 to bear on the evidence. Theories serve multiple purposes, among which further theoretical inspiration is not of small importance. Yet, if theories are to serve practical purposes, they must enable adequate testing and refuting.

In this section, I propose a way to test the theory presented in the previous chapter. The predictions drawn from the theory are numerous, and they are listed in Chapter 2 as predictions (a) through (f). This chapter, and those that follow, focus on the subset of predictions that are directly

---

[12] Latin American newspapers are plagued with periodic accounts of this dynamic, lending additional support to this approach.

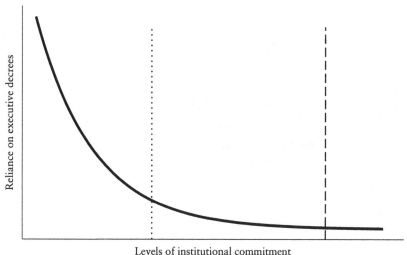

y-axis: Reliance on executive decrees

x-axis: Levels of institutional commitment

FIGURE 3.2. *Institutional commitment and decree reliance*
Source: Author's own elaboration.

relevant to the question of levels of reliance on decree authority and the choice between legislative instruments, namely predictions (b) and (c), in Chapter 2.

The first of these two predictions claims that the frequency of decrees is a function of institutional commitment such that (a) at low levels of institutional commitment we expect more unconstitutional decrees than otherwise, (b) when institutional commitment is lowest (i.e., equal to zero), we should expect enactment of decrees (regardless of their constitutionality), and (c) critical values of institutional commitment exist beyond which statutes are preferred to illegal decrees.[13] The second prediction is that statutes are the legislative instruments of choice, if and only if enacting the policy by decree is unconstitutional *and* institutional commitment is high enough that unconstitutional decrees become more expensive than statutes. In sum, I argue that there is an indirect relation between levels of institutional commitment and levels of reliance on decree authority, holding hurdle factors fixed, as suggested in Figure 3.2.

This figure seeks to convey how reliance on decrees is associated with levels of institutional commitment. For identical allocations of decision rights, countries have different values along the institutional commitment axis, and we can locate countries on different ranges along the curve in

[13] Chapter 6 tests these predictions.

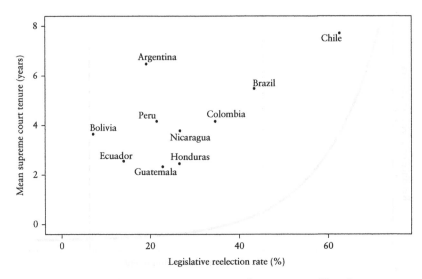

FIGURE 3.3. *Supreme Court tenure and experience of legislators*
Source: Elaborated from multiple sources (See Appendix 3.A for details).

Figure 3.2, depending on legislators' and supreme court justices' levels of institutional commitment. This allows us, in turn, to develop expectations regarding levels of reliance on decrees. The dotted and dashed lines seek to partition the space such that on the curve we may differentiate combinations of low levels of institutional commitment and high reliance on decrees, to the left of the dotted line, and combinations of high levels of institutional commitment and low reliance on decrees to the right of the dashed line. Because an institutional commitment scale does not exist, the exercise here is merely theoretical. The graph does not lend insight into the causal mechanisms highlighted above. Instead, it offers guidance into empirical expectations.

Figure 3.3 above is an empirical exercise. Using indicators of the two factors affecting institutional commitment highlighted above, legislators' and supreme court justices' job security, I establish a proxy for institutional commitment.

Figure 3.3 plots the average experience of legislators in their jobs against tenure of supreme court justices for nine Latin American countries with constitutional decree authority (Henisz 2000; Pérez Liñán 2011). The figure presents the location of the countries along an imaginary positive correlation line, with Chile at its upper right end and Bolivia and Ecuador close to its lower left end. If we take that imaginary line as providing levels along a continuum of institutional commitment, Bolivia and

Ecuador would be assigned relatively low levels, whereas Chile would receive the highest mark.

I use this rough indicator of levels of institutional commitment to locate the countries on the theoretical curve presented in Figure 3.2 above. Although I make no claims regarding the scale of the x-axis in Figure 3.2, it is fairly straightforward that Chile would fall on the higher end of the axis, quite possibly to the right of the dashed line, and, conversely, Bolivia and Ecuador to the left of the dotted line; all others would fall somewhere in between.

The prediction stemming from Figure 3.2 is that at high levels of institutional commitment, we expect policies to be enacted primarily by statute. That is precisely the observation in Chile, where only two decrees have been enacted by CDA since democracy was re-established in 1990. As levels of institutional commitment fall, reliance on executive decrees grows. To maintain emphasis on the cases discussed above, Argentina's location to the left of the dotted line says little in terms of just how often decrees are chosen over statutes there, but it suggests that on average it is quite often. We expect Brazil to rely on decrees less heavily than Argentina, based on this simple indicator of institutional commitment.

These implications are of direct applicability to the comparison across countries carried out in Chapter 6. The empirical analysis at that level is fairly straightforward, and requires knowledge of the allocation of decision rights in the legislative process to establish hurdle factors, and knowledge of levels of job insecurity of legislators and justices to establish levels of institutional commitment.

Regarding external agents' valuation of policy, we expect external agents to be equally vested in attaining their preferred policies across countries, and to put their resources to use equally. This is true at least in terms of using their resources toward achieving politicians' support for their preferred policies. So, although they may be more inclined to use those resources in one way than another in a given country, the underlying point remains that they are putting their resources to use to promote a policy, and that aspect does not vary across countries. So this variable is kept in the background in the comparative analysis, affecting motivations in a constant way. Chapter 6 tests the claims just presented.

When shifting attention to specific countries, the predictions stated above take different, and in some sense more precise, formulations. Assuming we know the level of legislators' and justices' institutional commitment (as derived from turnover rates), we hold these levels of institutional commitment fixed within different ranges: high, intermediate, and low. Given that the theory presented earlier predicts that at particularly high and low levels of institutional commitment, we expect particularly low and high levels of reliance on decrees, respectively, it makes sense to evaluate the theory at intermediate levels of institutional commitment, as this is where interesting variation emerges. By holding levels of institutional commitment fixed, and evaluating the choice game using specific allocations of decision rights in specific countries, we are in position to derive implications regarding the choice of decrees versus statutes that are specific for that level of institutional commitment and that specific allocation of decision rights. Changes to that allocation, usually in the form of constitutional amendments, are taken into account to assess the effect of changes in the rules. This is part of the exercise carried out in Chapters 4 and 5.

In countries with high levels of institutional commitment, we expect the enactment of statutes over unconstitutional decrees, and we expect only constitutional decrees to be enacted; this is so because at high levels of institutional commitment the cost of enacting unconstitutional decrees is higher than the cost of enacting statutes. When institutional commitment is lowest (i.e., equal to zero) we should expect enactment of decrees always, regardless of their constitutionality. At intermediate levels, between these extremes, we expect frequent, though not exclusive, enactment of unconstitutional decrees.

Yet, in addition to this, I have argued that different policy issues trigger institutional commitment more or less. High-stakes policy issues are more likely to lead to the defense of decision rights than low-stakes policy issues, as I have explained above. This effect is least likely to show in countries with low levels of institutional commitment since the cost of buying off legislators and justices is lower and decrees are simply always more likely (be they constitutional or not). In turn, the effect becomes more and more relevant as levels of institutional commitment rise. At very high levels of institutional commitment, decrees never occur and statutes are enacted always.

At the country level of analysis, I am able to summarize the predictions from Chapter 2 into two fundamental hypotheses, which are formulated as follows:

H1: Highly contested policy issues are enacted by statute.

H2: Uncontested policy issues are enacted by decree.

I test these claims by analyzing the choice of decrees versus statutes in countries that represent different levels of institutional commitment.

Brazil is an example of how the choice plays out at intermediate levels of institutional commitment, whereas Argentina represents a case of much lower (albeit above zero) commitment to institutions. Chile, where levels of institutional commitment are higher, is not analyzed in depth because, among other reasons, CDA has not been used at all in Chile during the current democratic period and thus we have no variation on the dependent variable.

3.3 EMPIRICAL ANALYSIS

In the chapters that ensue, the focus is placed on the analysis of the determinants of outcomes. This section provides the template used for analysis in Chapters 4 and 5, where I carry out within-country analyses. Details for the cross-country analysis vary to some extent, and are presented in more detail in Chapter 6.

Before moving on to explain the analysis carried out in Chapters 4 and 5, on Brazil and Argentina, respectively, a brief note on case selection. Testing the implications of the theory within countries requires selecting countries with sufficient variation in outcomes that it may be carried out. Most countries in the sample provide variation on the dependent variable, such that emphasis was placed on the main explanatory variable for the selection of the cases. While several countries show intermediate levels of institutional commitment as measured by supreme court tenure and legislative reelection rates (see Figure 3.2 above), these are not direct measures of the variable. Working with proxies of institutional commitment forces us to rely on additional knowledge of the cases as portrayed in the literature. Argentina and Brazil are probably the two most studied cases in Latin America and the specialized literature supports what the correlation shown in Figure 3.2 suggests, i.e., that the level of institutional commitment in Brazil is likely higher than in Argentina, despite the characterization of both as cases where legislators have progressive ambition (Jones et al. 2002; Samuels 2002). Reelection rates of legislators are higher in Brazil, tenure of supreme court justices is longer, and Brazil has not suffered from court-packing as has the Argentine Supreme Court, as the work of Chavez (2003), Helmke (2005), Iaryczower, Spiller and Tommasi (2002), Kapiszewski (2005), Scribner (2004), among others, suggests. Therefore, the case of Brazil allows testing the theory at a well-established intermediate level of institutional commitment, while the case of Argentina suggests lower levels of institutional commitment, possibly leading to higher overall prevalence of decrees. Relatively high levels of institutional commitment are present only in Chile among the countries analyzed in the book, yet carrying out in-depth analysis of the case is neither possible nor necessary as the very lack of variation in outcomes confirms the theoretical predictions made in this book.

For the analysis carried out in Chapter 4 for Brazil and Chapter 5 for Argentina, I construct the dependent variable as the dichotomous choice to enact decrees or statutes. The variable CHOICE takes the value 1 when a decree is chosen, and 0 when a statute is chosen.[14] Conceptually, this dichotomous choice is a measure of the enforcement of decision rights. Each time a policy is decided, whether by decree (1) or statute (0), legislators and supreme court justices are taking a stance on the enforcement of their decision rights in that specific case.

For the cross-national analysis carried out in Chapter 6, the dependent variable takes the form of a ratio, DECREE RELIANCE, which is the proportion of all decrees divided by the sum of all decrees and congressional statutes, $DR = d/(d+s)$, where d is the number of decrees enacted and s is the number of statutes. Taking values between zero and one, in the statistical analysis carried out in Chapter 6 it is calculated monthly, although its yearly values are also used in figures.

Testing the hypotheses presented above requires creating variables that measure both institutional variables and levels of institutional commitment. I present those variables next.

3.3.1 Independent Variables

3.3.1.1 *Proxies for Institutional Commitment*
Unfortunately, we are unable to observe institutional commitment directly. I have argued that we can infer overall levels from indirect measures such as turnover rates and other factors affecting job security, and I have explained why job security is of relevance to levels of institutional commitment. In the case of Chapter 6, since the main source of variation is cross national, I am able to rely on levels of rotation and reelection of politicians to construct proxies for institutional commitment. I also suggested that institutional commitment gets ignited more, and more often, when the stakes are high, that is, when the resources to be gained

---

[14] One might conceptualize this choice as including a third category: to do nothing. Measuring such a category would require including all bills that did not pass. Unfortunately, this is not possible, because there is no record of the planned executive decrees that were not enacted.

are abundant. I rely on this to create a proxy for levels of institutional commitment for Chapters 4 and 5. In what follows I explain how I constructed proxies for each of those two levels of analysis.

Proxies for Cross-Country Analysis. I have argued that we can infer politicians' overall levels of institutional commitment in each country by looking at indirect measures, such as reelection rates, and I have explained why job security is relevant to levels of institutional commitment. Chapter 6 uses the fairly conventional variables LEGISLATIVE RE-ELECTION and SUPREME COURT ROTATION or SUPREME COURT TENURE as proxies for the variation in institutional commitment across countries. LEGISLATIVE REELECTION is the percentage of legislators who were also legislators in the immediately preceding period. SUPREME COURT TENURE measures the average tenure of all justices on the Supreme Court or Constitutional Tribunal[15] in years, each year. SUPREME COURT ROTATION measures the proportion of justices who are removed on a yearly basis. For the same purpose, I also propose an INSTITUTIONAL COMMITMENT INDEX (ICI), which is a way to estimate the joint effect of institutional commitment playing out through the two branches of government charged with checking the executive. I created the index by rescaling LEGISLATIVE REELECTION and SUPREME COURT ROTATION into a common range (between 0 and 50) and then adding the value of each, such that the resulting variable ranges from 0–100. This index simplifies the interpretation of the results, while also capturing the joint effect of the two variables.

Proxies for Within-Country Analysis. Within any given country, policy areas are not equal in the resources they can mobilize, and some policy areas are more likely to generate higher levels of competition between agents with divergent policy preferences. These, I argue, are the areas that trigger higher levels of institutional commitment, because the gains to be made are higher. In this way, a correlation is established between types of policy issues, and levels of institutional commitment.

To test these claims, I construct for each country a set of variables identifying policy issues, which I classify into broader policy areas. These broader areas are then classified into three different categories (high,

---

[15] The term supreme court is used for simplicity, but this variable refers to tenure of supreme court justices as well as justices on constitutional tribunals. It captures tenure in the organization deciding the constitutionality of acts by the other branches (i.e., decree enactment). Countries place this responsibility with the supreme court or with a constitutional tribunal.

low, and political rights), depending on their ability to generate resource-mobilizing confrontation. The process is as follows:

- Step One: Identification of Policy issues

I code the policy area reported by the source[16] for each piece of legislation and produce a list of these policy areas. These issues are usually presented at a higher level of generality than the title of each piece of legislation, but still convey some detail regarding their specific matters. The final number and content of issues in each country is highly driven by the legislation enacted in each case, and varies considerably between countries.

- Step Two: Sorting into Policy Areas

Analysis of the list produced in step one reveals that the particular issues fit conventional policy areas (such as taxation, health policy, social policy, labor policy, social security, foreign affairs, trade policy, economic policy, financial policy, criminal law, civil law). I assign the items into these broad policy areas, adding areas to the list as needed. Given the nature of this process, the final list of policy areas may, but need not, be the same for all countries where one carries out this classification.[17]

- Step Three: Classification into Levels of Contestation

I create three categories – high, low, and political rights – to represent different groups of policies. I evaluate the policies on their relative capacity to provoke opposing views and contestation. When analyzing battles around policy decisions, different policy areas generate very different levels of conflict and contestation. Some policy areas present clearly differentiated groups defending conflicting views. I argue that when this is the case, the opposing groups tend to mobilize plentiful resources to promote their preferred policy (in the form of organizational resources, paid publicity, media coverage, and direct money contributions, among

---

[16] The sources used to collect bills and statutes were, SICON (Portal Legislação), Casa Civil da Presidência da República and Secretaria-Geral da Mesa do Senado in Brazil, and Dirección de Información Parlamentaria, Honorable Cámara de Diputados de la Nación in Argentina.

[17] The final number of areas considered in each country varies. The final list is provided within the context of each country chapter. As those chapters reveal, the total list includes 48 areas in Brazil and 52 in Argentina. While some of the categories may be grouped into broader ones (for example, I proceeded by including different industries in the industrial policy category in Argentina, but I kept some industries separate in Brazil), this difference does not affect results, as should become clear from the explanation of step three.

others). I refer to these policy areas as being high stakes. Other policy areas tend to be less confrontational, either because there is consensus on the matter or, more likely, because only one group is resourceful enough to promote its views. I refer to these policy areas as low-stakes. "High" and "low" refer not to the substantive importance of the policy under consideration, but to the gains that are at stake for lawmakers, which are high in the former case and low in the latter. I acknowledge that there is a subset of policies that affect political rights that are undoubtedly high stakes for lawmakers, but do not fit the pattern of external-agent promotion. While these policies are enacted almost exclusively using statutes (as my theory would predict high-stakes policies to be), they have the power to artificially inflate the effect of high-stakes policies. I create a separate category, political rights, to include these cases. After carrying out the classification, all pieces of legislation are classified as high-stakes, low-stakes, or political rights. Details of the construction of variables HIGH and LOW are included in the Section 3.A.2 in the Appendix to this chapter.

3.3.1.2 *Institutional Variables*

The effect of hurdle factors is most useful when comparing across institutional settings, as in Chapter 6. It is not directly tested in Chapters 4 and 5. Instead, the allocation of decision rights across the three branches is taken into account to generate predictions of expected behavior given the specific allocation. Some institutional effects, however, are tested directly in Chapters 4 and 5. In particular, I introduce indicator variables to account for changes in the allocation of decision rights, to assess whether the change in the rules significantly affects outcomes. Different variables are created in each country to account for these changes: EC32 in Brazil, which identifies observations passed after constitutional amendment No. 32 of 2001 in Brazil; CONSTITUTIONAL REFORM 94, which identifies observations enacted after the constitutional reform of 1994 in Argentina; and DNU COMMITTEE which identifies observations passed once the Bicameral Committee charged with approving or rejecting decrees was created in Argentina.[18]

Another institutional effect that we can test is that of the enforcement of the exclusion of certain policy areas from CDA. I construct the variable EXCLUDED CDA separately in each dataset to identify the policy

---

[18] Chapters 4 and 5 present more information regarding these variables.

areas that each constitution excludes from CDA in each case, as the areas excluded are different in Argentina and Brazil.[19] Ideally, we would not observe any decrees in areas excluded from CDA. However, as this book claims that the existence of rules *per se* does not ensure compliance with those rules, the variable serves as an indicator of enforcement. The expectation is that bills on policy areas excluded from decree authority should reduce the likelihood of decrees. Details regarding the construction of the variable for each country are included in each country-chapter.

3.3.1.3 *Economic Context Variables*

As described in Chapter 1, a prominent approach to the analysis of decree authority in Latin America has focused on the economy and factors related to economic crises. To test the effects of these factors, I include a set of economic variables that are the standard measures used in the literature. In both country analyses, I include INFLATION and ECONOMIC PACKAGE[20] to account for the alleged increase in decree enactment when hyper-inflationary crises strike, and emergency economic measures are taken by decree. While I include CURRENCY FLUCTUATION in Brazil to account for variations in the price of the Brazilian currency with respect to the US dollar, I do not include the variable in Argentina given the extended period of time during which Argentina artificially maintained parity between the two currencies. The distorting effect of this policy, as its termination gave way to the profound economic crisis of 2001, suggests it is better to exclude the variable from the analysis. To compensate for this absence in the case of Argentina, I include instead 2 different variables: COMMODITY INDEX and PUBLIC EXPENDITURES. The first is intended to capture the effect of international swings in food commodity prices, which are expected to affect Argentina's economy. Likewise, PUBLIC EXPENDITURES seeks to capture the effect of economic stimulation set off by public spending. Specific considerations of relevance to each measure, as well as the sources used in each case, are presented in the methodological Appendix included in each chapter.

[19] See Table 3.A.1 in Appendix 3.A for a detail of the areas excluded from CDA in each country.
[20] This variable is an indicator equal to 1 in months when the executive introduced a major stabilization package. Details regarding its construction are provided in the appendices of Chapters 4 and 5.

3.3.1.4 Political Context Variables

Theories of delegation, as well as unilateral action theories, have produced persuasive if contradictory claims regarding the conditions under which we should expect the executive to take on a greater role in the lawmaking process. I include a host of political context variables to account for the effects of parties, popularity, the timing of elections, and other time-specific variables that may explain the variation in the choice between decrees and statutes. Some of the variables used to test these effects are identical in both countries, such as DIVIDED GOVERNMENT, PRESIDENTIAL POPULARITY, and HONEYMOON. In other instances, I include variables that vary between Brazil and Argentina; however, the variables try to capture similar phenomena.

Because partisan coalitions have received great attention in the Brazilian legislature due to the highly fragmented nature of its party system and the virtual impossibility of single-party majorities, a series of measures have been developed to address these issues in Brazil that are not warranted in Argentina. I include LEGISLATIVE SUPPORT developed by CEBRAP,[21] and CABINET SIZE, CABINET COALESCENCE, and CABINET MANAGEMENT created by Octávio Amorim Neto (2002). No equivalent measures exist in the Argentine context.

Also, in order to capture some of the specificities of the cases, in each country I control for specific effects associated to the different presidencies, I control for the TRANSITION period between the prior constitutional regime and the one that took effect after Constitutional Amendment 32, and for the introduction of the presidential REELECTION clause that in Brazil originated in a separate constitutional amendment, and can therefore be accounted for separately.

The chapters that follow seek to test the theory laid out in the previous chapter through the lens provided in this one. The details and sources used in the construction of each of the variables mentioned here are found in the corresponding chapters.

---

[21] This variable, created by CEBRAP, is the percentage of legislators following the vote recommendation (*encaminhamento*) of the government's party coalition leader.

3.A APPENDIX: COMPLEMENTARY ANALYSIS AND SOURCES

3.A.1 Descriptions of Cases

TABLE 3.A.1. *Matters excluded from CDA, four cases*

Argentina[a] (DU)	Brazil (MPs)	Chile	Peru[b] (DNUs)
– penal	– nationality	– only places	All matters
– taxation	– citizenship	limit on	excluded, other
– electoral	– political rights	spending (2%	than
– political parties	– political parties	of budget	– economic and
	– electoral law	allocation)	financial, but
	– penal law		within these,
	– penal process		taxation is
	– civil process		excluded
	– organization of		
	Judiciary and		
	Public Service;		
	career and		
	guarantees to		
	members		
	– pluri-annual		
	budgets		
	– budgetary		
	process		
	– budget		
	– additional and		
	supplementary		
	credits (except		
	art 167 § 3)		

Sources: Bronfman Vargas and Martinez Estay (2005), Câmara dos Deputados da República Federativa do Brasil (2005), Landa Arroyo and Velazco Lozada (2005), Quinzio Figuerido), Zavalía (2001).
[a]CDA was not in the constitution prior to the 1994 Reform.
[b]CDA had no excluded areas in the 1979 Constitution.

3.A.2 Coding High and Low

The classification into these categories is bottom-up, that is, it is based on consideration of the specific issues (the specific subset in each country, available upon request), not on the connotation that ascribed policy areas may have. In order to distinguish between high and low-stakes policy issues, I ask a set of questions and code responses to these questions either o (negative) or 1 (affirmative). The analysis refers to conditions broadly prevalent between 1988–2007. Responses are based on an unstructured survey of the literature. The questions are as follows:

(1) Can we identify at least two agents with opposing interests on this issue? [o, 1]
(2) What resources does agent #1(#2) command?
   I. Is #1(#2) well organized?   [o, 1]
   II. Does #1(#2) have mobilization power?   [o, 1]
   III. Is #1(#2) wealthy?   [o, 1]

If the response to question (1) is negative, the policy area is coded "low," and no further question is asked. If the response to (1) is affirmative, the researcher moves on to question (2) and its components. If both sides to the issue have at least one affirmative response, the policy issue is coded "high." If this is true for only one group (or neither), it is coded "low."[22]

3.A.3 Country Sources of Data for Variables

The variable DECREE RELIANCE is calculated as the ratio of decrees to total legislation, calculated according to the following equation: dr = (decrees/(decrees+statutes)). Sources of decrees and statutes by country:

Argentina: DIP, Cámara de Diputados, HCN;

Brazil: SICON, Senado Federal http://legis.senado.gov.br/sicon/#/basica

Chile: Biblioteca del Congreso Nacional www.leychile.cl/Consulta/homebasico

Colombia: www.presidencia.gov.co/prensa_new/decretoslinea/ and http://web.presidencia.gov.co/leyes/archivo.htm;

Ecuador: www.lexis.com.ec/website/content/servicio/esilec.aspx

---

[22] Regarding ideology: In classifying policy areas into *high* and *low*, ideological divides are not taken into account. While ideological positions can give way to considerable preference divergence, the evidence regarding Brazil suggests that policy decisions are not made on an ideological basis (Desposato 2006; Zucco 2009). Zucco (2009) shows that while legislators in Brazil acknowledge the location of parties on the ideological spectrum in ways that are consistent through time, congressional votes on policy decisions do not coincide with ideological preferences. In their analysis of roll-call votes in the Argentine Lower Chamber, Jones and Hwang (2005) claim that distributive incentives easily dominate ideology and party reputation. I acknowledge that inclusion of other countries in the analysis may warrant reconsideration of this point.

Nicaragua: www.asamblea.gob.ni/index.php?option=com_wrapper& view=wrapper&Itemid=360;

Perú: www.congreso.gob.pe/ntley/LeyNumePP.htm

Legislative Reelection: percentage of re-elected legislators in the Lower Chamber, calculated after elections. Sources by Country:

Argentina: www.diputados.gov.ar/

Bolivia: www.oep.org.bo/, Tribunal Supremo Electoral 1997–2002 and 2002–2005, http://americo.usal.es/oir/legislatina/ for the period 2005-2010, and www.diputados.bo/ for the period 2010-2015.

Brazil: www2.camara.leg.br/deputados/pesquisa, and checked against Legislatina

Chile: www.elecciones.gov/.cl/, and www.camara.cl/

Colombia: http://web.registraduria.gov.co/; www.congresovisible.org/ and www.camara.gov.co/portal2011/

Guatemala: http://americo.usal.es/oir/legislatina/; www.congreso.gob .gt/, and http://200.12.63.122/gt/diputados.asp

Honduras: http://americo.usal.es/oir/legislatina/; www.congresona cional.hn/, www.revistazo.com/ene/doc1.html/ and http://voselsoberano .com/;

Nicaragua: http://americo.usal.es/oir/legislatina/, and www.asamblea .gob.ni/

Perú: http://americo.usal.es/oir/legislatina/, and www.congreso.gob .pe/; www.jne.gob.pe/; http://blog.pucp.edu.pe/fernandotuesta/files/2000- 2001%20Congresistas.pdf.

Supreme Court Tenure: Annual average tenure of Supreme Court or Constitutional Tribunal. Source: Dataset by Lara-Borges, Castagnola and Pérez Liñán (2012).

4

Reinstatement of Congressional Decision Rights

Brazil

Lawmaking in Brazil has made the limelight repeatedly due to what the literature has portrayed as the executive's ever-increasing use of *Medidas Provisórias* (MPV). As in other countries in the region, lawmaking by executive decree routinely trumps the congressional path to policymaking. Intended for use under dire circumstances, executive decrees have become a regular part of policymaking. This concentration of legislative power in executive hands seems to contradict the founding principles of presidential systems by altering the logic of checks and balances. By sidestepping congress in its fundamental legislative role, a key aspect of democratic representation is undermined, with consequences for the quality of policy and democracy.

Scholars of Brazil have approached the analysis of decrees – and more generally, policymaking – as a problem fundamentally pertaining to the executive's sphere of action. They posit that the president has an agenda, and the questions of relevance are whether and why she chooses to carry it out through the use of decrees rather than congressional statutes. Most of these studies are framed within the tenets of delegation theory, acknowledging that congress affects the enactment of decrees in several ways. Despite differences in the details, a consensus exists that what determines the frequency in use of decrees is the political context, with legislative support for the president playing a crucial role. However, when subjected to empirical scrutiny, political factors do not appear to have affected the frequency of decrees in systematic ways throughout the past two decades.

A fundamental limitation of the established literature is that it has fallen short of laying out a causal mechanism that can explain variations in the use of decree authority. Theoretical elusiveness spills over to the generation of hypotheses, ultimately leaving us with loosely specified tests and puzzling results. My analysis takes off where prior work remains inconclusive: What do legislators – and politicians in general – have to gain from enacting policies? By highlighting the motivations behind politicians' behavior, we gain insight into the fundamental tradeoffs underlying the choice of decrees versus statutes, a decision that is at the heart of policymaking in many countries.

In previous chapters, this book has set the basis for the analysis presented here. While Chapter 2 provides a parsimonious theory to explain the choice of decrees versus statutes, and Chapter 3 lays out how such a theory may be tested, this chapter tests this theory using a novel dataset of decree and statute enactment in Brazil. I provide an institutional explanation of reliance on decree authority while pointing to the conditions under which institutions fail to be enforced.

Briefly, my argument suggests that the choice to enact policies through decrees or congressional statutes is determined by the rules that govern the legislative process (decision rights), and, importantly, by politicians' valuation of those rules (institutional commitment). Although decision rights are set by the constitution, politicians' valuation of their rights, and their willingness to defend them from encroachment, depend on the gains they can extract from the legislative process. As put by a representative from the Brazilian Lower Chamber (Câmara dos Deputados) who I interviewed in November 2005:

"That also happens regarding legislative bills, because to the extent that nothing important comes through the legislature, who will owe me any favors? If I make privatizations happen, say, through the executive, that volume of interests will not come through me, so how can I place myself tomorrow, in the future, in a position to request electoral contributions, to be able to do things? So of course, that is an important factor in the process."[1] (Deputado interviewed in Brasilia, November 24, 2005)

Chapter 3 argues that the gain politicians can extract from the legislative process is fundamentally a function of job security, that is, their

---

[1] *"Isso também se dá na questão de projeto de lei, porque na medida em que nada importante passa pelo Legislativo, quem me deverá favores? Se eu faço privatizações passarem, é ... digamos assim, pelo Executivo, esse volume de interesses não vai passar por mim, como é que eu me situo amanhã, depois no cenário pra pedir contribuições eleitorais, pra poder fazer ... então claro, esse é um fator determinante do processo."* The deputado's identity is kept anonymous, as agreed before the interview.

expectation as to how long they are to remain in their jobs. In Brazil, this expectation stands at an intermediate level. Despite the fact that legislators in Brazil have been characterized as having progressive ambition (Samuels 2002), which provides incentives to pursue political careers beyond the hallways of the national congress, legislators' reelection rates are at intermediate levels for the region. Additionally, Brazilian Supreme Court justices enjoy reasonable levels of confidence that they will not be arbitrarily removed and that the composition of the court will not be politically manipulated.[2] This suggests that levels of institutional commitment are intermediate, following the presentation in Chapter 3. And at intermediate-to-high levels of institutional commitment we are able to draw the implication that when the prospects for gains are high, one expects policies to be enacted by statute; when those prospects are low, one expects enactment by decree.

The remainder of this chapter proceeds as follows. Section 4.1 reviews the literature on decree authority in Brazil and its fundamental findings, taking issue with some assumptions and approaches. Section 4.2 presents my own theoretical approach and draws implications for the analysis of Brazil. Section 4.3 presents the empirical analysis through a set of regressions. Section 4.4 draws conclusions.

4.1 DECREE AUTHORITY IN BRAZIL: MEDIDAS PROVISÓRIAS

Studies analyzing executive decree authority in Brazil are quick to note the country's history of executive dominance, and that the use of *medidas provisórias* stems from that tradition (Figueiredo and Limongi 1997; Power 1998; Merlin Clève 2000; de Abreu Junior 2002). This justification also figures prominently in government officials' discussions of concentration of power in presidential hands during interviews I conducted over the years.[3] While acknowledging that historical precedent, this chapter

---

[2] When asked about the stability of Supreme Court justices in Brazil, government officials interviewed in 2006 were firm in their opinion that politically motivated removal of members of the *Supremo Tribunal Federal* (STF, Supreme Federal Tribunal) was unthinkable. One high ranking congressional advisor declared that it was far more likely for presidents to be impeached, as presidents are part of a political struggle from which STF justices are removed. Chapter 6 discusses job security in different countries.

[3] Fieldwork for this chapter took place over the course of several years and different visits to the capital city of Brasília: November and December 2005, September 2006, and November 2012.

asserts that in recent years legislators have taken steps to reinstate their decision rights.

The Constitution of 1988 endows the executive with extensive legislative power, but it also manifests an underlying concern for the limits to these prerogatives. Decisions to lock-in certain policies by including them in the constitution itself, or to establish a specific type of law (*leis complementares*) to regulate certain policy areas and specific articles of the constitution, bear witness to this concern. The executive has undoubtedly gone to great lengths to stretch its own decision rights, but congress has reacted, proposing amendments to the constitution that more clearly draw the boundaries. Constitutional Amendment 32 (EC32), adopted in 2001, is commonly interpreted as a reform aimed at limiting the use of MPVs and their re-issuing by the executive. It may be understood more broadly as a move by the legislature to specify and reinstate its decision rights.

Early analyses of executive decrees in Brazil were concerned with the frequency of MPVs and their re-issuing by the executive (Figueiredo and Limongi 1997). It was clear that re-issuing decrees was at odds with the spirit of the constitution, and this attracted scholarly attention as well as several failed attempts at constitutional reform. Although the Constitution of 1988 established that MPVs would expire if not approved by congress within thirty days, it did not explicitly forbid the executive to re-issue MPVs once they expired. In 1989, President Sarney used the ambiguity in the text to his advantage and began to reissue MPVs (Figueiredo and Limongi 1997), a practice that became the *modus operandi* until Constitutional Amendment 32 was passed on September 11, 2001.[4]

This much-awaited amendment of article 62 of the Brazilian Constitution came to fruition toward the end of President Fernando Henrique Cardoso's second term. The reform put an end to the continual re-issuing of MPVs and limited the scope of matters on which presidents could issue decrees. Since then, when a president enacts an MPV, it immediately goes to Congress, which may reject it, amend it, or approve it as is. The new constitutional text establishes that if Congress does not act, an MPV's validity can only be extended *once* after sixty days of its

---

[4] The practice of reissuing MPVs began in 1989 when President José Sarney reissued MPV 29 (via MPV 39) once the period for a congressional decision had expired. This inaugurated a practice that was to stick, with presidents going as far as to reissue MPVs rejected by Congress. President Collor de Melo started this practice by reissuing MPV 185 (MPV 190), which congress had rejected by a close vote. Recall that President Collor de Melo resigned his position when faced with the specter of impeachment.

enactment, for an equal period of time. Forty-five days after its enactment, if congress has not given consideration to the MPV, it enters a special procedure known as *regime de urgência*, which displaces all other issues until a vote on the MPV is taken.[5] Importantly, MPVs come into effect immediately once enacted, even if a decision by congress is pending.

Tables 4.1 and 4.2 present the yearly frequency of statutes and of MPVs, respectively. Table 4.1 summarizes information on the approval of statutes (*leis ordinárias*) between 1988 and 2010. It distinguishes between projects originated in congress and those originated in the executive, and within the latter category, between MPVs and ordinary bills.[6] Table 4.2 presents information regarding the issuing of MPVs in the period starting in 1988 and leading up to EC 32/2001, as well as the trends inaugurated that year.

The distinction between original MPVs and re-issues (*reedições*, columns two, three, and four) illustrates why there was such concern regarding the re-issuing of decrees. Amendment 32 was intended to put an end to that practice, and it immediately succeeded at the task. The enactment of original MPVs, however, remained at levels comparable to the ones prevalent before the amendment (although a simple t-test reveals the difference in means before and after EC32 is statistically different from zero, the mean being higher in the latter period). And although pundits and laymen alike expected the number of decrees to decline with the amendment, my theory suggests that nothing in the amendment suggested that reliance on decrees would diminish. I return to this point in Section 4.3.

While Tables 4.1 and 4.2 present descriptive trends of the frequency of MPVs and statutes, Figure 4.1 contrasts the use of each instrument throughout the period.[7]

Early work on MPVs interpreted their enactment as a form of delegation that benefited members of congress by enabling policies that they favored while sparing them the costs linked to the policies (Figueiredo and Limongi 1997). There was also support for the notion that congress had delegated decree authority in 1988 to improve upon the experience with the decreto-lei,[8] without foreseeing that the executive would

---

[5] For an analysis of the constitution and is amendments, see Alexandre de Moraes (2006).

[6] Note that the MPVs reported in Table 4.1 are those that were passed into law during each year, not those enacted by the executive that year. So the yearly MPV figures in Table 4.1 and 4.2 need not coincide. Also, note that totals in these tables reflect a longer time period than the period of the sample used for regressions. I provide further detail of the sample used for regressions in Section 4.3.

[7] Note the negative correlation of −0.33 for the period 1988–2007.

[8] The *decreto-lei* was the type of executive decree established by the Constitution of 1937 (Estado Novo) and used until it was replaced by the *medida provisoria* in the Constitution

TABLE 4.1. *Congressional Statutes by Initiator, Brazil 1988–2010*[a]

Year	Executive MPV	Executive other	Congress	Other institution	Total
1988	11	41	15	1	68
1989	78	136	37	25	276
1990	66	76	19	5	166
1991	12	180	19	27	238
1992	7	158	22	35	222
1993	19	163	33	10	225
1994	44	35	45	7	131
1995	42	169	60	10	281
1996	16	127	31	3	177
1997	32	111	25	1	169
1998	38	106	24	10	178
1999	37	100	36	2	175
2000	17	166	28	6	217
2001 (total)	50	126	51	3	230
2001 (before EC32)	43	36	28	1	108
2001 (after EC32)	7	90	23	2	122
2002	54	126	50	7	237
2003	55	86	49	7	197
2004	69	152	23	8	252
2005	20	93	59	4	176
2006	59	64	44	10	177
2007	50	91	54	3	198
2008	15	116	119	9	259
2009	11	107	151	21	290
2010	10	73	99	9	191
TOTAL	812	2602	1093	223	4730

[a]Leis Ordinárias.
Source: SICON, Portal Legislação.

make abusive use of the prerogative (Power 1998). In an optimistic vein, Figueiredo and Limongi suggested that legislative prerogatives granted the executive the ability to induce cooperation from members of her coalition, and thus were the key to understanding law making and the

---

of 1988. While the two legislative instruments are similar, they bear some differences. *Medidas provisórias* require relevance *and* urgency to be valid, *decretos-lei* only required urgency *or* public interest, and *decretos lei* were limited in terms of the scope of decisions that could be made (importantly, spending decisions could not be made by decreto-lei), and they did not need congressional intervention of any type to become effective.

TABLE 4.2. *Medidas Provisórias, Brazil 1988–2010*

Year	Total	Original	Re-issued with amendments	Re-issued w/o amendments[a]	Passed into law	Rejected
1988	15	15	0	0	11	1
1989	95	83	2	10	80	6
1990	170	87	20	63	74	9
1991	11	8	2	1	7	1
1992	11	10	1	0	7	2
1993	96	47	12	37	28	0
1994	405	91	37	277	40	0
1995	438	30	86	322	45	0
1996	648	39	69	540	15	0
1997	716	33	71	612	31	0
1998	807	55	228	524	15	1
1999	1018	45	108	865	33	0
2000	1103	25	114	964	18	0
2001 (before EC32)	511	34	457[b]		45	1
2001 (after EC32)	20	20	–	14	18	2
2002	82	82	–	80	66	12
2003	58	58	–	56	57	0
2004	73	73	–	70	66	4
2005	42	42	–	42	34	3
2006	67	67	–	65	60	3
2007	70	70	–	70	60	2
2008	40	40	–	36	35	3
2009	27	27	–	26	24	0
2010	42	42	–	42	30	1

[a]After EC32, re-issuing *without* amendments implies a 60-day extension of the expiration date.
[b]With and without amendments.
– Cells with no possible cases.
Source: Casa Civil da Presidência da República (2017).

absence of institutional paralysis in Brazil's contemporary democracy (Figueiredo and Limongi 2000).

Following Figueiredo and Limongi's contribution, Amorim Neto and Tafner (2002) proposed that varying coalition formation styles imply

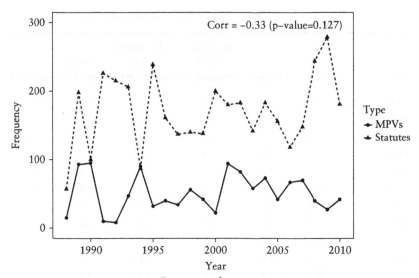

FIGURE 4.1. *Decrees and statutes, 1988–2010*
Source: SICON and Casa Civil da Presidência (2017).

different relationships between the executive and the legislative branches, and this ultimately affected the use of MPVs, their reissuing, and presidential initiation of bills in congress. It is most encouraging to find that Amorim Neto and Tafner's work is structured around the idea that the enactment of decrees and statutes are intrinsically related processes. They found that cabinet coalescence was inversely related to the enactment of original MPVs, but positively related to the number of bills sponsored by the executive and to the re-issuing of amended MPVs. But, although they acknowledge throughout that decrees and statutes are related outcomes, their analysis treats the outcomes as conforming to different processes. Later work by Amorim Neto (2006) again takes on the question regarding the choice of decrees versus statutes, albeit with focus on the president's strategies to attain his policy agenda.

More recently, two articles by Pereira, Power, and Rennó (2005, 2008) provide systematic analyses of the enactment of decrees *vis à vis* statutes during two distinct periods and posing two different if related sets of questions. They, too, emphasize the element of choice between legislative instruments, and refer to legislators' strategic calculations and utility-maximizing behavior. Politicians' motivations, however, are only loosely nested into their analysis, a point I return to briefly. Pereira, Power, and Rennó (2005) analyzed MPVs during 1988–1998 in an effort to adjudicate between the two prevailing explanations of the use of decrees:

unilateral action theory and delegation theory. They find inconsistent support for both theories, and, interestingly, that their analysis is highly sensitive to time and context,[9] which leads them to conclude "there is no one-size-fits-all" theory of presidential action. I return to this point below.

In their 2008 piece, Pereira, Power, and Rennó engage a different question, regarding how institutional change affects delegation of power and unilateral action in new democracies. They tackle the question by analyzing the effect of EC32 of 2001 on the number of decrees enacted monthly in Brazil. As in their previous work on decrees, their results are mixed. They hypothesize that (a) Amendment 32 would have a negative effect on the frequency of decrees, and (b) following the amendment, the frequency in the use of decrees would be closely associated to ongoing levels of congressional support for the president (since decrees can no longer be reissued, and congress *must* vote on them). Their findings suggest that the reform effectively did have an effect on the frequency of decrees, but that the effect is positive, not negative. And of the five variables they use to assess the effect of the political context, they find that only presidential popularity is significant and positive; other effects were not statistically significant. The fact that none of the explanations – economic, temporal or coalitional – can account for the variation in the use of MPVs during 1995–2005 suggests we have a puzzle in search of an explanation.

Taking these studies as a whole, several caveats are in order. It is difficult to establish causation from the measures that the diverse set of authors propose, especially given the loose fit between the empirics and the theoretical accounts they claim to test. Legislative support for the president, ultimately measuring concurrence in voting patterns, implies that the executive and a group of legislators are pursuing the same policy goal within the legislature. But it does not necessarily follow from that observation that this level of concurrence determines the executive's choice of decrees or statutes. Although we observe concurrence, we do not observe what has caused it: whether concurrence in voting patterns is caused by overlapping preferences, exchange of political favors, or outright bribes remains unclear. Work by Zucco (2009) focuses precisely on this point.[10] Congruence, I argue, is a result of the influence exerted by

---

[9] They find that the 1988–98 sample, when divided into two periods, shows different trends for each, which suggests that their choice of independent variables may not be adequate to explain the puzzle at hand, or that a key explanatory element is missing from their analysis.

[10] Zucco (2009) presents an account of the motivations guiding politicians' legislative behavior. Zucco's work focuses on a question that is related, though different, to the one

interest groups, but cannot itself predict the choice of legislative instrument as the influence is also present yet unobservable when decrees are enacted. We should expect this measurement to fare poorly as a predictor of the choice of legislative instrument. Likewise, cabinet size and its representation in congress may facilitate the policy process by making some coalitions more likely than others, but we need to know more about politicians' motivations to attribute causation to these variables.

Although this book concurs with much of the literature that has argued that institutions alone cannot explain political behavior in certain environments (Levitsky and Murillo 2005), and, specifically, with those arguing that levels of reliance on decrees cannot be explained by the mere existence of decree prerogatives (Carey and Shugart 1998; Pereira, Power, and Rennó 2008), it forcefully opposes the omission of institutional determinants.[11] While acknowledging the shortcomings related to dismissing non-institutional components of explanations, this chapter emphasizes the importance of maintaining institutions as a crucial part of the explanation, and argues against explanations of decree authority that are oblivious to institutional considerations.

4.2 CONFRONTING THE BRAZILIAN PUZZLE FROM A DIFFERENT STANDPOINT

I posit that the theory developed in Chapter 2 can help bring together claims in the preexisting literature and make sense of mixed results. My theory relies on some of the basic assumptions of delegation theories, and it clarifies otherwise contradictory observations by explicitly laying out assumptions and implications. Whereas previous analyses are well served by assuming utility-maximizing behavior on the part of politicians, it is useful to say more about what such maximization implies. Chapter 2 explicitly lays out politicians' utility functions, such that we gain a more precise picture of the behavior to expect from politicians, and, in turn, make clear predictions regarding the frequency of decrees.

If, as argued in Chapter 2, politicians derive their policy preferences from those of external agents (i.e., interest groups), we are encouraged to move away from the paradox imposed by assuming delegation à la

---

tackled in this book, and is highly compatible (and complementary) with the account I present herein.

[11] Note that the very powerful Chilean executive does not issue this type of decrees at all, providing evidence in support of these claims.

McCubbins and Schwartz (1984) while simultaneously assessing legislative choices as the sole function of the executive. From this perspective, the strategies and calculations of all politicians with prerogatives over the legislative process are taken into account. The puzzle no longer revolves around the choices presidents make, but around politicians' (including legislators and justices), and lobbyists' strategic calculations.

"Sometimes you make a political assessment and you find that if you go ahead with a medida provisória there will be reactions coming from society, you will face public outcry, so you need to wait and let things develop more, you see ... So what determines the choice for statutes? A need to avoid a strong retaliation in the case of a medida provisória ..."[12] [Deputado interviewed in Brasilia, November 24, 2005]

In the case of Brazil, given that the model is sensitive to changes in the allocation of decision rights, some expectations vary with the changes introduced by EC32. Most importantly, because after the reform all MPVs are forced to go through congress, legislators' levels of institutional commitment no longer affect the cost of enacting decrees.[13] But the game described in Chapter 2 emphasizes the role of the Supreme Court, given its review prerogatives. Supreme Court justices' levels of institutional commitment, unaffected by EC32, remain a concern. Constraints in terms of the policy areas enabled for enactment by decree affect the Supreme Court (*Supremo Tribunal Federal* or STF), which may overturn legislation, depending on its level of institutional commitment, l.[14]

Thus, both before and after Amendment 32, the choice of legislative instrument varies with levels of l. Following Chapter 2, the rules in place before EC32 determine four scenarios:

---

[12] "*Às vezes você faz uma avaliação política e acha, que se você baixar medida provisória vai haver reações da sociedade, é ... você vai ter uma grande gritaria, tem que esperar amadurecer mais, tá certo? ... O que determina a opção pela lei? A necessidade de você não ter uma represália muito dura, quando se tratar de uma medida provisória...*" The deputado's identity is kept anonymous, as agreed before the interview.

[13] In fact, assuming that statutes and decrees can be enacted with equal immediacy, Chapter 2 leads us to conclude that following the approval of EC32 legislators became indifferent between the two instruments. However, if we assume that policies may be enacted by decree to produce immediate effects that need not be sustained in time, legislators' concern for systematic exclusion from these negotiations would bring institutional commitment back to play.

[14] The STF has established through rulings that it will not go against political assessments of emergency; thus, it will not accept claims of unconstitutionality based on that prerequisite.

(a) At the lowest level of institutional commitment ($l = 0$), MPVs are preferred to statutes. They are enacted and re-issued indeterminately. Congress does not intervene, nor does the STF.

(b) When institutional commitment is positive but below the critical level at which the costs of decrees and statutes are identical ($c > l > 0$),[15] MPVs are preferred to statutes. The enactment and re-issuing of MPVs requires support from blocking coalitions in congress and the STF.[16] We should not observe explicit congressional approval of MPVs.

(c) When institutional commitment is positive and equal to the value c at which statutes and decrees impose equal costs ($c = l > 0$), external agents are indifferent between statutes and valid MPVs[17] (equivalent costs), but they prefer statutes to illegal MPVs, such that

(c.1) valid MPVs are approved with explicit congressional support,

(c.2) MPVs need not be re-issued, and

(c.3) unconstitutional MPVs are not enacted,

(d) When institutional commitment is high ($l > c$),[18] statutes are always preferred to illegal MPVs.

After Amendment 32, the effective enforcement of hurdle factors led legislators to be indifferent between decrees and statutes, as their payoffs do not vary with the choice of instrument. But STF calculations remained unaltered, and levels of l continue to determine the choice.[19] The distinction between valid and unconstitutional decrees remains relevant:

(a) If a policy makes for a constitutionally valid MPV, external agents are indifferent, and, absent concerns of immediacy, can choose one or the other instrument.

(b) If a policy makes for an unconstitutional MPV, despite legislators' indifference, forward looking external agents will need to secure a blocking coalition in the STF. Therefore,

(b.1) If institutional commitment is at its lowest ($l_j = 0$), MPVs do not imply additional costs, and agents remain indifferent.

(b.2) If institutional commitment is positive ($l_j > 0$), so is the cost of securing STF support, making statutes preferable.

---

[15] Below a certain critical level c, as suggested in Chapter 2.

[16] Congressional members are brought into the process to avoid reactions in defense of their decision rights (such as rejection of the MPV or impeachment of the president).

[17] The hurdle factor of passing a decree in congress is identical to that of passing a statute; decrees provide the additional advantage of immediate enactment. For simplicity, however, I assume both can be enacted with the same celerity given appropriate support.

[18] I.e., the enactment of statutes is cheaper than the passage of decrees.

[19] In particular, MPVs on subject matters explicitly excluded from CDA.

4.3 HYPOTHESES AND DATA

To assess the claims above, I have put together a dataset comprising all MPVs and statutes enacted between 1988 and 2005, a sample which is representative of the full period since Brazil's most recent democratization. The sample includes 8,910 observations.

In the previous section I proposed a theory of the determinants of the choice between decrees and statutes, and derived empirical implications. This section is devoted to testing the empirical validity of those claims. The choice between decrees and statutes is an indicator of the level of enforcement of decision rights. Politicians' decision to enforce their rights over the legislative process is made on a case-by-case basis, whenever a decision is made to enact a policy by statute or decree. The dependent variable in this chapter, CHOICE, is an indicator taking the value 1 each time an MPV is enacted, and the value zero each time a statute is enacted.[20]

A fundamental claim that I make is that the choice between decrees and statutes varies with levels of institutional commitment, and that the latter is not constant across policy issues. As stated above, higher-stakes policy issues that ignite competition between external agents will make legislators (politicians, more generally) want to defend those decision rights that lead to greater contributions, while the opposite is true of low-stakes policy areas. Consequently, we can expect high levels of correlation between levels of institutional commitment and policy issues.

Although we cannot observe levels of institutional commitment directly, we can observe the subject matter of each piece of legislation. Given the assumed correlation, this chapter and the next use the policy issues reported for each piece of legislation as proxies for levels of institutional commitment. With each piece of legislation's policy issue in hand, one can establish whether the policy in case belongs to the high-stakes or low-stakes category. In line with my claims, high-stakes policy issues are correlated with higher levels of contestation between interest groups, and, therefore, high levels of commitment to the prerogatives that provide access to the resources available. Likewise, low-stakes legislation should reflect low levels of commitment.

Based on the propositions above, I present the following hypotheses:

H1: Highly contested policy issues are enacted by statute.

H2: Uncontested policy issues are enacted by decree.

---

[20] All statutes are included, regardless of origin. I include bills that were successful only. The decision to assign the value 1 to MPVs and 0 to statutes is trivial.

To test these hypotheses, I grouped the 674 policy areas reported in congressional records into 48 broad categories, and classified each of these categories into either "high" or "low" stakes policy areas, which are proxies for high and low levels of institutional commitment. The variables HIGH and LOW are indicators, and I expect HIGH to diminish the likelihood of decrees, while LOW should have a positive effect on the choice.[21]

Among these policy issues, those affecting political rights are certainly high-stakes affairs (coincidentally legislated exclusively by statute). However, because these issues do not fit into the high stakes/low stakes divide in the sense that my model proposes (as confrontations led by external agents, not politicians), I placed them under a separate category, POLITICAL RIGHTS, and observations classified as such are neither classified as "high" or "low." POLITICAL RIGHTS is thus the omitted category of issues.[22]

As laid out previously, the other main determinant of the choice between decrees and statutes is the allocation of decision rights. This independent variable is fundamentally institutional, and refers to the set of rules that determines both the actors that intervene in the process and the rules that guide their voting rights. Additionally, constitutions may include clauses that enable the enforcement of the rules. While institutional variables are most relevant for cross-country comparisons, because they tend to remain constant within individual countries, the amendment to the rules enacted in Brazil in 2001 enables testing some institutional effects as well.

In this regard, I seek to establish whether the changes in the rules introduced through EC32 had an effect on the choice of decrees versus statutes.[23] The main proclaimed purpose of the amendment was to eliminate the reissuing of decrees (a problem with which this chapter does not take issue). This proclaimed purpose was met immediately. And, although reformers also proclaimed that the overall level of reliance on

---

[21] Refer to Appendix 4.A for details on the construction of these variables.

[22] An alternative construction is to include these observations under "high" and control for issues excluded from CDA (a control I include regardless). Such an approach would clearly strengthen the effect of the main independent variables, HIGH and LOW. By taking the three-category approach, I provide a more stringent measure of my variables of interest, increasing the difficulty of the test.

[23] Without denying the endogenous nature of changes in the rules introduced by the same actors who are later involved in the choice of decrees versus statutes, I do not find that this precludes the possibility of analyzing the effects of this reform on the choice, given the goal of the reform was to end re-issues, something not analyzed here.

decrees would decrease, the rationality behind such expectation merits scrutiny. I argue that legislators' rights over the legislative process were reinstated by the requirement that all decrees be approved by congress to remain effective. Note that the enactment of MPVs *per se*, if approved by congress, does not violate congressional decision rights, as legislators are part of the decision-making process. Moreover, because legislators' payoffs from enacting decrees and statutes are equivalent under the new setting, we have no reason to assume that legislators would prefer *fewer* decrees. In fact, while Pereira, Power, and Rennó argue that the amendment implied agency loss for members of congress, I hold the opposite view, i.e., that agency was gained. Therefore, whether the amendment should have caused an increase or a decrease in levels of reliance on decrees is under debate. I constructed an indicator variable, EC32, to test these claims. The indicator is equal to 1 if the piece of legislation was enacted after the new institutions put forth by the amendment were in effect, and 0 otherwise.

As I proposed in the previous section, we expect the effect of institutional commitment to hold equally before and after the amendment. This is so because even if, under the new institutional setting, legislators need not worry about encroachment on their decision rights, the Supreme Court's willingness to react against violations to the rules remains unchanged. Therefore, the same hypotheses apply before and after EC32; the main difference is that after the reform they apply to the choice of unconstitutional MPVs only (recall that before the reform, due to the possibility of indefinite re-issues, even constitutional decrees often did not go through congress).

To account for the exclusion of issue areas from CDA (a clear determinant of the constitutionality of decrees) I created the indicator variable EXCLUDED CDA, which equals 1 when the reported policy area of the piece of legislation is excluded from CDA. We expect the effect of EXCLUDED CDA to be negative, that is, that the rule that excludes certain issues from enactment by decree would decrease the likelihood that policies on those issues be enacted by MPV.

Stemming from a similar concern, I created the indicator TAXES to account for the effects of a set of constitutional rules that explicitly prevent tax policy from being enacted by ordinary statutes (*leis ordinárias*). The Brazilian constitution establishes that the most significant tax policies are to be enacted by *lei complementar*, while explicitly enabling the executive to modify tax rates by decree. Given these prerogatives, a huge proportion of the laws included in the category "taxes" are precisely changes in tax rates enacted by decree, while a substantial part of what the legislature has preserved for congressional enactment is excluded here because it was passed as *lei complementar*. In fact, 15 out of the 70 *leis complementares* enacted between 1988 and 2007 are tax policies – a striking 21 percent of all *leis complementares*, while the remaining 79 percent is distributed among twenty-nine different policy areas.

Regarding alternative explanations, previous work on the use of MPVs pays close attention to factors related to the economic and political contexts. To assess the competing claims, I include economic and political variables in my analysis. I replicated the set of variables used by Pereira, Power, and Rennó to control for the political context. PRESIDENTIAL POPULARITY is a measure taken from public opinion polls, and is expressed as a percentage of positive appraisal of presidential performance; LEGISLATIVE SUPPORT for the president is a measure created at CEBRAP,[24] and is expressed as the percentage of legislators following the vote recommendation (*encaminhamento*) of the leader of the governmental coalition in the Lower Chamber.[25] Two variables and an interaction are used to get at the president's capacity to manage the coalition on the floor, Amorim Neto's (2002) measures of CABINET SIZE (which is expressed in terms of the percentage of the seats held in the Câmara by parties represented in the presidential cabinet) and CABINET COALESCENCE (a rate ranging between 0 – no correspondence between legislative seats and ministerial payoffs – and 1 – perfect correspondence; following Pereira, Power, and Rennó I multiply the rate by 100 for ease of computing), and the interaction of the two, CABINET MANAGEMENT, which tries to convey the notion that the utility of the nominal size of the coalition is conditional on the proportionality with which coalition parties are represented in the cabinet. All of these variables are lagged in the analysis.

---

[24] See Appendix 4.A for details of the sources and operationalization of variables.

[25] Note that my criticism of this variable is that observed variations in levels of support for executive policies tell us nothing about what causes the variation. While Pereira, Power, and Rennó use it to indicate variations in the relationship between the president and congress, and as such, a predictor of the extent to which the president will rely on decrees, I argue that it cannot predict the choice between decrees and statutes (recall that decree enactment also requires high levels of congruence, even if before EC32 such congruence was not observable). If what underlies congruence is interest group pressure, one may feel inclined to use this variable as a measure of such pressure, but that would be problematic because this measure is a monthly average, while I argue that interest group pressure varies with policy issues. In this sense, increased congruence would be measuring a higher proportion of high-stakes policies under consideration in congress, but this can hardly predict the choice of one legislative instrument over the other, especially since there are no temporal constraints to the choice.

Following Pereira, Power, and Rennó, I control for additional contextual variables that measure diverse political factors, which may have an impact on the choice between decrees and statutes. ELECTIONS, an indicator that takes the value 1 during the three months preceding presidential elections, seeks to account for the change in pace that may accompany presidential campaigns, when lame-duck presidents may alter their legislative behavior, while legislators may feel less obliged toward the outgoing president, two dynamics which could affect the choice of legislative instruments. TRANSITION, an indicator of the weeks preceding the date EC32 went into effect, is used to control for the increase in MPV enactment that preceded the amendment: during those six weeks. 72 decrees were enacted that would not be subjected to the new approval rules and would be effective indeterminately. LULA, an indicator for President Lula da Silva's time at the *Palácio da Alvorada*, controls for any leadership characteristics associated to Lula, who has been accused of increasing the use of MPVs in an unprecedented way. HONEYMOON, an indicator for the first three months of presidential office, controls for any patterns altered as a consequence of the favorable public opinion presidents enjoy during the beginning of their terms. Finally, REELECTION is an indicator that represents the constitutional amendment of 1997 to allow presidential reelection, controls for the fact that presidents that face the possibility of reelection may make a different use of their prerogatives.

The economic context, which has been less unstable in recent years, provided an excellent justification for the enactment of MPVs during junctures of dire economic crises. Decrees were used to stabilize the economy and to implement shock measures. I control for variation due to economic developments by using, also following Pereira, Power, and Rennó, common measures of INFLATION (INPC, the monthly accumulated changes in consumer prices), and CURRENCY FLUCTUATION, expressed as monthly percent change in the value of Brazilian currency with respect to the US dollar. ECONOMIC PACKAGE, an indicator coded 1 in months during which there was a major stabilization package introduced by the executive, is also intended to tackle the economic context.

4.3.1 Empirical Testing

The sample I consider includes all MPVs and leis enacted in 1988–2005[26], a total of 8,910 observations, of which 2,920 are statutes and 5,990 are

---

[26] Note that Tables 4.1 and 4.2 present data until 2010. However, the statistical analysis includes observations until 2005 as other variables were only collected for that period.

MPVs. The large number of MPVs is due to the multiple instances in which certain MPVs are counted because of the practice of re-issuing expired decrees. The analysis, however, counts each MPV only once (i.e., MPVs that are repetitions of expired MPVs are excluded), pulling 5,107 MPVs out of the sample. The reduced sample has 3,803 observations, of which 2,920 are statutes and 883 are decrees.[27]

The analysis of the data[28] is carried out using maximum likelihood estimation. Given the limited nature of my dependent variable, and the inherent element of choice, I implement a logit model. The dichotomous nature of my dependent variable merits further justification, since the legislative process I seek to represent may in fact be interpreted as a three-pronged process (enact a decree, enact a statute, do nothing), which would call for different coding of the choice and a different model.

The theory I lay out makes a point of the relevance of this question by design, by placing a strong status quo bias on the policy enacting process. Nothing happens, that is, no policies are enacted, unless an agent seeking a change in policy has the resources to overcome the impetus of the agent that stands in defense of the status quo. Acknowledging this, one may choose to measure the choice to do nothing and a way to do so would be to gather information on all proposals, successful or not – in other words, to take into account the dogs that don't bark. This chapter suggests that decisions to do nothing imply that agents have concluded that they lack sufficient resources to beat the status quo; given complete information, proposals that are not approved are miscalculations that we should not observe in equilibrium. Empirically, taking into account attempts that failed is not possible, since there is no public record on MPVs that fail to be enacted. Therefore, while collecting data on failed congressional bills is feasible, the equivalent for MPVs is not, and any attempt to include a third category to represent "failed attempts/status quo" would be biased. This rules out a strict multinomial logit type of approach to the problem.

Table 4.3 presents the results of a set of specifications designed to assess the validity of the different explanations: (1) presents a specification including institutional commitment variables HIGH and LOW, and

---

[27] Including the excluded MPVs would fictitiously increase the instances in which there was a choice between decrees and statutes; before EC32, once a decree was in place, and as long as it was not rejected, it was considered fully valid, such that re-issuing the decree was the natural course of things (as opposed to a new instance in which actors make calculations).

[28] Table 4.A.2 in Appendix 4.A presents the descriptive statistics of the variables included in the regression analysis.

TABLE 4.3. *Logistic analysis of choice between decrees and statutes,*
Brazil 1988–2005

	(1)	(2)	(3)
High	−0.335*	−0.379*	−0.404*
	(0.193)	(0.210)	(0.217)
Low	0.939***	0.869***	0.762***
	(0.199)	(0.216)	(0.224)
EC32	0.930***	1.623***	1.987***
	(0.103)	(0.136)	(0.171)
Excluded CDA	−2.576***	−2.662***	−2.640***
	(0.171)	(0.184)	(0.191)
Taxes	1.997***	2.052***	2.058***
	(0.184)	(0.202)	(0.211)
Inflation (Lagged)		−0.040***	−0.035***
		(0.011)	(0.012)
Currency Fluct. (Lagged)		0.052***	0.036***
		(0.011)	(0.011)
Economic Package		0.522**	0.642**
		(0.236)	(0.255)
Legislative Support (Lagged)		0.010***	−0.001
		(0.003)	(0.004)
Presidential Popularity (Lagged)		−0.008***	−0.008***
		(0.002)	(0.003)
Cabinet Size (Lagged)		0.102***	0.062
		(0.031)	(0.040)
Cabinet Coalescence (Lagged)		0.021	−0.037
		(0.034)	(0.045)
Cabinet Management		−0.001	−0.000
		(0.001)	(0.001)
Transition			4.039***
			(0.477)
Honeymoon Effect			2.332***
			(0.271)
Lula's Presidency			0.388*
			(0.223)
Reelection			−0.330*
			(0.200)

(continued)

TABLE 4.3. *(continued)*

	(1)	(2)	(3)
Elections			1.178***
			(0.245)
Constant	−1.052***	−6.095***	−3.033
	(0.184)	(1.633)	(2.098)
McFadden Pseudo R^2	0.2	0.3	0.3
Log-likelihood	−1571.0	−1403.4	−1286.3
Likelihood-ratio test	979.6	1104.5	1338.6
p-value	0.0	0.0	0.0
AIC	3154.1	2834.8	2610.6
BIC	3191.5	2921.7	2728.5
Observations	3803	3655	3655

*** $p < 0.01$, ** $p < 0.05$, * $p < 0.1$; Standard errors in parentheses.

the effect of rules EC32, EXCLUDED CDA, and TAXES; (2) adds the traditional political and economic context variables; and (3) adds a host of contextual controls.

The empirical analysis supports the main tenets of my theory, confirming that there is reason to remain cautious regarding explanations based on economic crises, and shedding new light on the effects of the political context. The analysis of the effect of my main explanatory variables HIGH and LOW, and institutional variables EC32, EXCLUDED CDA, and TAXES, yields statistically significant coefficients in the expected directions. It is noteworthy that these effects are consistent throughout the different specifications.

My proxies for institutional commitment, variables HIGH and LOW, consistently yield coefficients in the predicted direction: HIGH negatively affects the likelihood of decrees, while LOW affects that likelihood positively.[29] This implies that when high-stakes policies (that is, policies that ignite high levels of institutional commitment) are considered, the likelihood that these policies will be enacted by decree diminishes, whereas it increases if the policies are of the low-stakes type. Substantively, high stakes policies ignite institutional commitment, such that politicians are more likely to enforce their decisions rights – and fewer decrees are enacted

---

[29] I conduct z-tests to check the difference of coefficients for these two variables. The tests allow me to reject the null hypothesis of no difference in all of the models presented in Table 4.3 and Table 4.4.

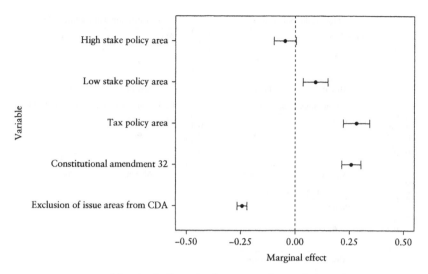

FIGURE 4.2. *Marginal effects for logistic analysis of choice between decrees and statutes, Brazil 1988–2005*
Note: Average partial effects. 95% confidence intervals.

on these issues. The analysis that follows focuses on model 3, which provides the best fit between the three models presented in Table 4.3.[30] Figure 4.2 presents marginal effects of the main explanatory variables, and Figure 4.3 presents a graphical depiction of predicted probabilities.[31]

The inclusion of the dummy variable TAXES proves to be necessary, affecting levels of significance of HIGH, where tax policy is included.[32] TAXES captures the effect of the problematic category, taking away some of the noise in the specification.

Regarding institutional variables and their effects, it is interesting to note that the constitutional exclusion of certain policy areas from constitutional decree authority, EXCLUDED CDA, effectively precludes decrees from being enacted, in likelihood. This effect holds consistently across specifications and is significant at the 0.01 level. In turn, EC32, which I anticipated should not impact decree enactment negatively, consistently

[30] A likelihood ratio test between models 2 and 3 reveals that model 3 provides a better fit for the data (LR = 234.19). The test cannot be performed between models 1 and 3 given the different sample sizes.

[31] In Appendix 4.A, I include three tables, Table 4.A.3, Table 4.A.4, and Table 4.A.5, which present odds ratios, marginal effects, and predicted probabilities estimated on the basis of the regressions in model 3 of Table 4.3.

[32] Recall that important tax policy is enacted via congressional *leis complementares* (not included in this analysis) and only minor tax policy is enacted by decree.

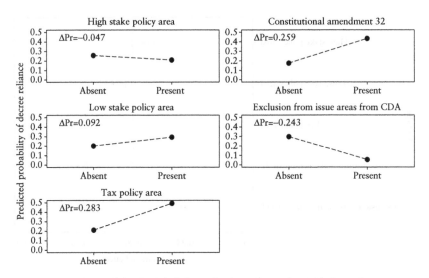

FIGURE 4.3. *Predicted probabilities for logistic analysis of choice between decrees and statutes, Brazil 1988–2005*
Note: Preditied probability with obsereved value approach.

yields positive coefficients that are statistically significant in the fully specified models (in line with Pereira, Power, and Rennó's 2008 findings). The famous constitutional amendment has not decreased decree enactment.

Economic context variables, which previous theories have associated with promoting concentration of power in the executive and facilitating the enactment of decrees, do not produce consistent effects across specifications. Furthermore, when evaluated as the sole determinants of the outcome (results not shown here), all three variables yield coefficients that are not statistically significant. They perform better when included in less-restricted models (such as 2 and 3), but it remains puzzling that while ECONOMIC PLAN and CURRENCY FLUCTUATION increase the likelihood of enacting decrees, INFLATION, which seeks to get at the same economic crisis phenomenon, yields a negative effect.[33] Dropping INFLATION from specifications does not alter the results, but dropping CURRENCY FLUCTUATION causes INFLATION to change the direction of its effect while losing statistical significance. These results make it difficult to interpret

---

[33] Note that while INFLATION and CURRENCY FLUCTUATION are highly correlated (.95), T-tests between the two and of each with ECONOMIC PACKAGE reveal that the difference between their means is statistically different from zero at the .01 level.

the effect of the economic context, casting doubt on the generalizability of O'Donnell's (1993, 1994) famous claims.

Stabilization packages, and other policies approved around the time these packages are passed, appear to increase the likelihood of decrees. Although it is important to note that this variable is highly contextual and provides little in the way of explaining the choice between legislative instruments more broadly,[34] economic packages are undoubtedly high stakes policies. However, institutional commitment may very well be at the core of this effect. Given that stabilization packages are rare and extraordinary events, their capacity to create precedents for the future may be limited and legislators may not perceive risk in ceding legislative prerogatives to the executive on these policy packages.

Political context variables are also included in models 2 and 3. In previous research, the effects of these variables were elusive. But evaluated here as determinants of the dichotomous variable CHOICE, more robust effects emerge. This is possibly a result of improved research design. Unfortunately, the effects of several political context variables differ across specifications.

In these models, the effect of Legislative SUPPORT, the variable created with data from CEBRAP, which seeks to get at the congressional support for the president by measuring concurrence in voting patterns, alternates between positive and negative effects. It is ultimately not statistically significant when evaluated in the unrestricted model 3 (and variations on model 3 not presented here). The effects of LEGISLATIVE SUPPORT for the president merit additional comment. Recall that LEGISLATIVE SUPPORT captures the lagged effect of levels of congruence in voting patterns, both regarding votes on statutes as well as on MPVs, and as such, it is an *ex post* measurement of concurrence. We have no theoretical reason to believe that concurrence should affect the choice of decrees versus statutes, even if it could prove useful in anticipating future levels of concurrence. Moreover, I propose that inter-branch agreements are necessary even when we do not observe votes on MPVs, such as before EC32. So, it is reasonable to see why the contextual variables added in model 3 drive away the effect of LEGISLATIVE SUPPORT *per se*, as they identify moments during which levels of concurrence between the branches are higher. Whether it is the effect of honeymoons, Lula's mensalão, or some other factor, there appears to be overlap in what this important variable

---

[34] And in fact, it drops from specifications in the period after EC32.

measures and what the more easily constructed dummies capture, and these effects merit further analysis. The same applies to cabinet variables.

Cabinet related variables, which also try to capture executive-legislative party-based relations, present a problematic scenario, too, since they yield significant results only when institutional variables are kept out of specifications. This suggests that they may be capturing some of the institutional effects that are more explicitly modeled by the institutional variables. When included in the fully specified model, only CABINET SIZE (the percentage of seats held in the Lower Chamber by parties represented in the presidential cabinet) yields a statistically significant positive effect, suggesting that higher percentages of seats held in congress by cabinet parties make it more likely for decrees to be enacted. This result is compatible with Amorim Neto's (2006) finding that presidents holding decree powers appoint a lower share of non-partisan members to the cabinet than otherwise, which in turn would support the relevance of congress for decree enactment, with parties as mediators.[35] The coefficients on CABINET COALESCENCE and CABINET MANAGEMENT are not statistically significant.[36]

Variables introduced as controls for different contextual factors that may impact the likelihood of decrees seem to have more uniform effects across specifications. PRESIDENTIAL POPULARITY affects the likelihood of decrees negatively. That this effect is negative, suggesting that popular presidents are less likely to enact decrees (as delegation theories predict) is also compatible with the theory described throughout this book. And while the theory put forth in this book does not make any claims regarding the effect of presidential popularity, there is no question that it is a powerful resource in hands of the executive (Canes Wrone 2001). Whether it can benefit agents seeking policies by reducing the cost of contributions to politicians that do not want to be identified as opposing the president (public appeals by the president playing some role) is an interesting question, one that may merit further attention.

TRANSITION, the variable that reflects the increase in decree enactment that immediately preceded EC32, yields a positive effect, as expected. The HONEYMOON effect on the choice of decrees versus statutes is

---

[35] This literature claims that cabinet appointments are done with a partisan logic in mind, to help manage congressional votes. Lower shares of non-partisan members when presidents hold decree power suggests that far from leading the president to ignore partisan appointments and dismiss congressional support, decrees require support from congress.

[36] A t-test of CABINET SIZE and CABINET COALESCENCE leads me to reject the null that there is no difference between their means.

also positive, as is the effect of ELECTIONS and President LULA's effect, although the latter does not yield significant results systematically across specifications. Together, these controls reassure us that during presidential honeymoons, during electoral campaigns, and if President Lula is in office, decrees are more likely. REELECTION, in turn, yields a negative effect in the specification included here; its effect varies across additional specifications not included here. In the fully specified model above, its negative effect suggests that the prospect of running for reelection decreases the likelihood of decrees.[37] Regardless of the many stories we can tell from these results, what we should note is that none of these controls alter the expected effects of institutional variables.

The picture we take away suggests that there is substantial support for an institutionally motivated explanation of the choice of legislative instruments even when contextual factors impact the choice in various ways. This is forcefully so given that even when the effects of contextual variables vary across specifications, the effect of the five core variables that test my theory remain basically unaltered across specifications.

While specifying the causal mechanisms through which political and economic variables affect the choice between decrees and statutes is beyond the scope of what this chapter sets out to do, it certainly constitutes a dilemma in search of more appropriate theorizing and testing. This chapter advances that research agenda by operationalizing the dependent variable as a dichotomous choice between legislative instruments and showing that much is gained by this approach, as the effects of political and economic variables at least become more stable. However, more detailed theorizing and especially more attention to identifying the precise measures that can allow us to distinguish between party-centered and context driven explanations are in order.

To test the theoretical claims of this project further, I estimated the specifications in (1) and (3) of Table 4.3 interacting the variables in each with EC32 to check whether the effects are different in the period after the amendment. The exercise is interesting, as it helps disentangle the unique effect of my key variables HIGH, LOW, TAXES, and EXCLUDED CDA before and after EC32. I report the results in Table 4.4, which shows that the main trends presented above are replicated here for the period before

---

[37] Given the nature of variables REELECTION and LULA, which are simply dummies identifying different portions of the data (from mid-1997 and 2003 onwards, respectively) that could be capturing all sorts of effects, I tested dropping both from model 5 and also each alternatively, with no substantive differences in the effects of the remaining variables.

EC32. Next, I interpret these results, with emphasis on understanding the effects after the amendment took place.

The first model in Table 4.4 presents the restricted model that tests institutional commitment variables (HIGH and LOW) and institutional variables (EXCLUDED CDA and TAXES) fully interacted with EC32, while model 2, in the last column, adds contextual controls while also interacting all variables with EC32. In each model, the coefficient for each individual variable represents the unique effect of that variable before the amendment, when EC32 = 0, while the coefficient of each variable interacted with EC32 represents the unique effect of that variable after the amendment, when EC32 = 1.

Briefly summarized, these results show that the main explanatory variables created to test my theory have a strongly significant effect in the expected directions in the period before EC32. Their effects after EC32, however, are not all aligned with my theoretical expectations. The effect of HIGH on the likelihood of decree enactment changes direction and becomes positive after EC32, implying that decree enactment becomes more likely when dealing with high-stakes issues. Arguably, this is a consequence of the fact that after EC32 all decrees forcibly go through congress for approval or rejection within a maximum period of 120 days, which cuts losses for legislators, as they are now part of the support coalition of decrees. My predictions for the period after the enactment of EC32 suggest that legislators are left indifferent between enacting policies by decree or by statute, quite simply because the payoffs they extract in the opposing scenarios are identical. Legislators, now equally compensated whether enacting decrees or statutes, are indifferent between the two legislative instruments, and less inclined to go out of their way to maintain a strong grip on high-stakes policies.

On the other hand, LOW and EXCLUDED CDA, while positive and negative, as expected, do not yield statistically significant effects after EC32. TAXES, instead, is both statistically significant and in the expected direction. The effects of economic context variables[38] and political context variables are maintained in the pre EC32 period to resemble effects in Table 4.3, but are not statistically significant post EC32, with the exception of INFLATION.

Overall, the results in Table 4.4, and especially what we see after EC32, make sense within the framework provided by this book, and they offer reassurance that the empirical support for my theory is robust and that

---

[38] ECONOMIC PLAN is correlated with EC32 and was dropped from specifications.

TABLE 4.4. *Logistic analysis of choice between decrees and statutes, Brazil 1988–2000*

	(1)	(2)
EC32	−0.373	544.679
	(0.674)	(15715.627)
High	−0.547***	−0.666***
	(0.202)	(0.232)
Low	0.848***	0.629***
	(0.208)	(0.240)
Excl.CDA	−2.467***	−2.543***
	(0.195)	(0.220)
Taxes	2.197***	2.278***
	(0.207)	(0.242)
Inflation (Lagged)		−0.040**
		(0.017)
Current Fluct. (Lagged)		0.036**
		(0.016)
Economic Plan		0.516**
		(0.259)
Legislative Support (Lagged)		−0.008*
		(0.005)
President Popularity (Lagged)		−0.005
		(0.003)
Cabinet Size (Lagged)		0.124***
		(0.041)
Cabinet Coalescence (Lagged)		0.055
		(0.050)
Transition		3.603***
		(0.473)
Honeymoon Effect		2.163***
		(0.283)
Lula's Presidency		−17.196
		(330.052)
Reelection		0.775***
		(0.257)
Elections		1.103***
		(0.260)
Cabinet Management		−0.002**
		(0.001)

(continued)

TABLE 4.4 *(continued)*

	(1)	(2)
High × EC32	1.569**	2.237**
	(0.686)	(1.078)
Low × EC32	1.099	1.785
	(0.700)	(1.087)
Excl.CDA × EC32	−0.399	−0.588
	(0.406)	(0.569)
Taxes × EC32	−0.896**	−1.332**
	(0.437)	(0.530)
Inflation (Lagged) × EC32		0.571***
		(0.213)
Elections × EC32		1.851*
		(1.113)
Constant	−0.920***	−5.341**
	(0.190)	(2.245)
McFadden Pseudo R²	0.241	0.412
Log-Likelihood	−1564.772	−1150.315
Likelihood-ratio test	992.272	1610.662
p-value	0.000	0.000
AIC	3149.444	2366.630
BIC	3211.879	2571.357
Number of observations	3803	3655

Note 1: Interactions with the variables CURRENCY FLUCTUATION (lagged), LEGISLATIVE SUPPORT lagged), PRESIDENTIAL POPULARITY (lagged), CABINET SIZE (lagged), CABINET COALESCENCE (lagged), CABINET MANAGEMENT, HONEYMOON EFFECT, and LULA, although not reported in this table, were included in the specification in model 2. None of them is statistically significant.
Note 2: *** $p < 0.01$, **$p < 0.05$, *$p < 0.1$; Standard errors in parentheses.

it provides a framework to understand the determinants of the choice between decrees and statutes in Brazil, even when important institutional change such as the amendment of 2001 are enacted.

4.4 CONCLUSIONS

Given the ongoing concern regarding the concentration of power in executive hands in democracies new and old around the globe, and the shortcomings of the theories that have set out to explain encroachment of prerogatives in the past, the evidence put forth in this chapter fills a long-sustained vacuum.

The empirical findings presented in this chapter lend credit to the claim that the established theoretical accounts place disproportionate emphasis on contextual factors, and for that reason they fall short of providing comprehensive explanations. Contextual economic and political factors certainly affect law-making decisions, and in that vein, they should have an effect on the choice of decrees versus statutes. Yet unless one presumes that the political and economic forces behind the enactment of laws are different to the ones affecting decrees, these factors can, at best, provide contextual information to a more systematic explanation of the determinants of the choice between the two instruments. Variables such as presidential popularity or the proportionality with which legislative parties are represented in the cabinet intervene in complex ways and affect levels of reliance on decrees, but they probably affect statutory agreements in similar ways.

This chapter analyzes the enactment of decrees and statutes jointly, to test the validity of my claims in the case of Brazil, showing that rules, and the extent to which politicians value the rules and enforce them, provide a fairly consistent explanation of the choice of legislative instrument. By focusing on the effects of the rules within Brazil, and explaining how institutional commitment affects politicians' behavior and plays out in the choice of decrees versus statutes, this chapter has shed new light on a persistent problem. The findings support the claim that institutions and levels of institutional commitment affect the choice to legislate by decree. This chapter finds that at the intermediate level of institutional commitment at which Brazil is located, high-stakes issues effectively ignite institutional commitment in a way that leads to an increased likelihood that those topics will be legislated by statute, whereas low-stakes issues have the opposite effect, and are more likely to be enacted by decree.

An additional contribution lies in the design of the empirical tests. The construction of the dichotomous dependent variable adequately fits the choice decision, and the construction of empirical measurements of the independent variables fit the problem at hand. This all adds up to improved tests of all variables, including contextual variables (both political and economic), such that their contributions to the likelihood of decrees are better assessed.

Taking a step back from the narrow issue of the choice between legislative instruments to reflect upon its implications, the chapter shows that the Brazilian executive is far from legislating at whim, despite the broad prerogatives and the stream of resources within reach. Yet, while the consensus has been that any and all constraints on decree enactment come from party and coalition related determinants, the theory put forth in this book emphasizes, and the evidence supports, that the main determinant is *not* organizational or contextual: It is institutional. It is by enforcing the legislative prerogatives that allow them continued access to the resources that ensure their long-term goals that politicians (legislators, justices) effectively limit encroachment by the executive, and they strengthen legislative institutions in the process. The fact that the crucial variables tested above, HIGH and LOW, provide consistent results in support of the theoretical account guiding this chapter provides substantial support for this account of lawmaking, and sheds light on our understanding of the much convoluted legislative-executive relations in Brazil.

This chapter also provides a different approach to our understanding of Constitutional Amendment 32, adopted in 2001, which is often interpreted as aimed at limiting the use of MPVs and their re-issuing by the executive. I propose that instead, it was a move by the legislature to specify and reinstate its decision rights. By changing the rules of decree enactment such that legislators would necessarily have to step in to approve or reject MPVs, they gained decision rights in the decree realm. Under the new scenario, the effective enforcement of hurdle factors led legislators to be indifferent between decrees and statutes, as their payoffs do not vary with the choice of instrument. This explains the otherwise puzzling finding that decree enactment increased after the amendment: after EC32 the executive is no longer encroaching upon legislative decision rights the way she did before, so it is reasonable that more decrees are enacted.

In terms of Tsebelis' (2002) veto players, what Brazilian legislators did by means of Constitutional Amendment 32 was to become veto players in a process in which they were previously not. This book highlights the mechanisms behind such decisions, and argues that job security, which in Brazil take the form of relatively higher levels of legislative reelection and longer tenures in the Supreme Court, by leading to the enforcement of decision rights, ultimately defines the relevant or effective set of veto players in the policymaking arena.

Interestingly, the findings suggest that the Brazilian Congress, having reasserted its decision rights through the enactment of EC32 in 2001, has possibly entered a virtuous cycle. That it is not exclusively altruism that generates the cycle is a normative concern, and as such should be dealt with separately. I come back to this in Chapter 7.

4.A APPENDIX: COMPLEMENTARY ANALYSIS AND SOURCES

4.A.1 Operationalization of Variables and Sources

CHOICE: Indicator equal to 1 if the observation is a *Medida Provisória*, and equal to zero if it is a congressional statute. Source: SICON, Senado Federal.

CABINET COALESCENCE: expressed as an index multiplied by 100. This measures the disproportionality between the share of cabinet portfolios and the share of intra-coalitional legislative seats held by parties. The coalescence rate for a given cabinet is arrived at by adding the absolute value of the difference between the percentage of portfolios and the percentage of legislative seats, for all parties in the cabinet (whether or not they have seats in the House) and for all ministries (whether or not they are party members), and then dividing the total by two, and subtracting the total from one. The index ranges from zero (no correspondence) to one (perfect correspondence). Cabinet variable in Amorim Neto 2002.

CABINET MANAGEMENT: an interaction term that multiplies cabinet size and cabinet coalescence.

CABINET SIZE: size of the cabinet's political coverage, expressed in terms of the percentage of legislative seats held in the Lower House by the parties represented in the cabinet. Source: Cabsize variable in Amorim Neto 2002.

CURRENCY FLUCTUATION: expressed as monthly percent change in the value of Brazilian currency with respect to the US dollar. Source: BCB Boletim/BP (IPEADATA).

EC32: Indicator equal to 1 when the observation was enacted after September 11, 2001, when Constitutional Amendment 32 was passed.

ECONOMIC PACKAGE: Indicator equal to 1 in months in which there was a major stabilization package introduced by the executive: January 1989 (Plano Verão), part of March 1990 (Plano Collor), December 1990 (Plano Collor II), December 1993 (Fundo Social de Emergência/URV), and June 1994 (Plano Real).

ELECTIONS: Indicator equal to 1 during the months preceding presidential or legislative elections. Coded 1 for September, October, and November 1989 and 1994, September and October 1998 and 2002, 2006.

EXCLUDED CDA: Indicator equal to 1 when the reported policy issue is among those excluded from executive decree authority by the constitution, and equal to zero otherwise.

HIGH: Indicator equal to 1 when the observation's policy issue falls under the "high stakes" category, and equal to zero otherwise. See Chapter 3 for a full explanation of this categorization. Source: SICON, Senado Federal.

HONEYMOON: Indicator equal to 1 during the first three months in office of each president inaugurated during the period analyzed in this chapter.

INFLATION: monthly accumulated changes in consumer prices, expressed as a percentage (INPC), takes negative and positive values). Source: IBGE/SNIPC (IPEADATA).

LEGISLATIVE SUPPORT: Monthly average of the percentage of legislators following the floor recommendation of the Leader of Government in the Lower Chamber. When the executive recommends a negative vote, the denominator is the total of votes cast in the House. When the executive recommends an affirmative vote, the denominator is the total number of seats in the house. In months with no floor votes, the last value available is carried forward. Source: Banco de Dados Legislativos, CEBRAP.

LOW: Indicator equal to 1 when the observation's policy issue falls under the "low stakes" category, and equal to zero otherwise. See Chapter 3 for a full explanation of this categorization. Source: SICON, Senado Federal.

LULA: Indicator equal to 1 from January 2003 onwards, while President Lula holds office.

PRESIDENTIAL POPULARITY: percentage of positive appraisal of presidential performance, replicating the measure used in Pereira, Power, and Rennó 2008. The data come from the three main pollsters in Brazil: DataFolha (1988–2008), Vox Populi/Sensus (1995–2008), CNI/Ibope (1995–2008). Respondents are asked to rate presidential performance as excellent (ótimo), good (bom), average (regular), bad (ruim), or awful (péssimo). The average shown is a result of subtracting the negatives (bad/awful) from the positives (excellent/good) and ignoring the intermediate category. Source: Fernando Rodrigues, UOL.

REELECTION: Indicator equal to 1 from June 1997 onwards, representing the period during which reelection of the executive has been possible.

TAXES: Indicator equal to 1 when an observation is classified by the source as a tax policy (*tributos*).

TRANSITION: Indicator equal to 1 for August 2001 and the first ten days of September, the weeks preceding the date EC32 took effect, on September 11 of that year.

4.A.2 Codification of High/Low Variables

TABLE 4.A.1. *Classification of policy areas of bills in Brazil*

High	Low	Political rights
1. Taxes	4. Housing	5. Executive
2. Transportation	8. Bureaucracy/	7. STF
3. Business associations	administration	26. Judicial system
6. Education	9. Crimes	27. Electoral
12. Real estate	10. Social security	31. Constitution
13. Defense	11. Police/homeland	35. Legislative branch
14. Health	security	41. Attorney general
15. Consumer defense	16. Foreign trade	
17. Regional	18. Public service	
22. Telecommunications	19. Economic policy	
23. Fishing	20. Financial policy	
25. Labor	21. Social policy	
28. Political parties	24. Science and	
29. Environment	technology	
30. Land rights	33. IR	
32. Energy and mining	34. Criminal law	
36. Agriculture	39. Symbolic	
38. Urban matters	40. Civil law	
42. Information technology	43. Sports	
44. Industrial policy	47. Culture	
45. Public spending/works	48. Minorities	
46. Food	49. Subsidies to	
	individuals	

4.A.3 Complementary Analysis

TABLE 4.A.2. *Summary statistics Brazil dataset*

Variable	Obs	Freq = 0	Freq. = 1	Min	Max	Range	Median	Mean	Standard deviation
Choice	3803	76.78	23.22	–	–	–	–	–	–
High	3803	27.56	72.44	–	–	–	–	–	–
Low	3803	79.33	20.67	–	–	–	–	–	–
EC32	3803	81.23	18.77	–	–	–	–	–	–
Excluded CDA	3803	63.21	36.79	–	–	–	–	–	–
Taxes	3803	95.77	4.23	–	–	–	–	–	–
Economic Package	3803	93.79	6.21	–	–	–	–	–	–
Transition	3803	98	2	–	–	–	–	–	–
Honeymoon	3803	96.03	3.97	–	–	–	–	–	–
Lula	3803	83.43	16.57	–	–	–	–	–	–
Reelection	3803	49.3	50.7	–	–	–	–	–	–
Elections	3803	96.42	3.58	–	–	–	–	–	–
Inflation	3803	–	–	-0.49	82.18	82.67	1.21	10.64	15.64
Currency Fluctuation	3800	–	–	-10.69	65.31	76	1.83	10.19	15.33
Legislative Support	3670	–	–	26.67	99.5	72.83	62.31	67.04	16.62
Presidential Popularity	3721	–	–	-63	67	130	0	-4.65	28.05
Cabinet Size	3736	–	–	26.2	76.6	50.4	61.6	58.5	12.77
Cabinet Coalescence	3736	–	–	22	70	48	57	51.92	10.72
Cabinet Management	3736	–	–	786	5201	4415	3155.2	3122.67	1117.08

Source: Author's own calculation based on SICON (2010).

TABLE 4.A.3. *Odds ratio analysis for logistic model (3) of choice between statutes and decrees, Brazil 1988–2005*

Variable	Type	Change	Odds ratio	Standard error	CI (95%)	Variation (%)
High	Dichotomous	1	0.67	0.14	[0.44, 1.03]	−33.25
Low	Dichotomous	1	2.14	0.48	[1.4, 3.36]	114.27
EC32	Dichotomous	1	7.29	1.25	[5.23, 10.22]	629.17
Excluded CDA	Dichotomous	1	0.07	0.01	[0.05, 0.1]	−92.86
Taxes	Dichotomous	1	7.83	1.65	[5.21, 11.92]	682.86
Inflation	Continuous	10.6	0.69	0.01	[0.53, 0.89]	−31
Currency Fluctuation	Continuous	10.2	1.44	0.02	[1.15, 1.81]	44.2
Economic Package	Dichotomous	1	1.9	0.48	[1.15, 3.12]	89.94
Legislative Support	Continuous	67	0.91	0	[0.55, 1.53]	−8.62
Presidential Popularity	Continuous	−4.7	1.04	0	[1.07, 1.01]	3.99
Cabinet Size	Continuous	58.5	37.19	1.47	[0.44, 3834.79]	3619.06
Cabinet Coalescence	Continuous	51.9	0.15	0.01	[0, 14.83]	−84.99
Cabinet Management	Continuous	3123	0.91	0	[0.01, 107.69]	−8.55
Transition	Dichotomous	1	56.76	27.07	[24.03, 159.78]	5575.71
Honeymoon	Dichotomous	1	10.3	2.79	[6.11, 17.73]	929.85
Lula	Dichotomous	1	1.47	0.33	[0.95, 2.28]	47.37
Reelection	Dichotomous	1	0.72	0.14	[0.49, 1.07]	−28.1
Elections	Dichotomous	1	3.25	0.79	[2.01, 5.26]	224.95

Note: Results are based on model (3) of Table 4.3. Change indicates the magnitude of change used for the calculation of odds ratios. For Dichotomous variables it is their range, and for continuous variables it is their mean. Variation (%) describes the percentage change associated (100*(OR−1)).

TABLE 4.A.4. *Marginal effects for logistic model (3) of choice between statutes and decrees, Brazil 1988–2005*

Variable	Marginal Effects at Means				Average Marginal Effects			
	Effect	Standard error	p-Value	Significance	Effect	Standard error	p-Value	Significance
High	−0.045	0.026	0.082	<0.1	−0.047	0.026	0.071	<0.1
Low	0.095	0.033	0.004	<0.01	0.092	0.029	0.001	<0.01
EC32	0.316	0.036	0	<0.001	0.258	0.023	0	<0.001
Excluded CDA	−0.241	0.012	0	<0.001	−0.243	0.012	0	<0.001
Taxes	0.382	0.052	0	<0.001	0.282	0.031	0	<0.001
Inflation (Lag)	−0.004	0.001	0.005	<0.01	−0.004	0.001	0.005	<0.01
Currency Fluctuation (Lag)	0.004	0.001	0.002	<0.01	0.004	0.001	0.002	<0.01
Economic Package	0.083	0.04	0.037	<0.05	0.078	0.033	0.018	<0.05
Legislative Support (Lag)	0	0	0.731		0	0	0.731	
President Popularity (Lag)	−0.001	0	0.004	<0.01	−0.001	0	0.004	<0.01
Cabinet Size (Lag)	0.006	0.004	0.117		0.007	0.004	0.119	
Cabinet Coalescence (Lag)	−0.004	0.005	0.413		−0.004	0.005	0.413	
Cabinet Management (Lag)	0	0	0.971		0	0	0.971	
Transition (pre-EC32)	0.765	0.052	0	<0.001	0.551	0.057	0	<0.001
Honeymoon	0.452	0.066	0	<0.001	0.321	0.039	0	<0.001
Lula	0.045	0.028	0.115		0.045	0.027	0.093	<0.1
Reelection	−0.035	0.021	0.104		−0.037	0.022	0.098	<0.1
Elections	0.181	0.05	0	<0.001	0.151	0.034	0	<0.001

Note: Results are based on model (3) of Table 4.3. For dichotomous variables it shows the partial change from zero to one.

TABLE 4.A.5. *Predicted probabilities for logistic model (3) of choice of statutes and decrees, Brazil 1988–2005*

Variables	Minimum	Predicted probability at min.	Maximum	Predicted probability at max.	Difference in probability
High	0	0.257	1	0.21	−0.047
Low	0	0.201	1	0.293	0.092
EC32	0	0.176	1	0.435	0.259
Excluded CDA	0	0.298	1	0.055	−0.243
Taxes	0	0.211	1	0.494	0.283
Inflation (Lag)	−0.49	0.27	73.99	0.066	−0.204
Currency Fluctuation (Lag)	−10.691	0.158	65.309	0.496	0.338
Economic Package	0	0.223	1	0.301	0.078
Legislative Support (Lag)	26.67	0.233	99.5	0.222	−0.011
President Popularity (Lag)	−63	0.286	67	0.167	−0.119
Cabinet Size (Lag)	26.2	0.079	76.6	0.371	0.292
Cabinet Coalescence (Lag)	22	0.371	70	0.156	−0.215
Transition (pre EC32)	0	0.213	1	0.764	0.551
Honeymoon	0	0.215	1	0.536	0.321
Lula	0	0.219	1	0.264	0.045
Reelection	0	0.249	1	0.212	−0.037
Elections	0	0.22	1	0.371	0.151

Note: Results are based on model (3) of Table 4.3. Calculation of probabilities uses the observed value approach (Hanmer & Kalkan 2013).

5

A Corollary of Low Levels of Institutional Commitment

Argentina

5.1 INTRODUCTION

This chapter addresses the debate on executive decree authority in the case of Argentina. Much has been written on the limitations of Argentina's democratic regime since its return to democracy in 1983, and much of the distrust regarding the quality of Argentine democracy and the strength of its institutions has sprouted from the ever-increasing use of decrees, or *Decretos de Necesidad y Urgencia* (DNU) as they are known in Argentina. While, during the eighties, President Alfonsín resorted to decrees far less than his successors would, at the time his level of reliance on decrees was exceptional if compared to earlier democratic periods. Under President Menem, however, the enactment of decrees exploded to unprecedented levels, and President Kirchner would later rely on decrees even more heavily. Under President Fernández, the use of decrees declined considerably, only to rise again during President Macri.

The dynamics described in the previous chapters are present in the enactment of all policies (if not always observable), and results are greatly affected by the muscle of external agents with strong policy preferences. The example presented in Chapter 1 regarding Resolución 125/2008,[1] shows a huge miscalculation on the executive's part, as she was unable to accurately assess farmers' valuation of the policy and to what extent they would affect decisions in Congress and the Supreme Court. In equilibrium, we would not have observed this decree – only decrees that garner enough support to withstand opposition.

---

[1] While this is not strictly a decree of the CDA type, the fact that the inter-branch dynamics apply to the more secluded presidential domain of *resoluciones* reinforces my point.

In the Argentine context, the research focusing on DNUs initially set out to make sense of what was considered a political innovation introduced by President Carlos Menem: the use for normal policymaking of what had until then been an extremely exceptional legislative resource. By the time Carey and Shugart (1998) put out their volume on executive decree authority, a constitutional reform had taken place in Argentina, making it obvious that DNUs would be a permanent part of the Argentine legislative landscape. During the same turbulent period, however, important pieces of legislation were passed by Congress (and not enacted by decree), and in a few outstanding cases, the Argentine Congress blocked key presidential initiatives or reversed highly contested policies enacted by DNU.[2]

Periodic confrontations between the executive and Congress in Argentina suggest that although the use of DNUs has advanced considerably on congressional decision rights, legislators are not indifferent regarding their role in the decision-making process. I have argued that this is so because decision rights provide a unique tool that allows politicians to tap into valuable resources. By presenting the implications for Argentina of the theory laid out in Chapter 2, this chapter seeks to provide an explanation of the determinants of the choice of decrees versus statutes that goes beyond the role of contextual factors to point out the causal mechanisms that underlie observed behavior.

This chapter assumes that low levels of institutional commitment are present in Argentina, as a function of the high levels of job insecurity that result from high turnover of legislators and Supreme Court justices. The findings suggest that overall low levels of institutional commitment in Argentina effectively influence the extent to which decrees are favored over statutes. Legislators and Supreme Court justices, lacking the long-term horizons that would move them to defend their decision rights, are content to extract whatever they may from the legislative process in the present. Whereas policies on a handful of areas most dear to the legislature's heart seem to be less likely to be enacted by decrees (those excluded from constitutional decree authority), even policies affecting political rights and basic elements of checks and balances are more likely to be enacted by decree than by statute.

This does not suggest, by any means, that the legislature is oblivious to policy decisions. The fact that policies that are excluded from CDA have

---

[2] Some privatizations, and labor reform during the 90s, as well as the 2008 reversal of *retenciones móviles* (an incremental tax on agricultural exports), are cases in point.

an increased likelihood of being enacted by statute reveals that, however small, there is a turf that legislators and Supreme Court justices are willing to defend from executive encroachment. Legislators and Supreme Court justices remain an irreplaceable component of law-making coalitions, although more often than not their participation is paid off at devalued prices.

The chapter proceeds as follows. Section 5.2 provides an overview of the evolution of decree authority in Argentina, it presents the facts regarding the enactment of decrees *vis à vis* congressional statutes in the current democratic period, reviews the literature on the topic, and offers an assessment of the level of institutional commitment in the country. Section 5.3 presents the implications of my theoretical approach for the analysis of Argentina. Section 5.4 presents the empirical analysis and Section 5.5 draws conclusions.

5.2 EXECUTIVE DECREES

Characterizing Argentina, together with other Latin American democracies, as having reactive assemblies and proactive presidents (Cox and Morgenstern 2001), analyses of the lawmaking process in Argentina have focused heavily on partisan dynamics and the degree to which parties aid or hinder the policymaking process. At the heart of these analyses, however, it is rare to find work focusing on legislative agendas other than the executive's. The research on the country's use of executive decrees (Ferreira Rubio and Goretti 1998; Maurich and Liendo 1998) and on the executive's legislative success rates (Calvo 2007; Alemán and Calvo 2010; Laurentiu 2008[3]), as well as a host of works on policymaking and inter-branch relations in Argentina, bear witness to this trend. And while the executive's policy agenda has occupied central concern, so have institutional determinants weighing in on the polity's ability to further policy goals. Jones et al. (2002), Jones and Hwang (2005), Kim (2006), Magar (2001), Spiller and Tommasi (2007), among many others, are valuable contributions to our understanding of the interplay of the institutional setting in Argentina and its implications for lawmaking.

This chapter adds to this literature by bringing institutions to play with external determinants on the policymaking process, an approach

---

[3] Stinga, Lauretiu. 2008. "Revisiting Governance by Decree in Argentina: political culture or structure?" Presented at the 2nd ECPR Graduate Conference in Barcelona, 24–26 August 2008.

that enables me to examine the legislative process as permeable to external influence. It offers a different perspective on policymaking, one that moves away from notions that equate policymaking with enacting the executive's policy agenda. By bringing together the enactment of congressional statutes and executive decrees as competing instruments in the law-making process, I bridge the disjuncture prevalent in a literature that has analyzed these law-making tools as only loosely related.

5.2.1 Decree Authority in Argentina: *Decretos de Necesidad y Urgencia*

Before 1994 executive decree authority had not been constitutionally established in Argentina. The use of DNUs had emerged out of severe and exceptional circumstances that required swift executive decisions. Their use was very sporadic throughout most of the country's history, but it picked up after 1983, with the inauguration of the country's most recent experience with democracy, which came in hand with unprecedented economic woes. Between 1853 and 1983, a total of fifteen DNUs had been issued in Argentina. Yet the inauguration of the current democratic period witnessed a shift: between 1983 and 1989, President Raúl Alfonsín enacted eleven DNUs, an amount then considered unacceptably high. His successor, President Menem, enacted a total of 152 decrees between July 9, 1989, and August 23, 1994, a brief five-year period.[4] Astonished by this expansion in legislative prerogatives, scholars initially analyzed it as stemming from the leadership style of Carlos Menem. Menem had not only expanded the use of DNUs to non-emergencies, but also carried out a serious attack on the set of institutions most essential to checks and balances. Immediately after taking office, he promoted an expansion of the Supreme Court that allowed him to appoint (with senate consent) six of its nine members between April and May of 1990. The Constitutional Reform of 1994 congealed other assaults on the system of checks and balances that had *de facto* been in place during his presidency. By the time

---

[4] Throughout this section, the figures on DNUs that I use are those reported by the *Dirección de Información Parlamentaria*, Molinelli, Palanza, and Sin (1999). The very history of DNU origination, added to the government's lack of interest in (or explicit strategy to avoid) clarifying the institutional status of decrees, and establishing a clear categorization procedure by which they can be easily identified, has created a debate on the actual number of decrees enacted. While there seems to be grounds for claims that the numbers reported by official sources are deflated, the proliferation of individually preferred lists does not seem helpful. As others before me, I choose to use the official numbers provided by congress, while acknowledging (as does the source) that the list is not exhaustive.

the new constitution was in effect, DNUs had become an enduring part of the institutional system – albeit a part resented by many.[5] The presidents that came after President Menem would not shy away from using decrees, though there have been interesting fluctuations in the proportion of decrees and statutes.

The Constitutional Reform of 1994 was expansive in its goals. Motivated by President Menem's ambition to stay in office for an additional period, it was facilitated by an agreement between President Menem and President Alfonsín known as the "*Pacto de Olivos,*" in reference to the location where the pact was sealed, the presidential residence in Olivos. The pact involved a negotiation between the two leaders of Argentina's then most prominent parties, the *Partido Justicialista* (PJ or Peronism) and the *Unión Cívica Radical* (UCR). In Argentina, the constitution can only be amended by a convention once congress establishes the need through law. Once it comes together, the constitutional convention has the prerogative to decide on constitutional issues with absolute sovereignty. So, because no fixed agenda could be imposed on the convention, to a large extent the pact was intended as a way to guide the reform process to ensure that there would be compliance with the main bargaining chips on each of the two sides of the agreement. The pact included what became known as the core of basic agreements (*núcleo de coincidencias básicas*) and a set of additional clauses enabling the delegates to the convention to discuss other specific issues,[6] and on 29 December 1993, congress ratified the pact.[7] The reform was expansive, and combined, importantly, the reduction of the presidential mandate from six to four years with the possibility of a consecutive reelection. Among the changes introduced by the reform,[8] the single most important change for the

---

[5] See Ferreira Rubio and Goretti (1998) for a detailed account of the evolution of events regarding DNUs between 1989 and 1993.

[6] Mainly as a result of the requests of provincial party leaders, who saw the opportunity to revise the procedures to establish and reform the federal fiscal regime in the constitution. They made their support in congress conditional on the inclusion of this subject among those to be reformed. Menem and Alfonsín were compelled to accept these terms.

[7] Law 24309: "*Constitución Nacional: Declaración de la necesidad de su reforma*" (National Constitution: Declaration of the need of its reform).

[8] The creation of a Chief of Cabinet position, direct election of senators combined with a reduction of their mandates and partial renovation of the Senate, the adoption of direct election of president and vice-president with a second round to replace the electoral college, direct election of the Chief of Government of the City of Buenos Aires (which was granted autonomy), several changes to the legislative process in the form of regulations to partial vetoes, a reduction of the number of times each chamber could revise bills, and the establishment of qualified majorities for bills changing the electoral system or

purpose of this book is that the prerogative to enact decrees, until then not established in the constitution, was included in the constitutional text along with conditions for its restraint.

In what follows, I present evidence of the evolution of legislation passed using each of the two legislative instruments, congressional statutes and decrees, since the inauguration of democracy in 1983. Table 5.1 presents a yearly detail of statutes passed by the Argentine Congress, providing total and partial amounts to distinguish bills by origin. Table 5.2 presents DNU approval by year and president. The difference between Alfonsín's years and those that followed is quite stark, with only 3 years during Menem's tenure resembling the pre-Menem era.

The variation presented in these tables has attracted plenty of scholarly attention, yet, just as the two separate tables in this chapter, analyses of congressional law making and the use of executive decrees have been carried out separately (valuable exceptions are Kim 2006 and Magar 2001) as if decrees and statutes pertained to different spheres of affairs. Figure 5.1, in contrast, is an invitation to think about decrees and statutes as being linked in important ways, as the figure contrasts the use of each instrument throughout the period. This figure shows the variation over time of the two legislative instruments.[9] It suggests that analyzing lawmaking as a two-pronged process that leads to policy enactment by statutes or decrees is a reasonable approach, especially considering that statutes and decrees modify each other interchangeably and for all practical purposes have equal legislative status.

The predominant view among scholars, however, was that DNUs were an extraordinary resource in hands of the executive – even when presidents had been using them routinely for years. Ferreira Rubio and Goretti's (1998) analysis provides an excellent look into the way in which Menem used decree authority, and how the other two branches interacted with the executive in the process. They provide several detailed examples that stress different aspects of decree use during those years. These illustrate the variation in topics and importance of DNUs, ranging from key pieces of legislation to minor laws that could hardly pass the

---

political parties, reforms intended to increase controls on the bureaucracy, reforms to change appointment and removal procedures in the judiciary, the reform of the procedure of federal intervention, along with changes intended to strengthen the federal system and municipal autonomy, and mechanisms of direct democracy (DIP, HCDN).

[9] The yearly enactment of statutes and decrees shows different levels of correlation by period: The correlation for the entire period is 0.76, but between 1984 and 1989 it is 0.11, and between 1990–2007 it is 0.79.

TABLE 5.1. *Congressional statutes by initiator, Argentina 1983–2007*

Year[a]	Deputies	Senate	Executive	Other	Total
1983	0	0	1	0	1
1984	34	27	68	0	129
1985	45	19	69	9	142
1986	48	25	111	4	188
1987	10	3	31	6	50
1988	39	22	52	4	117
1989	30	14	66	3	113
1990	0	37	77	2	166
1991	44	20	143	1	208
1992	52	33	86	1	172
1993	27	25	69	2	123
1994	37	17	79	2	135
1995	66	41	84	1	192
1996	56	32	73	2	163
1997	64	37	78	2	181
1998	53	33	81	0	167
1999	69	33	113	0	215
2000	43	27	95	1	166
2001	61	33	86	1	181
2002	72	29	163	0	264
2003	42	34	166	1	243
2004	59	27	130	0	216
2005	27	29	59	0	115
2006	29	32	123	2	186
2007	50	33	76	2	161
Total	662	1107	1481	50	3300

Note 1: Laws passed per year.
Note 2: The empirical analysis in this chapter goes up to 2007 and includes 12 laws that were passed in 2007 but signed by the president in 2008.
[a]Calendar year (1983 begins on Dec 10).
Source: Dirección de Información Parlamentaria, HCDN (2017).

TABLE 5.2. *Decretos de Necesidad y Urgencia, Argentina 1983–2010*

Year	Alfonsín	Menem	De La Rúa	R.Saa	Duhalde	Kirchner	Fernández	Total
1983	–	–	–	–	–	–	–	–
1984	3	–	–	–	–	–	–	3
1985	1	–	–	–	–	–	–	1
1986	3	–	–	–	–	–	–	3
1987	1	–	–	–	–	–	–	1
1988	1	–	–	–	–	–	–	1
1989	2	6	–	–	–	–	–	8
1990	–	29	–	–	–	–	–	29
1991	–	59	–	–	–	–	–	59
1992	–	32	–	–	–	–	–	32
1993	–	18	–	–	–	–	–	18
1994	–	8	–	–	–	–	–	8
1995	–	6	–	–	–	–	–	6
1996	–	8	–	–	–	–	–	8
1997	–	23	–	–	–	–	–	23
1998	–	21	–	–	–	–	–	21
1999	–	37	5	–	–	–	–	42
2000	–	–	23	–	–	–	–	23
2001	–	–	29	6	–	–	–	35

(continued)

TABLE 5.2 *(continued)*

Year	Alfonsín	Menem	De La Rúa	R.Saa	Duhalde	Kirchner	Fernández	Total
2002	–	–	–	–	105	–	–	105
2003	–	–	–	–	46	47	–	93
2004	–	–	–	–	–	63	–	63
2005	–	–	–	–	–	36	–	36
2006	–	–	–	–	–	56	–	56
2007	–	–	–	–	–	20	–	20
2008	–	–	–	–	–	–	3	3
2009	–	–	–	–	–	–	10	10
2010	–	–	–	–	–	–	10	10
Total	11	247	57	6	151	222	23	717

Source: Dirección de Información Parlamentaria, HCDN (2017).

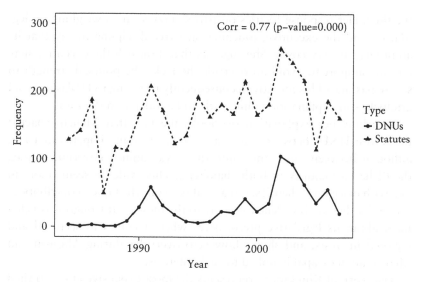

FIGURE 5.1. *Decrees and statutes, 1984–2007*

urgency test; variation in the way the executive communicated the enactment of DNUs to Congress, which among other things generated the
confusion surrounding their numbers: and the strategic variation across
Supreme Court decisions.

These accounts provide the reader with a sharp picture of the usage
made of decrees, but they provide less guidance in terms of the underlying
determinants of the increase and variation in their use, stating toward the
end of the chapter that Congress had lost legitimacy, which had reduced
its ability to confront the executive. Whether congressional inaction facing
decrees led to such legitimacy loss, and what may have caused inaction in
the first place, are questions unanswered by that early article on DNUs.
Later work would seek responses.

Work by Ana María Mustapic (2002) emphasizes the use of DNUs
as a tool enabling the executive to overcome the institutional paraly-
ses to which presidentialism is prone by design. Her work suggests that
absent executive decree authority, Argentina would have faced gridlock
in several circumstances, and that the threat of decree enactment helped
push forward legislation that was otherwise highly contested.[10] In try-
ing to make sense of decrees more broadly, she asks why Menem relied
on decrees so frequently, despite his near majority in congress most of

---

[10] Interestingly, however, the contested legislation she mentions was enacted by statute.

the time. Her response focuses on partisan constraints weighing on legislators and the executive, touching on party discipline to say that its
attainment is very costly. She suggests that although the executive may
rely on support to avoid an override, he lacks the political strength to
secure passage of his initiatives, consequently resorting to DNUs to avoid
gridlock – an explanation in line with unilateral action theories.

Somehow her explanation overlooks the fact that Menem enacted
the fewest DNUs between 1994 and 1996, regaining impetus in 1997,
although between 1996 and 1998 there was unified government (i.e.,
the PJ had a majority in both chambers). This evidence seems more in
line with delegation theories. On a final note on Mustapic's contribution,
I note that her analysis lends support to the thesis that Congress is vehe-
ment about its legislative prerogatives when it comes to sectorial and
regional interests, and shows how veto overrides during Alfonsín and
Menem are inescapably linked to such interests.

The work of Kim (2007) represents the most expansive effort to shed
light on the puzzle surrounding executive decrees in Argentina, analyzing the determinants of reliance on decrees during the period between
1916–2004. His work is innovative in his view of decrees as the result
of interactions among the three branches of government, which leads
him to take into account the president's influence on the Supreme Court
as well as his partisan alignment with Congress. In response to previous work, which was inconclusive regarding the prevalence of unilateral
action theory or delegation theory to explain levels of decree reliance in
Argentina, he takes on this debate. Kim emphasizes as his main finding
that Argentine presidents are "less inclined to issue decrees when the relative size of the pro-government or the opposition party in the legislature
is small, and if the president can secure majority support in the Supreme
Court" (Kim 2007: 128).

A setback of his empirical approach, however, is his choice to model the
problem of decree enactment as being separate from statute enactment.
Using the number of DNUs enacted at a given time as the dependent
variable, he accounts for legislative production (enactment of statutes)
by including it, together with other explanatory variables, on the right-
hand side. In fact, he motivates the inclusion of legislative production
and divided government by citing studies that have suggested that levels
of reliance on decree authority were related to presidential attempts to
avoid gridlock. He finds, however, that legislative productivity is not a
significant determinant of decree enactment. My approach would suggest
that decree enactment and statutory enactment (the latter being legislative

productivity in Kim's wording) are components of the same process, and as I present below, the modeling strategy should be a different one.

Argentina's Low Level of Institutional Commitment

An important assumption that I make is that the overall level of institutional commitment in Argentina is low. Those who believe that Argentina, like most other new democracies, suffers from institutional weakness may be inclined to accept my claim at face value. Yet, by referring to varying levels of institutional commitment, I refer to something quite specific. There appears to be certain consensus that Latin American democracies suffer from institutional weakness (O'Donnell 1993, 1994; Levitsky and Murillo 2005).[11] I emphasize, as others have before me, that considerable variation exists among weakly institutionalized democracies.[12] In my view, this is because levels of institutional commitment vary across cases – and admittedly, this, too, is a product of rules, only different ones, not the ones being characterized.

Chapter 3 describes institutional commitment as a function of legislators' time horizons, which implies their job security. Recent research has pointed out repeatedly that legislators who do not see a future in the legislature will not make investments in congress as an institution (Jones et al. 2002; Jones and Saiegh 2007; Samuels 2002). Adding to this view, I suggest that legislators who believe they will be in possession of their decision rights briefly have limited incentives to defend these rights from encroachment. If, instead, they expected to be in their jobs for longer periods of time, they would defend the long-term gains to be derived from their decision rights, and, in so doing, congress would be strengthened.

[11] I find the profusely adopted terminology of *institutional weakness* to be problematic, as it suggests that it is the institutions that are weak, and at the most basic level, confounds two diverse definitions of institutions. By one definition, an institution (a rule) is strong if it has the capacity to bind the actors affected by it to act in specific ways, which maximizes a set of long-term goals (federalism, democracy, etc.). In a different use of the word, congress and the executive are considered institutions – the problem with this use being that it has the potential to conflate rules, actors, and organizations. Typically, when references are made to weak institutions in Latin America, what seems to be implied is often that congress is weak because it fails to check the executive, or even that the political system is weak because it fails to enforce democracy. In this sense, in the case of Latin American institutional settings, one would perhaps be better served by referring to sub-optimal institutional arrangements leading to poor democracy, than to institutional weakness in a given democracy.

[12] Levitsky and Murillo (2005) attribute this variation to two factors, enforcement and stability. While they seem to get at important characteristics of institutions, in their characterization enforcement is not necessarily a quality of the institution under analysis but often a result of the effects of other institutions that play into political behavior.

Specifically, I claim that legislators' decision rights endow them with access to resources to which they would not have access absent their prerogatives. For example, when seeking the enactment of a given policy, proponents of that policy (and those opposing it) will approach the broad array of actors with decision rights over policy approval to get their support. In the case of Argentina, this includes the executive and legislators (and, sometimes, Supreme Court justices). We expect supporters of, and opponents to, that policy to use their resources – public visibility, organizational resources, and money, among others – to attain political support for their preferred policy.

As pointed out in Chapter 3, if a politician (a legislator) expects to be out of office soon, he will try to maximize the gains he can extract from his decision rights in the present because once his term ends, he will no longer be in possession of those prerogatives. Yet a legislator who expects to remain in his job for more than one term, and believes that what he does in his current term will affect that probability, will be less inclined to maximize current gains in detriment of long term gains. In other words, the latter would be less inclined to accept violations of his decision rights today that would undermine the very prerogatives that guarantee him continued access to those gains. In sum, the legislator with a longer time horizon is more likely to defend his decision rights from encroachment than is his short-term counterpart.

This account of legislators' motivations applies equally to other politicians, including presidents and supreme court justices. These actors behave in accordance with the incentives they face, making decisions in view of broader determinants on their career paths and long-term interests (Spiller and Tommasi 2000, 2007). Argentine legislators' career perspectives are well documented in Jones et al. (2002) and Jones and Saiegh (2007), which describe the adverse electoral and partisan incentives weighing on legislators, and more recently in the work of Micozzi (2013, 2014). While there are no formal constraints on the reelection of legislators in Argentina (as there are in Mexico and Costa Rica), their careers in congress are limited by electoral rules, party dynamics, and local interests that maximize goals other than permanence in congress, hence weakening the structure of checks and balances.

Regarding the judiciary, Helmke (2002, 2005), Iaryczower, Spiller, and Tommasi (2002), among others, document the effect of job insecurity on Argentina's judicial decision-making.[13] As in the case of legislators, the

---

[13] See Kapiszewski (2012) for an account that highlights multiple motivations apart from job security.

constitution places minimal limits on Supreme Court justices' tenure,[14] yet turnover in the Supreme Court has been constant (see Helmke 2002), casting serious doubt on its independence, despite significant evidence showing that the court has ruled independently in a number of cases comparable to the US Supreme Court.[15] The work of Iaryczower, Spiller, and Tommasi highlights precisely this independence.

This briefly illustrates a scenario in which key political actors' temporal horizons are shortened by the effects of institutions and dynamics foreign to congress or the Supreme Court per se, yet nonetheless very powerful. It is on the basis of this evidence that I classify Argentina as having low levels of institutional commitment. Analysis of turnover rates in the Argentine legislature, as well as in the Supreme Court, reveal that Argentina has one of the highest turnover rates in the region (Molinelli, Palanza, and Sin 1999).

5.3 CONFRONTING THE ARGENTINE PUZZLE FROM A DIFFERENT STANDPOINT

The theory presented in Chapter 2 allows us to make sense of empirical regularities in the preexisting literature on the use of decree authority in Argentina. Recall that Chapter 2 claims that the choice of legislative instrument is made by external agents, and is a function of their valuation of the policy at stake, the allocation of decision rights (i.e., the hurdle factors related to each instrument), and politicians' institutional commitment. Formally, the choice is a function of four factors:

$$\text{Choice} = f(r, l, V, W)$$

where r is the hurdle factor given by the allocation of decision rights, l is the level of institutional commitment, and V and W are the two external agents' respective valuations of policies. The empirical work in this chapter focuses mainly on formal rules r, and on levels of institutional commitment l. Variables V and W are not directly observable.

---

[14] Once justices reach the age of seventy-five, a new presidential nomination and senatorial confirmation is required every five years.

[15] Regarding executive manipulation of the Supreme Court (Corte Suprema de la Nación) by DNU, it is interesting to note that when President Menem issued DNU 2071/91, which targeted Supreme Court autarchy by suspending the court's ability to determine compensation for members and employees of the judiciary, the otherwise permissive court issued Acordada 42/91 declaring DNU 2071/91 null and void. In response, the executive issued a new decree a month later to reestablish the Supreme Court's authority on the matter.

Given that the model is sensitive to changes in the allocation of decision rights, expectations should vary before and after the Constitutional Reform of 1994. However, because the constitutional text established in Argentina in 1994 was enforced minimally (at least until 2006 – when the Bicameral Committee was created – and arguably also after that landmark), the *de facto* situation in Argentina after the 1994 reform resembles that of Brazil prior to the *Emenda Constitucional* 32 of 2001, i.e., during the period analyzed here congressional participation in the approval of DNUs is mandated, but not exercised. Before the reform, DNUs in Argentina were simply unconstitutional.

Both before and after the expansive Constitutional Reform (hereafter CR94), legislators' and Supreme Court justices' levels of institutional commitment are central to the possibility of sustaining decrees,[16] since we expect politicians to react to the encroachment of their decision rights at sufficiently high levels of institutional commitment. The effect of the Reform (until 2006) was to constrain the scope of decrees that could be disputed on constitutional grounds, i.e., it shrunk the universe of potentially unconstitutional DNUs.

To understand the implications of the reform, in what follows I present the expectations before and after. Before the CR94:

(a) At the lowest level of institutional commitment ($l = 0$), DNUs are preferred to statutes.

(b) When institutional commitment is positive but below the critical level at which the costs of decrees and statutes are identical ($c > l > 0$),[17] DNUs are preferred to statutes.

(c) When institutional commitment is positive and equal to the value c at which statutes and decrees impose qual costs ($c = l > 0$), external agents are indifferent between the two, hence:

    (c.1) DNUs are approved without observable intervention by congress, and

    (c.2) Impeachment attempts may occur but do not succeed.

(d) When institutional commitment is high ($l > c$),[18] statutes are preferred to DNUs.

After the CR94, the main innovation is that of legal and illegal DNUs. Before the reform all DNUs were illegal, as there was no mention of them

---

[16] Menem's packing of the Supreme Court certainly played a role in the way the Court overlooked the constitutionality of decrees before 1994.

[17] As presented in Chapter 2.

[18] I.e., the enactment of statutes is cheaper than the passage of decrees.

in the constitution. After the reform, some DNUs may conform to the constitutional rule, while others do not; many do not satisfy the requirement of need and urgency, and some disregard limitations imposed on some topics. These changes affect expectations, such that (a)–(c) below refer to illegal decrees (as opposed to decrees in general before CR94), (d) is identical to what it was before the reform and (e) is the only new condition. Therefore, after the CR94:

(a) At the lowest level of institutional commitment $(l = 0)$, *illegal* DNUs are preferred to statutes.

(b) When institutional commitment is positive but below the critical level at which the costs of decrees and statutes are identical $(c > l > 0)$, *illegal* DNUs are preferred to statutes

(c) When institutional commitment is positive and equal to the value c at which statutes and *illegal* decrees impose equal costs $(c = l > 0)$, external agents are indifferent between the two:

(c.1) *Illegal* DNUs are approved without observable intervention by congress, and

(c.2) Impeachment attempts may occur but do not succeed.

(d) When institutional commitment is high $(l > c)$, statutes are preferred to DNUs.

(e) At any level of institutional commitment, *legal* DNUs are preferred to statutes.

With the establishment of the Bicameral Committee on July 27, 2006, the cost of decree enactment was effectively altered. Whereas under the previous situation the main deterrent to decree enactment coming from congress was impeachment, once the Bicameral Committee was established, the strategic implications of the impeachment process are virtually replaced by those of the *resolución* process. And, as is always the case with less restrictive voting requirements, blocking decisions is more costly[19] under the *resolución* process than under the impeachment process. This implies that under the new scheme, external agents seeking to sustain a decree need to secure a larger coalition to block its rejection (i.e., ½ + 1 of the Senate), whereas in the previous scheme they needed to secure a smaller coalition to block impeachment (1/3 + 1 of the Senate). On the other hand, external agents seeking to reverse decrees, and legislators acting to reject decrees out of a desire to defend their prerogatives,

[19] Whereas $1/3 + \varepsilon$ is all that is necessary to block a $2/3$ majority, $1/2 + \varepsilon$ is needed to block a simple majority.

experience no difference in their payoffs under the two schemes, since these coalitions are determined fundamentally by levels of institutional commitment, as explained in Chapter 2.[20]

The implications of the creation of the Bicameral Committee in 2006 are as follows:

(a) At the lowest level of institutional commitment ($l = 0$), DNUs are preferred to statutes.

(b) When institutional commitment is positive but below the critical level at which the costs of decrees and statutes are identical ($c > l > 0$), DNUs are preferred to statutes, and DNU approval is tacit (failure to reject).

(c) When institutional commitment is positive and equal to the value c at which statutes and decrees impose equal costs ($c = l > 0$), external agents are indifferent between statutes and valid DNUs[21] (equivalent costs), but they prefer statutes to illegal DNUs that could be struck down by the Supreme Court, such that:

   (c.1) Valid DNUs are approved with tacit congressional support, and

   (c.2) Unconstitutional DNUs are not enacted,

(d) When institutional commitment is high ($l > c$),[22] statutes are preferred to illegal DNUs.

(e) Congressional rejections of DNUs do not occur in equilibrium.

5.4 HYPOTHESES AND DATA

With the previous expectations in mind, this section tests a set of hypotheses. The main hypotheses, however, are identical to those tested in the previous chapter regarding the influence of high and low stakes policy issues on the choice of legislative instrument:

---

[20] The fact that congress put in place a procedure that makes avoiding congressional rejection of DNUs more difficult simply insures that a larger fraction of the senate is needed in deals to uphold decrees, which may have a partisan explanation given the decades-long dominance of the PJ (the party in government when the law was passed) in the senate.

[21] The hurdle factor of blocking congressional rejection to a decree is identical to that of passing a statute. Although one may argue that decrees have the advantage of immediate enactment, I assume for simplicity that both can be enacted with the same celerity given appropriate support.

[22] I.e., the enactment of statutes is cheaper than the passage of decrees.

H1: Highly contested policy issues are enacted by statute.

H2: Uncontested policy issues are enacted by decree.

Note that the overall level of institutional commitment in a given country is fixed, determined by the overarching institutional setting that affects politicians' time horizons. Within countries, levels of institutional commitment, while constant, are activated differently across policy issues, and this affects the choice of legislative instrument, which will vary depending on whether high or low-stakes policies are at play. In other words, at any level of overall institutional commitment, legislators would care more to legislate on high-stakes policies than they would to pass low-stakes policies. In the case of Argentina, this means that legislators are less likely to look the other way if the president issues a decree on labor policy than on other less salient topics (Etchemendy and Palermo 1998).[23]

5.4.1 Dataset and Variables

In the previous section, I proposed a theory of the determinants of the choice between decrees and statutes, and derived empirical implications. This section is devoted to testing the empirical validity of those claims. For these reasons, I have assembled a dataset comprising all DNUs and statutes enacted in Argentina between 1983 and 2007, a sample representative of the full period since Argentina's most recent democratization. The sample includes 4,006 observations.[24] My dependent variable, CHOICE, is an indicator taking the value 1 each time a DNU is enacted, and the value zero each time a statute is enacted.[25] Conceptually, this dichotomous choice is a measure of the enforcement of decision rights. Each time a policy is decided, whether by decree (1) or statute (0), legislators and Supreme Court justices are taking a stance on the enforcement of their decision rights in that specific case.

---

[23] The exception to this claim is when exceedingly low levels of overall institutional commitment occur: in this case, the theory predicts that decrees would always be the preferred outcome, and we would never observe statutes. This sets a low bar to test that levels of institutional commitment are effectively always greater than zero, as we observe the enactment of statutes in every Latin American democracy that enacts executive decrees of the CDA type.

[24] Note that Tables 5.1 and 5.2 present data until 2010. However, the statistical analysis includes observations until 2007 as other variables were only collected for that period.

[25] All statutes are included, regardless of origin. I include bills that were successful only. See Chapter 4 for a discussion of the obstacles to including unsuccessful cases and the implications of that choice. The decision to assign the value 1 to DNUs and 0 to statutes is trivial.

A fundamental claim that I make is that the choice between decrees and statutes varies with levels of institutional commitment, and that the latter varies with issues. Given this claim, we should expect high levels of correlation between institutional commitment and policy issues. And although we cannot observe levels of institutional commitment directly, we do observe the subject matter of each piece of legislation. I use the policy issues reported for each piece of legislation as a proxy for high and low levels of institutional commitment.

To test my claims, I follow the guidelines laid out in the previous chapter. While identical variables as those used in the case of Brazil were used in this chapter when these were available, a few changes were required due to the uniqueness of some of the variables used to analyze the political context in Brazil. Also, the specificity of each country's institutional settings and constitutional reforms called for the use of different variables.[26] I test a few more economic variables in the case of Argentina than I do in Brazil, but the inclusion of these variables does not alter the general results.

As in the previous chapter, I group the 4,483 policy classifiers reported by the Argentine government into distinct broad policy area categories (53), and classify each of these into either "high" or "low" stakes policy areas, which I take to be proxies for high and low levels of institutional commitment. The variables HIGH and LOW are indicators, and I expect HIGH to decrease the likelihood of decrees, while LOW should have a positive effect on the choice.[27]

I recognize that policies dealing with political rights are high-stakes affairs (not coincidentally legislated exclusively by statute). But because these issues do not fit into the high-stakes/low-stakes divide in the sense that my model proposes, as confrontations led by external agents, not politicians, I do not include them in HIGH. Instead, I place them under a separate category, POLITICAL RIGHTS, and observations classified as such are neither classified as "high" or "low."

As I have claimed repeatedly, the other fundamental determinant of the choice between decrees and statutes is the allocation of decision rights. This independent variable refers to the set of rules that determine

---

[26] As an example, in Argentina I include an indicator for the creation of the bicameral committee charged with overseeing the enactment of decrees. In Brazil the constitutional reform and the establishment of the committee happened at the same time, but the two events had to be included separately in Argentina given the twelve-year delay in the establishment of the committee.

[27] I include details on the construction of variables in the Section 5.A.1 in Appendix 5.A.

both the actors that intervene in the process and the rules that determine their voting rights. While fixed components of the institutional setting are not testable in individual case analyses, changes in the rules may provide insight to some of the effects of those institutions. The constitutional reform enacted in Argentina in 1994 together with the creation of the Bicameral Committee charged with enforcing some of the changes are two such examples.

I seek to establish whether the institutional changes introduced through the CR94 had an effect on the choice of decrees versus statutes. This constitutional reform was broad-ranging, and included presidential reelection perhaps as its main goal. Regarding executive decree authority, the publicly stated purpose of the amendment was to limit its use by explicitly stating its bounds and regulating its use in the Constitution.[28] While the sheer incidence of decrees was certainly a concern at the time, the reform would make legal what had until then occurred *de facto*. The issues on which DNUs were enacted had also become of huge concern, given the expansion of the policy areas affected by DNUs and the circumstances under which they were being used. Apart from including DNUs, the constitution made explicit note of the areas excluded from constitutional decree authority.

To test these claims, I constructed a set of indicator variables. To examine the effect of the constitutional reform itself, I created CONSTITUTIONAL REFORM 94 – which takes the value 1 once the new constitution is in effect. The variable BICAMERAL COMMITTEE is constructed to assess the effect of the creation of the committee charged with the enforcement of the role of Congress in the DNU approval process, and EXCLUDED CDA seeks to test if the exclusion of certain policy areas from decree authority has any effect on the choice of decrees.

While I argue that we should not expect significant differences in the choice of decrees and statutes before and after CR94 (especially absent the necessary mechanisms regulating congressional intervention, which were not established until 2006), I also claim that legislators' rights over the legislative process were advanced by the requirement that certain policy

---

[28] Concerns for endogeneity seem unwarranted. The inclusion of DNUs in the constitution came as a bargaining chip that Menem conceded, among others, in exchange for reelection. It has been broadly acknowledged that the inclusion of DNUs occurred at the request of Alfonsín, who had made minimal use of the unconstitutional decrees during his administration (Acuña 1995; Sabsay 1995; Smulovitz 1995). Alfonsín believed that given his party's difficulty to attain unified government, if the Unión Cívica Radical were to gain the presidency in the future it would benefit from having this prerogative.

areas be excluded from CDA. In this limited terrain, agency was gained. The reform wrote into the constitution executive prerogatives that were until then absent, retracting congressional legislative prerogatives in a formal sense, while providing a legal framework to a *de facto* legislative instrument that had been of common usage for several years. By setting such minimal guidelines, the reform had no effect on the allocation of decision rights other than making an unconstitutional practice legal. But if institutions do impact the choice of decrees versus statutes, we should expect the effect of CONSTITUTIONAL REFORM 94 to increase the likelihood of decrees, and that of excluding topics from CDA to diminish it.

The creation in 2006 of the Bicameral Committee mandated by the Constitution is in some sense more transcendent, as it effectively altered the allocation of decision rights. Yet, while the Constitution established that a Bicameral Committee was to decide on the validity of decrees, it did not provide much detail in terms of establishing the precise criteria the committee would be expected to use or how it was to function. These details regarding the design of the committee and how it was to operate were left for congress to fine-tune.[29] In deciding the composition of the committee and the criteria used to decide the validity of DNUs, congress delegated substantial influence to the committee, which hands its report to each of the chambers for an up or down vote. Furthermore, the procedures agreed upon to regulate congressional participation in the approval of DNUs made explicit congressional approval unnecessary, as single-chamber approval is sufficient for DNUs to hold (the rejection by one chamber does not strike down the DNU). Under these rules, rejecting decrees by means of a *resolución* is just as costly as an impeachment process was under the previous scheme: it requires a majority in each of the chambers.

Regarding alternative explanations, previous work on reliance on decree authority in Argentina and elsewhere pays close attention to factors related to the economic and political contexts. I include a set of variables to examine the competing claims. I created the variable DIVIDED GOVERNMENT to indicate when a party or coalition different to the president's has the majority in at least one chamber. Party discipline has long been used to explain behavior in Argentine politics, and DIVIDED GOVERNMENT provides a way to test whether losing partisan dominance

---

[29] Congress passed Law 26.122 on 20 July 2006. See Posdeley (2016) for a detailed account of the early decisions surrounding the creation of the Bicameral Committee and its establishment of procedures.

in at least one chamber has effects on the legislative process. The established literature has found that party discipline and unified government are important for advancing the executive's policy agenda. This chapter looks at the policymaking process from a different set of assumptions that shift focus away from the executive (and her agenda). Consequently, the purpose of including DIVIDED GOVERNMENT here is to examine whether it plays a role in the choice of legislative instruments, regardless of who the formal initiator of the legislation is. In my approach, the effect of partisan variables is at best contextual (i.e., only important sometimes), and in consequence, I expect DIVIDED GOVERNMENT to have no significant effect overall, even if it appears to have some effect when evaluated in samples representing different periods.

I use the variable PRESIDENTIAL APPROVAL to examine whether variations in the public's appreciation of the president affect the chances that policies are enacted by decree or statute. While my theory does not make any claims regarding the effect of this variable, an important and growing literature emphasizes its role. In the case of Argentina, Calvo (2007) finds that presidential approval increases the success rate of executive bills in congress. Related to presidential approval, yet arguably capturing additional factors such as general goodwill to an incoming president, the variable HONEYMOON is an indicator of the first three months of each presidency. I include the variable to account for any effect this special period may have on the choice of decrees versus statutes. I also control for the days remaining until the next election, DAYS TO ELECTION, as a way to get at the lame duck effect, which is credited for diminishing executive influence.

Finally, I created a host of indicators of different presidential periods, to control for what may be considered different leadership styles, and distinguish them from other more stable determinants. While Alfonsín's term is too different from the remainder to prove revealing (and I try to control for this by looking at post-Alfonsín years separately), the dummies for Menem, De La Rúa, Duhalde, and Kirchner are included in the specifications.[30]

The economic context has repeatedly provided justification for the enactment of DNUs during dire economic crises. Decrees were used in Argentina to implement shock measures to stabilize the economy, adjust fiscal deficits, and alternatively deregulate and re-regulate sectors of the

---

[30] Puerta and Rodríguez Saá are not included because their time in office is so brief that very little gets done.

economy. The main tenets of Guillermo O'Donnell's (1993, 1994) explanation are linked to the economy, as he suggests that economic shocks have the power to alter expectations and allow for concentration of power in the executive. I control for variation due to economic developments by using common measures of INFLATION (based on the IPC, the consumer price index), PUBLIC EXPENDITURE, and COMMODITY INDEX, which is a commodity price index for a set of food items that compose an important part of Argentine exports.[31] ECONOMIC PACKAGE, an indicator coded 1 in months during which the executive introduced a major stabilization package, also tackles the economic context.

5.4.2 Empirical Analysis

The dataset[32] constructed for this chapter includes all *DNUs* and *leyes* enacted between 1983 and 2007, i.e., 4,006 observations,[33] 17.3 percent of which are decrees. The analysis of the data is carried out using maximum likelihood estimation. Given the limited nature of my dependent variable, and the inherent element of choice, I implement logit models. A justification of this choice is included in Chapter 4.

Table 5.3 presents a set of specifications designed to examine the validity of the different explanations. Model (1) presents a restricted specification including institutional commitment variables HIGH and LOW, and the effect of rules EXCLUDED CDA, CONSTITUTIONAL REFORM 94, and BICAMERAL COMMITTEE; (2) adds a set of frequently used political and economic context variables; (3) incorporates additional political and economic controls; and (4) adds indicators for Menem, De La Rúa, and Kirchner, to assess the effect of these three presidents on the choice of decrees versus statutes.

The empirical analysis reveals support for the main tenets of my theory, confirming that the effects of institutional commitment variables HIGH and LOW, together with other institutional variables, are significant, and that they behave in the way expected given Argentina's low level of institutional commitment. Institutional variables EXCLUDED CDA, and CONSTITUTIONAL REFORM 94, together with institutional commitment

---

[31] Indices for other commodities were also tested, with similar results.

[32] The Table 5.A.2 in Appendix 5.A presents the descriptive statistics of the variables included in the regression analysis.

[33] As mentioned previously in this chapter, the statistical analysis includes observations until 2007, as other variables were only collected for that period.

TABLE 5.3. *Logistic analysis of choice between decrees and statutes, Argentina 1983–2007*

	(1)	(2)	(3)	(4)
High	1.559***	2.154***	2.211***	2.105***
	(0.251)	(0.329)	(0.331)	(0.334)
Low	0.846***	1.394***	1.424***	1.325***
	(0.253)	(0.331)	(0.333)	(0.336)
Excl.CDA	−0.357**	−0.322*	−0.343*	−0.409**
	(0.176)	(0.179)	(0.181)	(0.187)
Constitutional Reform 1994	0.802***	1.346***	0.897***	−0.290
	(0.099)	(0.158)	(0.166)	(0.258)
DNU Bicameral Committee	−0.357**	0.247	1.274***	−0.475
	(0.173)	(0.227)	(0.274)	(0.331)
Economic Package		0.782***	0.429***	0.842***
		(0.110)	(0.125)	(0.213)
Inflation		−0.001	−0.001	
		(0.004)	(0.004)	
Inflation (% Change)				−0.349*
				(0.211)
Commodity Index			−0.015**	0.007
			(0.007)	(0.006)
Public Expenditure			−0.000***	−0.036***
			(0.000)	(0.008)
Divided Government		0.240	−0.190	0.000**
		(0.159)	(0.198)	(0.000)
Presidential Approval		0.008**	0.004	−0.002
		(0.004)	(0.004)	(0.209)
Honeymoon Effect			0.011	0.036**
			(0.187)	(0.016)
Days to Election			0.004	−0.001***
			(0.011)	(0.000)
Menem's Presidency				3.340***
				(0.437)
De La Rúa's Presidency				2.295***
				(0.512)
Duhalde's Presidency				4.644***
				(0.597)

(continued)

TABLE 5.3 *(continued)*

	(1)	(2)	(3)	(4)
Kirchner's Presidency				4.725***
				(0.481)
Constant	−3.229***	−5.011***	0.467	−5.092***
	(0.254)	(0.423)	(0.984)	(1.238)
McFadden Pseudo R^2	0.047	0.076	0.105	0.162
Log likelihood	−1759.153	−1664.961	−1612.456	−1509.896
Likelihood-ratio test	175.121	272.424	377.435	582.556
p-value	0.000	0.000	0.000	0.000
AIC	3530.31	3349.923	3252.912	3055.791
BIC	3568.08	3412.502	3340.523	3168.434
Observations	4006	3858	3858	3858

Note: *** $p < 0.01$, **$p < 0.05$, *$p < 0.1$; Standard errors in parentheses.

variables HIGH and LOW, reveal consistent effects across specifications, whether controls are included or not. While the inclusion of political and economic context variables improves the fit of the model to the data, their effects and levels of significance differ across specifications.

The analysis that follows is based mainly on the results of model 4, since likelihood ratio tests reveal that it is the one that best fits the data; I make specific indications when I consider results from other models.[34] The Figures 5.2 and 5.3 graph effects from model 4 in Table 5.3. The full list of marginal effects and predicted probabilities are presented in Appendix 5.A (Tables 5.A.3 and 5.A.4 respectively).

At a basic level, the results reveal that categories HIGH and LOW do affect the likelihood that policies are enacted by decree in ways that are statistically discernible from zero ($p < 0.001$).[35] This result may seem counter to expectations upon first view, yet it is exactly what we would expect at lower levels of institutional commitment. While at intermediate levels of institutional commitment we expect the enactment of policies

---

[34] Likelihood ratios between models 2, 3, and 4 reveal that model 4 provides the best fit. Model 3 provides a better fit than model 2 (LR = 105.01), while model 4 improves both on model 2 (LR = 310.13) and on model 3 (LR = 205.12). AIC and BIC confirm this.

[35] The two variables are highly correlated (−0.86), as expected, yet they yield effects in the same direction. I conducted z-tests to check the difference in coefficients for HIGH and LOW. The tests allow me to reject the null hypothesis of no differences between the coefficients of HIGH and LOW in these and all other regressions included in this chapter.

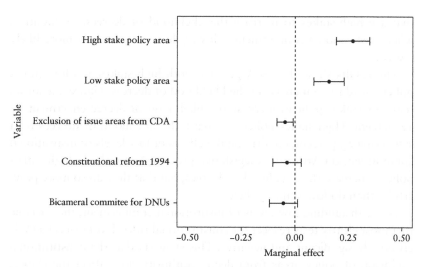

FIGURE 5.2. *Marginal effects for logistic analysis of choice between decrees and statutes, Argentina 1983–2007*
Note: Average partial effects. 95% confidence intervals.

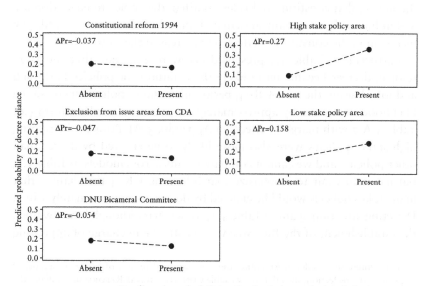

FIGURE 5.3. *Predicted probabilities for logistic analysis of choice between decrees and statutes, Argentina 1983–2007*
Note: Predicted probability with observed V.

that are high-stakes to increase the likelihood of decrees, in countries where institutional commitment is lower, decrees are simply more likely always.

The results show that in Argentina, both high-stakes and low-stakes policies lead to an increase in the likelihood of decrees. Figure 5.2 shows that low-stakes policies increase the likelihood of decree enactment by 12 percent. High-stakes policies increase the likelihood of decrees by a staggering 23 percent, confirming the effects of low levels of institutional commitment on Argentina's legislative process. Not only do high-stakes policies increase the likelihood of decrees, but that they do so more powerfully than do low-stakes policies.

Notwithstanding low levels of institutional commitment, the variable that most clearly tests respect for constitutional rules, EXCLUDED CDA, is effectively significant and negative. This suggests that the constitutional exclusion of policy areas from decree authority does affect the choice, making decrees less likely in excluded areas, even if its marginal effect is small (5 percent), as we would expect in contexts where institutional commitment is low.

The remaining institutional variables confirm our expectations as well: Constitutional Reform 94 increases the likelihood that policies are enacted by DNU by about 10 percent.[36] This particular result supports the notion that constitutional rules do affect the choice to enact decrees, and in line with what many anticipated, that the legalization of DNUs by inclusion in the constitution effectively increased their use.

Furthermore, Table 5.5 presented below reveals that after the 1994 reform, decrees became more likely than statutes for policies both high and low. During the post-CR94, period high-stakes policies increase the likelihood of decrees by approximately 35 percent after the reform (see Table 5.A.7 with marginal effects in Appendix 5.A). Prior to the reform, high-stakes policies were also more likely to be enacted by decree than other policies, and we cannot compare results across models in Table 5.5, but it remains fair to emphasize that following CR94 the chances that high-stakes policies would be enacted by decree are approximately 1 in 3. Directing attention again to Table 5.3, we see that although long-awaited, the establishment of the BICAMERAL COMMITTEE in charge of approving

---

[36] As an interesting aside, in Argentina the constitutional reform of '94 also established presidential reelection, such that the variable CONSTITUTIONAL REFORM 94 conflates the effect of REELECTION, a variable taken into account in the chapter on Brazil. Interestingly, while REELECTION has a negative effect on the choice of decrees in Brazil, the effect of CR94 in Argentina is positive.

or rejecting DNUs yields no significant effect on decree enactment, as expected – and the additional fact that we observe no rejections in the senate provides further support to institutional variables.

Regarding the effect of economic context variables, we find that during periods of economic turmoil, in which extraordinary economic packages where passed, policies were more likely to be passed by decree. Specifically, policies enacted during these periods were approximately 11 percent more likely to be DNUs than otherwise ($p < 0.001$). That decrees are passed in response to economic emergencies is no surprise, as these circumstances originally spawned the use of decrees.

Interpretation of the effects of other economic context variables is not as straightforward.[37] Most interestingly, inflation does not yield a statistically significant effect on the likelihood of decrees in any specification. Only the variable INFLATION2, which represents the change in the consumer price index with respect to December of the previous year, yields a significant yet tiny negative coefficient, which contradicts O'Donnell's (1993, 1994) famous claim that inflation and economic turmoil increase executive influence and the use of decrees. Yet, other economic indicators suggest different dynamics. From O'Donnell's perspective, negative shocks from the economy impact the political structure and promote concentration of power in the executive, so we would expect the effect of variables as COMMODITY INDEX and PUBLIC EXPENDITURES, two variables whose increases should decompress the economy, to have negative effects on the likelihood of decree enactment. Both the effect of increases in food commodity prices and of PUBLIC EXPENDITURES lead to a lower likelihood of decrees (albeit by a very small margin of less than 1 percent). Table 5.3 reveals that increases in levels of public spending decrease the likelihood of decrees. However, Tables 5.4 (analyzing the post Alfonsín era) and 5.5 (analyzing periods pre- and post-CR94) show the effect of public spending to be in the opposite direction, increasing the likelihood of decrees in all cases except before CR94 (model 3) in Table 5.5.[38] These contradictory effects leave us with uncertainty regarding the effect of the economy on the choice between decrees and statutes.

Traditional political context variables, such as DIVIDED GOVERNMENT, PRESIDENTIAL APPROVAL, HONEYMOON, and DAYS TO ELECTION also

---

[37] Lagged effects of all economic variables were tested; they were not statistically significant and did not alter other effects significantly. Those specifications are not presented here.

[38] I acknowledge there is an endogenous element in this variable. Spending is partly determined by levels of tax collection, but undoubtedly the government has some discretion in the decision.

TABLE 5.4. *Logistic analysis of choice between decrees and statutes, Argentina Post Alfonsín Era*

	(1) Post-1989	(2) Post-1989
High	2.121***	2.123***
Low	1.365***	1.344***
	(0.331)	(0.336)
Excluded.CDA	−0.343*	−0.426**
	(0.179)	(0.187)
Constitutional Reform 1994	0.232**	−0.305
	(0.105)	(0.249)
DNU Committee	−0.373**	−0.461
	(0.173)	(0.329)
Economic Package		0.701***
		(0.210)
Inflation2		−0.001***
		(0.000)
Commodity Index		−0.038***
		(0.009)
Public Expenditure		0.000**
		(0.000)
Divided Government		−0.426**
		(0.213)
Presidential Approval		0.015**
		(0.006)
Honeymoon Effect		0.056
		(0.209)
Days to Election		0.032*
		(0.016)
Menem		0.268
		(0.505)
De La Rúa		−0.583
		(0.512)
Duhalde		1.730***
		(0.608)
Kirchner		1.517***
		(0.582)

	(1) Post-1989	(2) Post-1989
Constant	−3.174***	−1.835
	(0.334)	(1.289)
McFadden Pseudo R²	0.039	0.111
Log likelihood	−1625.164	−1492.567
Likelihood-ratio test	131.241	373.789
p-value	0.000	0.000
AIC	3262.328	3021.135
BIC	3299.001	3130.888
Observations	3335	3286

Note: *** p < 0.01, ** p < 0.05, * p < 0.1; Standard errors in parentheses.

reveal unstable results across specifications, and in so doing reinforce the idea that they fall short of providing an expansive explanation of the choice of decrees versus statutes. This is so notwithstanding that partisan considerations may be of weight when putting together coalitions around projects. While their inclusion with economic context variables improves the model's fit to the data, their effects, when significant, are inconsistent across specifications.

All four variables reproduce the unstable pattern, which is magnified if Tables 5.3–5.5 are analyzed together. Table 5.3 reveals (taking only into account the unrestricted model 4) that DIVIDED GOVERNMENT yields a small negative effect on the likelihood that decrees will be chosen over statutes – approximately 5 percent when considering its marginal effect. This result merits emphasis, since it is the only effect that is consistently negative and significant across Tables 5.3, 5.4, and 5.5. PRESIDENTIAL APPROVAL is not significant most of the time, and alters signs between specifications when it is significant. Because it is not statistically significant in the less restrictive models, I am inclined to say that such is its prevalent effect. The specifications in which PRESIDENTIAL APPROVAL yields statistically significant results are model 2 in the post-1989 era (Table 5.4) and models 3 and 5 in Table 5.5; its minuscule effect switches direction. HONEYMOON, which gets at a related phenomenon of favor toward the president, presents an unstable pattern as well. Its effect, when significant, is positive and of a larger magnitude than that of PRESIDENTIAL APPROVAL. Lastly, DAYS TO ELECTION yields significant results more often than not, but the direction of the effect varies between specifications. Table 5.3 would suggest a minuscule negative effect on the choice.

TABLE 5.5. *Logistic analysis of choice between decrees and statutes, Argentina pre and post-Constitutional Reform of 1994*

	(1) Pre-CR94	(2) Post-CR94	(3) Pre-CR94	(4) Post-CR94	(5) Post-CR94
High	0.494	2.440***	1.645***	2.482***	2.481***
	(0.325)	(0.421)	(0.545)	(0.426)	(0.430)
Low	−0.056	1.665***	1.022*	1.666***	1.658***
	(0.335)	(0.423)	(0.552)	(0.428)	(0.431)
Excluded CDA	1.019***	−1.437***	1.238***	−1.518***	−1.535***
	(0.236)	(0.295)	(0.284)	(0.302)	(0.305)
DNU Committee		−0.371**		−0.111	−0.515
		(0.174)		(0.312)	(0.336)
Economic Package			0.413	−0.235	−0.398
			(0.308)	(0.260)	(0.431)
Inflation2 (% Change)			−0.091**	0.341	−0.181
			(0.035)	(0.693)	(0.720)
Commodity Index			−0.024	−0.028***	−0.043***
			(0.025)	(0.010)	(0.010)
Public Expenditure			−0.051***	−0.004***	0.003*
			(0.007)	(0.001)	(0.002)
Presidential Approval			−0.018*	0.013	0.016*
			(0.010)	(0.009)	(0.009)
Honeymoon Effect			4.210***	0.244	−0.088
			(1.054)	(0.223)	(0.245)
Days to Election			−0.060	−0.046***	0.020
			(0.043)	(0.015)	(0.018)
Divided Government				−0.577**	−0.535**
				(0.227)	(0.227)
Menem				−1.076***	−2.129***
				(0.244)	(0.732)
De La Rúa					−1.987***
					(0.615)
Duhalde					0.435
					(0.685)
Kirchner					−0.771
					(0.748)

	(1) Pre-CR94	(2) Post-CR94	(3) Pre-CR94	(4) Post-CR94	(5) Post-CR94
Constant	−2.429***	−3.213***	21.348***	1.936	0.679
	(0.306)	(0.416)	(4.105)	(1.203)	(1.421)
McFadden Pseudo R^2	0.029	0.052	0.222	0.122	0.138
Log likelihood	−495.344	−1234.310	−372.924	−1126.127	−1105.024
Likelihood-ratio test	30.021	135.269	213.377	312.247	354.453
p-value	0.000	0.000	0.000	0.000	0.000
AIC	998.688	2478.621	767.849	2280.255	2244.049
BIC	1019.868	2507.807	825.590	2361.514	2342.721
Observations	1473	2533	1407	2451	2451

Note: *** $p < 0.01$, **$p < 0.05$, *$p < 0.1$; Standard errors in parentheses.

Instead, the variables included to assess the effect of individual presidents on the choice of decrees versus statutes produce results that are significant at the 0.01 level. Importantly, note that when these variables are excluded from an otherwise identical specification, political variables yield results that are not statistically significant (this is true for all political variables except PRESIDENTIAL APPROVAL).[39] President MENEM, known for increasing reliance on decrees to unprecedented levels, along with including the prerogative in the 1994 Constitution, in fact affects the likelihood of decree enactment by approximately 33 percent (as compared to times when he was not in office). KIRCHNER, however, belittles Menem's infamous *decretazo*: Nestor Kirchner's tenure in office increases the likelihood of decree enactment by an impressive 61 percent as compared to times when others were in charge of the executive. In Table 5.3 the effect of President DE LA RÚA is similar to Menem's. President DE LA RÚA, who unsuccessfully governed over part of the country's deepest economic crisis yet, in Table 5.5 has a negative effect on the likelihood of decree enactment (which Kim (2007) has linked to the fact that he is the only president since 1983 to have faced an unfriendly supreme

[39] A likelihood ratio test between model 4 and its equivalent without the presidential dummies reveals that the unrestricted model provides a better fit, and justifies the inclusion of these variables in the specification.

court). However, all presidents examined seem to have a positive effect on decrees (as opposed to when they were not in office). This is likely an artifice of the very low levels of reliance on decrees under Alfonsín, as the direction of the effect of Menem and De La Rúa changes to negative when only considering the post CR94 period. Admittedly, post hoc generalizations of individual presidents' impact is of limited theoretical value, and similar conclusions could be reached by simple observation of the descriptive data in Table 5.2.

As anticipated above, I estimated the models in Table 5.3 using different sub-samples. The period-wise analyses allow me to (a) focus attention on the post-Alfonsín era, when enactment of decrees is comparable across presidents, and (b) compare effects before and after the CR94. I present these results in Tables 5.4 and 5.5, respectively.

Table 5.4 presents two models. The first is restricted to institutional and institutional commitment variables, and the second incorporates contextual controls. The columns in Table 5.4 evaluate Table 5.3's models 1 and 4 in the years after the end of the Alfonsín administration in 1989. Importantly, the effects of my key explanatory variables remain largely unaltered, despite the larger effects when Alfonsín's so-called "institutionalist" period is excluded from the sample (see Table 5.A.7 in Appendix 5.A).[40] Note that there are no significant differences regarding the effects of institutional commitment variables HIGH and LOW, nor regarding EXCLUDED CDA. The dummy CR94 is not significant in the less restrictive model when considered in this period, which suggests that enactment of decrees during Menem was similar before and after the reform (i.e., it is likely that the lower incidence of decrees during the Alfonsín years is driving part of the effect of CONSTITUTIONAL REFORM 94 in the full sample).

Regarding economic context variables, the effect of ECONOMIC PACKAGE remains positive and significant. The effect of monthly inflation (not shown) is not significant, but that of INFLATION2 yields a tiny and significant negative effect on the choice. The impact of rises in prices of food commodities, as measured by COMMODITY INDEX, is the same in this shorter time frame as it is in the full sample, but the direction of the effect of PUBLIC EXPENDITURES is reversed, which is less consistent with O'Donnell's explanation.

---

[40] I use this terminology as it is commonly used in Argentina, to characterize Alfonsín and UCR leaders in general as having above-average regard for the rule of law.

The effects of political context variables, as I anticipated, vary considerably when evaluated in the post-1989 period. Importantly, the effect of DIVIDED GOVERNMENT remains significant and negative, lending support to delegation theories of decree enactment, which would suggest that decrees occur as a consequence of congressional delegation, be it explicit or implicit. A change from unified to divided government decreases the likelihood that a policy is enacted by decree by approximately 7 percent. Note that there was unified government only during a brief two-year period, 1995 to 1997, during Menem's second term in office, and then not again until 2005, so I do not discard that peculiarities of those years may be guiding this effect. However, that decrees are more likely, all else equal, during unified government implies that partisan liaisons may in fact diminish the cost of including legislators in coalitions. In contrast to findings for the full sample, this period also reveals a statistically significant, albeit tiny, positive effect of PRESIDENTIAL APPROVAL, while the effect of HONEYMOON remains not significant, and that of DAYS TO ELECTION switches to positive when considered in the post-1989 period. Controls for different presidents show that the effects of DUHALDE and KIRCHNER are significant and positive, with smaller marginal effects than when evaluated in the full sample, 32 and 25 percent, respectively. The effects of DE LA RÚA and MENEM are not statistically significant in this analysis.

In a different approach to the analysis, Table 5.5 presents results for the different periods before and after the constitutional reform of 1994. Models 1 and 2 present a restricted model that includes only institutional commitment and strictly institutional variables before and after the reform, respectively. Models 3, 4, and 5 present less restrictive models including political and economic context controls, before the reform (model 3) and after the reform (models 4 and 5).

Contrasting the restricted model in the two periods (models 1 and 2), they appear to show different dynamics.[41] A likelihood ratio test for structural breaks leads us, in fact, to reject the null that there are no breaks.[42] The sets of coefficients before and after the reform are

---

[41] Pooling different periods in a regression imposes the restriction that an independent variable has the same effect on the dependent variable for different groups of data.

[42] I conducted tests on several specifications, with no substantive variations in results. For practical reasons, I report only two specifications here. One is a LR test of the pooled sample against the two regressions for each of the partial periods (including independent variables HIGH, LOW, EXCLUDED CDA, ECONOMIC PACKAGE, INFLATION2,

statistically different. Interestingly, however, while the effects of economic and political context variables vary between periods, the effects of my key variables remain largely unaltered across specifications when they are significant. In what follows I analyze the results in Table 5.5 and reflect on the implications of this for Table 5.3.

Before the reform, critical policy areas within the realm of criminal law, taxation, electoral matters, and political parties (policy areas which the reform would later exclude from decree authority) appear to increase the likelihood that decrees are chosen over statutes. (Note that there were no explicit exclusions before, so the enactment of decrees on these salient topics was as illegal as the enactment of decrees on any other topic.) After the reform and the establishment of clear restrictions to these policy domains, inclusion in the category EXCLUDED CDA decreases the likelihood of enactment by decree by 16 percent. Along with the institutional change, the effect of institutional commitment variables HIGH and LOW also yield statistically significant and positive effects, as in the previous tables, after the reform – with magnitudes similar to those in Tables 5.3 and 5.4. Note that the residual category is POLITICAL RIGHTS, so one could say that when compared to the enactment of laws affecting political rights, high and low stakes policies both are more likely to be enacted by decree. As I highlighted before, this result is in line with expectations in settings where institutional commitment is low.

Models 3–5,[43] which incorporate controls, essentially replicate the effects of my key explanatory variables, and as in model 2 in this same table, present magnitudes that are larger than those in the pooled regressions, as if the effects were concentrated in this period. This is the case with variables HIGH, LOW, and EXCLUDED CDA. The effect of DNU COMMITTEE, though negative, is hardly statistically significant.[44]

COMMODITY INDEX, PUBLIC EXPENDITURES, DIVIDED GOVERNMENT, PRESIDENTIAL APPROVAL, HONEYMOON, DAYS TO ELECTION – plus two indicators in the pooled sample: CONSTITUTIONAL REFORM 94, and a dummy for the structural reforms of the 1990s (STRUCTURAL REFORM 90, to account for the reforms carried out during the nineties, which I believe is what is behind the break). This test has 9 degrees of freedom and LR = 68.17, which is larger than the critical value, enabling a rejection of the null that there are no structural breaks. The second LR test I report was carried out on the same specification, but excluding the years before Menem (i.e., before May 13, 1989); LR = 62.90, with 9 degrees of freedom; same substantive result.

[43] A likelihood ratio test shows model 5 provides a better fit than model 4 (LR = 42.21).

[44] Because the committee came into existence in 2006, the limited time period during which it could affect outcomes may explain this result.

Economic context variables do not fare as consistently. COMMODITY INDEX and PUBLIC EXPENDITURES both yield statistically significant results across specifications. The effect of COMMODITY INDEX, when statistically significant, is consistently negative, suggesting that increases in the prices of food commodities (which benefit the Argentine economy) reduce the likelihood of decrees. PUBLIC EXPENDITURES have a similar effect, although the direction of the effect changes to positive when including Presidents DUHALDE and KIRCHNER in the equation. This suggests that a favorable economic landscape and higher levels of public spending tend to decrease the likelihood of decrees, all else equal. INFLATION and ECONOMIC PACKAGE do not yield statistically significant results.

Less consistent still are the results yielded by political context variables. The effect of DIVIDED GOVERNMENT, as mentioned, proves to be the most consistent across specifications and samples, even if it is not always statistically significant (note that the variable drops in several specifications because there is no variation until December 1995). In the specification in model 5, a switch from unified to divided government decreases the likelihood that a policy is enacted by DNU by approximately 8 percent.

The effect of PRESIDENTIAL APPROVAL is hardly statistically significant, and switches signs from negative in the period preceding the reform to positive after the reform. The effect of HONEYMOON appears to have a strong positive effect before the reform only. It seems, then, that the early years are driving the effect in the full sample; during the post-Alfonsín era and after the constitutional reform, the effects are small and lack statistical significance.

Inclusion of dummies for presidents MENEM, DE LA RÚA, DUHALDE, and KIRCHNER reveal an interesting dynamic: the effect of MENEM is negative, as is DE LA RÚA's. This places Menem's strong reliance on decrees in a different light, as the years following his would witness even higher levels of reliance on decrees. The effects for DUHALDE and KIRCHNER, however, are not statistically significant.

Overall, Table 5.5 suggests that while the effects of institutional variables and institutional commitment variables are consistent across the two periods, the effect of the alternative explanations varies. While the economy appears to have an effect on the likelihood of decrees that is the same before and after the reform, coefficients on variables testing the effects of economic shocks and policy reactions to those shocks are minuscule and often not significant in either period. Among political variables, DIVIDED GOVERNMENT produces a negative effect in the post

CR94 period (note that this variable lacks variation in the earlier period), while PRESIDENTIAL APPROVAL and the HONEYMOON effect are significant in the earlier period, albeit in opposite directions. This suggests that in the earlier period, while levels of approval for the president decreased the likelihood of decrees, the chance that decrees are enacted during the beginning of a presidential term are higher.

5.4.3 A Structural Break Around 1994

Given the results in Table 5.5, in this section I return to issues surrounding the effects of the constitutional and structural reforms of the nineties. While it is possible that it is the constitutional reform itself that causes the break (as a consequence of the change in rules), there are reasons to doubt that the constitution is the cause. For this reason, Table 5.6 presents two models analyzing different dynamics in the full sample. The first interacts all variables with the indicator variable CONSTITUTIONAL REFORM 94, and the second interacts all variables with the indicator STRUCTURAL REFORMS '90S, as an alternative to splitting the samples in each case to evaluate the effect of the independent variables in the periods following the constitutional reform and the structural reforms, alternatively.

The purpose of these models is to test whether the two most likely culprits for the structural break do indeed provide leverage on the differences between periods. Both models in Table 5.6 replicate the nonrestrictive specifications in the previous tables, and add interaction terms to disentangle the effects of different periods. Model 1 interacts all independent variables with the dummy variable CONSTITUTIONAL REFORM 94 and Model 2 does the same with the dummy variable STRUCTURAL REFORMS 90S to account for these competing possibilities.

In these models, which allow us to disentangle the effects of the independent variables in different temporal scenarios, the effects remain statistically significant and consistent with previous specifications when evaluated individually, as in Table 5.3, yet the interaction terms are not always statistically significant. I analyze models 1 and 2 separately next, and then compare the models to get at the broader question of the effect of the constitutional reform versus the structural reforms of the nineties.

In model 1, which gets at the specificities of the post CR94 period, the effects of interaction terms HIGH*CONSTITUTIONAL REFORM 94 and LOW*CONSTITUTIONAL REFORM 94 are not statistically significant. However, the added effect of the coefficient of HIGH (given the interaction term, this is the unique effect of HIGH when CONSTITUTIONAL

TABLE 5.6. *Logistic analysis – choice between decrees and statutes, Argentina pooled sample, interacted models for structural break*

	(1) Constitutional Reform 94		(2) Structural Reforms 90's	
	Coefficients	Standard errors	Coefficients	Standard errors
High	1.473***	(0.546)	2.595***	(0.425)
Low	0.842	(0.553)	1.739***	(0.427)
Excl.CDA	1.210***	(0.292)	−1.094***	(0.256)
Constitutional Reform 1994	1.346	(5.626)	0.659***	(0.240)
Structural Reforms of 90s	−0.468	(0.479)	−1.770	(6.941)
Economic Package	1.309***	(0.494)	0.635***	(0.174)
Inflation (% Change)	−0.086***	(0.030)	0.889	(0.680)
Commodity Index	0.027	(0.034)	−0.035***	(0.009)
Public Expenditure	−0.012	(0.009)	−0.004***	(0.001)
Divided Government	−0.815***	(0.210)	−0.792***	(0.209)
President Popularity	0.004	(0.011)	0.041***	(0.006)
Honeymoon Effect	1.853*	(1.008)	0.576***	(0.199)
Days to Election	−0.032	(0.056)	−0.027**	(0.013)
High × Constitutional Reform 94	1.045	(0.693)		
Low × Constitutional Reform 94	0.862	(0.699)		
Excluded CDA × Constitutional Reform 94	−2.704***	(0.419)		
Econ. Plan × Constitutional Reform 94	−0.667	(0.524)		

(continued)

TABLE 5.6 (*continued*)

	(1) Constitutional Reform 94		(2) Structural Reforms 90's	
	Coefficients	Standard errors	Coefficients	Standard errors
Inflation × Constitutional Reform 94	0.944	(0.683)		
Commodity I. × Constitutional Reform 94	−0.064*	(0.035)		
Public Exp. × Constitutional Reform 94	0.007	(0.009)		
Pres Pop. × Constitutional Reform 94	0.039***	(0.012)		
Honeymoon × Constitutional Reform 94	−1.262	(1.028)		
Days to Election × Constitutional Reform 94	0.002	(0.057)		
High × Structural Reforms 90s			−1.512**	(0.703)
Low × Structural Reforms 90s			−1.031	(0.707)
Excluded CDA × Structural Reforms 90s			2.187***	(0.415)
Econ. Plan × Structural Reforms 90s			0.809	(0.560)
Inflation × Structural Reforms 90s			−0.975	(0.680)
Commodity I. × Structural Reforms 90s			0.067*	(0.039)

	(1) Constitutional Reform 94		(2) Structural Reforms 90's	
	Coefficients	Standard errors	Coefficients	Standard errors
Public Exp. × Structural Reforms 90s			−0.006	(0.010)
Pres Pop. × Structural Reforms 90s			−0.034***	(0.012)
Honeymoon × Structural Reforms 90s			1.238	(1.034)
Days to Election × Structural Reforms 90s			−0.025	(0.061)
Constant	−0.057	(5.547)	0.433	(1.126)
McFadden Pseudo R²	0.112		0.107	
Log likelihood	−1491.013		−1499.853	
Likelihood-ratio test	376.897		359.218	
p-value	0.000		0.000	
AIC	3030.027		3047.706	
BIC	3176.365		3194.044	
Observations	3286		3286	

Note: *** $p < 0.01$, **$p < 0.05$, *$p < 0.1$; Standard errors in parentheses.

REFORM 94 = 0) plus that of the interaction term HIGH*CONSTITUTIONAL REFORM 94, which is the effect of HIGH when CONSTITUTIONAL REFORM 94 = 1, is positive, comparable and slightly bigger than the effect of HIGH when only evaluating the post-CR94 period (as in the reduced sample of model 2 in Table 5.5). These results are in line with those in previous tables. Among the main explanatory variables, only EXCLUDED CDA*CONSTITUTIONAL REFORM 94 yields a significant result, and the effect after the CR94 is in the expected negative direction. These are interesting findings, as the CR94 could have deterred the use of decrees, but this is not what the data suggest. However, the constitutional exclusion of certain topics from decree authority did have an effect and after the constitutional reform policy on those issues has been systematically more likely to be legislated by congressional statutes. The other interaction term that yields statistically significant coefficients is PRESIDENTIAL POPULARITY* CONSTITUTIONAL REFORM.

In model 2, which seeks to identify the specific effects associated to the structural reforms of the 90s, the effect of HIGH*STRUCTURAL REFORMS 90S is both significant and negative, but when this coefficient is added to the unique effect of HIGH outside of the structural reforms period, to get at the effect for all HIGH when STRUCTURAL REFORMS 90S = 1, the resulting effect on the likelihood of decrees versus statutes is positive, as elsewhere. Interestingly, the effect of EXCLUDED CDA*STRUCTURAL REFORMS 90S is positive, and remains positive when added to the unique effect of EXCLUDED CDA on the likelihood of decrees, which suggests that during structural reforms Excluded CDA did not deter the likelihood of policy enactment by decree as it does over the course of the post CR94 period. Argentina's structural reforms included the privatization of highly lucrative areas of the Argentine economy (energy, communications, and transportation, to name a few), high-stakes policies that could have ignited defensive actions by legislators, but the data suggest that they did not do so systematically.

The results do not lend much support to the intuition that the structural reforms of the 90s affected the likelihood of decree enactment differently. During the period that structural reforms were being adopted, the likelihood that decrees were chosen over statutes is affected in the same direction as it is during normal times. The only exception to this is EXCLUDED CDA, which only during structural reforms carries a positive effect on the likelihood of decrees.

I find that, in most cases, coefficients of my main explanatory variables remain consistent across specifications in their individual effects; that is, before the constitutional reform of 1994 and under times when structural reforms are not taking place, but also after CR94 and during the structural reforms period (although some lose statistical significance in the latter scenarios).

5.5 CONCLUSIONS

The findings in this chapter advance our understanding of decree authority both in the sphere of Argentine politics and in comparative perspective. Within Argentine politics, the findings confirm the expectation that where levels of institutional commitment are low, the choice of statutes will occur less frequently, and high-stakes policies will hold the interest of politicians with less force. This appears to be the dynamic at play. High-stakes and low-stakes policies, which are proxies for higher and lower levels of institutional commitment around those policies, are significantly associated to increases in the likelihood of decrees (as opposed to the null of no effects). However, low levels overall of institutional commitment (institutional near-sightedness) in Argentina prevents the directionality of effects to be what we might expect it to be in polities were levels of institutional commitment are higher. Interestingly, the years during which Argentina underwent structural reforms, perhaps years in which high-stakes took a dimension all of its own, the effect is what one would expect at higher levels of institutional commitment. Additionally, the analysis of the case of Argentina provides a benchmark against which to assess the explanatory value of the theory of legislative choice in a comparative perspective.

That low levels of institutional commitment in Argentina are at the core of the choice between legislative instruments, while not an optimistic assessment, should nonetheless aid our understanding of the determinants of policy choices in the country. It emphasizes the point that the enforcement of decision rights lies at the heart of any chance at checking presidential encroachment of legislative decision rights. Interestingly, it also indicates that political rights, the residual category against which we analyze the effects of HIGH and LOW in the regressions, are unlikely to be legislated by decree.

In this regard, the literature has alerted to the consequences of low levels of institutional commitment repeatedly. Within that body of work, my focus on the legislative process and congress seeks to emphasize the effects of a specific subset of institutions surrounding the long-term motivations of legislators. That is, a mix of electoral rules and partisan regulations that drive legislators away from the legislature also affects their willingness to enforce their decision rights. This is to say, it avoids the activation of mechanisms of accountability and the possibility to create autonomous reputations and spheres of influence that may assist in the long-term valuation of legislative jobs. The mix of institutions at the root, however, has proven to be quite stable and effectively enforced.

Not only legislators would benefit from longer tenures and increased enforcement of decision rights. Higher levels of institutional commitment lower the relative weight of external agents' contributions. So, while higher levels of institutional commitment lead to a more balanced system of separation of powers, they also lead to a system in which interest groups have less say in the decision of legislative instruments, which, in turn, could lead to more stable decision-making.

Regarding levels of reliance on decree authority in particular, this chapter stresses that analyses of the choice between statutes and decrees should focus less on partisan and economic variables. While these variables may appear to carry explanatory weight under particular circumstances and for a number of years at a time, the effects are short-lived. My claim that legislators respond to external contributions rather than partisan calls is backed by several findings, and importantly the result of HIGH during the structural reforms period of the 90s. The fact that high-stakes policies and low-stakes policies,[45] despite yielding effects in the same direction, each have individually significant effects on the choice of decrees over statutes, suggests that the variables effectively capture a commonality among those policy issues, which I argue is the level of contestation that surrounds them, and that this commonality has explanatory weight. This is, admittedly, an indirect test. Well-known case studies, such as the evidence surrounding labor reforms (Etchemendy and Palermo 1998) or privatizations (Llanos 2002), as well as my analysis of the case of *Retenciones Móviles*, provide less systematic yet persuasive support for my claim. Additionally, the results yielded by variables testing alternative explanations vary a great deal from one specification to another, suggesting that, at best, their effects are contextual but fall short of providing an explanation to the phenomenon of interest. The results yielded by variables such as DIVIDED GOVERNMENT and HONEYMOON, which are not always significant, provide additional credit to my explanation.

Shifting toward the comparative sphere, an important point made in this chapter is that institutional rules, while important in explaining political behavior, are not sufficient when political actors are not committed to defending their decision rights. Argentina, equipped with a set of institutions quite similar to those of its neighboring countries (and in fact, until 1994, more restrictive rules regarding CDA), presents behavior that shows very low levels of concern for the long-term gains that politicians can extract from their decision rights. Placed in comparative perspective, Argentina provides an example of how the choice between decrees and statutes plays out in countries with low levels of institutional

---

[45] Which I used to get at institutional commitment by constructing variables HIGH and Low from highly conflictive (high-stakes) and little conflictive (low-stakes) policy issues, under the assumption that these issues are correlated with high and low levels of institutional commitment (in its variation across policy issues). Recall that these variables yield statistically significant results in the expected direction and are highly consistent across specifications.

commitment. Politicians' temporal horizons are constrained in a way that long-term gains that they would derive from enforcing their decision rights and avoiding violations by competing actors, cannot offset gains to be perceived in the short term. When politicians loosen their grasp on their decision rights, congress and the supreme court as collective bodies are weakened.

This illustrates the way in which the individual decision to enforce decision rights has the first order effect of checking the executive, but associated, the second order effect of virtually delineating the form taken by the system of checks and balances. In terms of veto players, the enforcement of decision rights is what holds veto players as such. Absent a sufficient level of institutional commitment, the player ceases to exist as a veto player (Tsebelis 2002), virtually abandoning the policymaking arena.

5.A APPENDIX: COMPLEMENTARY ANALYSIS AND SOURCES

5.A.1 Operationalization of Variables and Sources

CHOICE: Indicator equal to 1 if the observation is a *Decreto de Necesidad y Urgencia*, and equal to zero if it is a congressional statute. Source: Dirección de Información Parlamentaria, HCDN.

HIGH: Indicator equal to 1 when the observation's policy issue falls under the "high-stakes" category, and equal to zero otherwise. See Chapter 3 for a full explanation of this categorization. Source: InfoLEG (Centro de Documentación e Información del Miniterio de Economía y Finanzas Públicas).

LOW: Indicator equal to 1 when the observation's policy issue falls under the "low-stakes" category, and equal to zero otherwise. See Chapter 3 for a full explanation of this categorization. Source: InfoLEG (Centro de Documentación e Información del Ministerio de Economía y Finanzas Públicas).

EXCLUDED CDA: Indicator equal to 1 when the reported policy issue is among those excluded from executive decree authority by the constitution, and equal to zero otherwise.

CONSTITUTIONAL REFORM 94: Indicator equal to 1 when the observation was enacted after August 23, 1994, the date the text resulting from the constitutional reform was published.

BICAMERAL COMMITTEE: Indicator equal to 1 when the observations occur after July 27, 2006, the date of enactment of the law that established the Bicameral Committee.

ECONOMIC PACKAGE: Indicator equal to 1 in times in which there was a major stabilization package introduced by the executive: 1 Jan 1985–1 Jan 1986, 1 June 1988–15 Aug 1989, 15 Aug 1989–15 Aug 1992, and 1 June 2000–1 June 2003.

INFLATION: Percent change in the IPC (consumer price index) with respect to previous month. Base: June 1999 = 100. Source: INDEC, Dirección de Índices de Precios de Consumo.

INFLATION2: Percent change in the IPC (consumer price index) with respect to the month of December of the previous year. Base: 1999 = 100. Source: INDEC, Dirección de Índices de Precios de Consumo.

COMMODITY INDEX: Commodity price indices (for cereals, vegetable oils, protein meals, meats, seafood, sugar, bananas, and oranges), taken from the International Monetary Fund's monthly series for 8 price indices, available at www.imf.org/external/np/res/commod/index .asp

PUBLIC EXPENDITURE: Total expenditure by the national government in millions of pesos 2001. Source: Dirección de Análisis de Gasto Público y Programas Sociales - Secretaría de Política Económica.

STRREF90: Indicator equal to 1 between the inauguration of President Menem and the end of 1992.

DIVIDED GOVERNMENT: Indicator equal to 1 if a party or coalition different from the president's dominates at least one of the two congressional chambers.

PRESIDENTIAL APPROVAL: percentage of positive appraisal of presidential performance, Nueva Mayoría.

HONEYMOON: Indicator equal to 1 during each president's first three months in office.

DAYS TO ELECTIONS: Number of days remaining to the next presidential election.

MENEM: Indicator equal to 1 if Carlos Menem is in office.

DUHALDE: Indicator equal to 1 if Eduardo Duhalde is in office.

KIRCHNER: Indicator equal to 1 if Nestor Kirchner is in office.

5.A.2 Codification of High/Low Variables

TABLE 5.A.1. *Classification of policy areas of bills in Argentina*

High	Low	Political rights
2) Labor	1) Symbolic	4) Constitutional affairs
3) Social Security	12) Bureaucracy/administration	5) Executive
13) Financial policy	14) Economic policy	6) Authorization to travel
15) Budget & public spending	20) IR	7) Legislative branch
16) Emergencies	21) Foreign trade	8) Legislative delegation
17) Taxes	22) Police/homeland security	9) Checks and balances
18) Ports & shipping	26) Social policy	10) Electoral affairs
19) Industrial policy	30) Justice	11) Political parties
23) Arms	33) Law: civil, criminal, etc.	31) Supreme court
24) Defense/armed forces	36) National cultural heritage	32) Judicial branch
25) Health policy	39) Professions	
27) Agriculture & farming	46) Subsidies to individuals (benefits, pensions, and transfers)	
28) Public services	48) Science & technology	
29) Energy & mining	50) Environment	
34) Commercial law	51) Housing	
35) Regions, provinces, & municipalities	52) Cinematography	
37) Education		
38) Universities & degrees		
40) Roads & transportation		
41) Railroads		
42) Airports & a transport		
43) Automotive industry		
44) Broadcasting & media		
45) Telecommunications		
47) Fishing		
49) Sports		

Complementary Analysis

TABLE 5.A.2. *Summary statistics Argentina dataset*

Variable*	N	Freq. = 0	Freq. = 1	Min	Max	Range	Median	Mean	Standard deviation
Choice	4006	82.68	17.32	–	–	–	–	–	–
High	4006	56.12	43.88	–	–	–	–	–	–
Low	4006	51.37	48.63	–	–	–	–	–	–
Const Reform 94	4006	36.77	63.23	–	–	–	–	–	–
Excluded CDA	4006	92.74	7.26	–	–	–	–	–	–
Bicameral Committee	4006	93.16	6.84	–	–	–	–	–	–
Economic Package	4006	62.73	37.27	–	–	–	–	–	–
Divided Government	3918	16.39	83.61	–	–	–	–	–	–
Honeymoon	4006	93.78	6.22	–	–	–	–	–	–
Alfonsín	4006	83.75	16.25	–	–	–	–	–	–
Menem	4006	56.69	43.31	–	–	–	–	–	–
De La Rúa	4006	90.71	9.29	–	–	–	–	–	–
Duhalde	4006	91.01	8.99	–	–	–	–	–	–
Kirchner	4006	80.38	19.62	–	–	–	–	–	–
Inflation	3956	–	–	-0.8	196.6	197.4	0.6	4.16	13.02
Inflation2 (Δ)	3956	–	–	-1.8	4923.6	4925.4	4.4	155.43	520.02

Commodity Index	3956	–	–	75.39	153.02	77.63	96.42	97.42	12.65
Public Expenditure	3994	–	–	31065	63768	32703	43701	43101.89	6825.59
Presidential Approval	3907	–	–	8	84	76	40	38.23	18.84
Days to Election	3956	–	–	2	2173	2171	946	923.75	529.03

Note: *In some models variables are divided by 100 (Inflation, Inflation 2, Public Expenditure and Days to Election) for visualization purposes.

TABLE 5.A.3. *Marginal effects for logistic models of Table 5.3 of choice between decrees and statutes, Argentina 1983–2007*

	\multicolumn{8}{c}{Average marginal effects}							
	(1)		(2)		(3)		(4)	
Variable	Effect	p	Effect	p	Effect	p	Effect	p
High	0.226	<0.001	0.306	<0.001	0.304	<0.001	0.270	<0.001
Low	0.117	<0.001	0.186	<0.001	0.185	<0.001	0.158	<0.001
Excluded CDA	-0.045	<0.05	-0.040	<0.1	-0.041	<0.05	-0.047	<0.05
Const Reform 1994	0.102	<0.001	0.163	<0.001	0.110	<0.001	-0.037	
Bicameral Committee	-0.045	<0.05	0.036		0.213	<0.001	-0.054	
Economic Package	–		0.112	<0.001	0.058	<0.001	0.110	<0.001
Inflation	–		-0.000		-0.000		–	
Inflation2 (% Change)	–		–		–		-0.000	<0.001
Commodity Index	–		–		-0.002	<0.05	-0.005	<0.001
Public Expenditure	–		–		0	<0.001	0	<0.05
Divided Government	–		0.031		-0.026		-0.046	

Presidential Approval	–	0.001	<0.05	0.001		0.001
Honeymoon Effect	–	–		0.001		-0.000
Days to Election	–	–		0.001	0.005	<0.05
Menem	–	–		–	0.328	<0.001
De La Rúa	–	–		–	0.353	<0.001
Duhalde	–	–		–	0.670	<0.001
Kirchner	–	–		–	0.607	<0.001

Note: Results are average partial effects. For dichotomous variables, it shows the partial change from 0 to 1.

TABLE 5.A.4. *Predicted probabilites for logistic model (4) of choice between decrees and statutes, Argentina 1983–2007*

Variables	Minimum	Predicted probability at min.	Maximum	Predicted probability at max.	Difference in probability
High	0	0.09	1	0.36	0.27
Low	0	0.131	1	0.289	0.158
Excluded CDA	0	0.181	1	0.134	−0.047
Const Reform 94	0	0.206	1	0.169	−0.037
Bicameral Committee	0	0.182	1	0.128	−0.054
Economic Package	0	0.139	1	0.249	0.11
Inflation	−1.8	0.19	4923.6	0.008	−0.182
Commodity Index	75.39	0.289	145.97	0.04	−0.249
Public Expenditure	31065	0.138	63768	0.292	0.154
Divided Government	0	0.216	1	0.17	−0.046
Presidential Popularity	8	0.155	84	0.226	0.071
Honeymoon Effect	0	0.177	1	0.177	0
Days to Election	0.02	0.142	21.73	0.241	0.099
Menem	0	0.116	1	0.444	0.328
De La Rúa	0	0.164	1	0.517	0.353
Duhalde	0	0.139	1	0.808	0.669
Kirchner	0	0.12	1	0.727	0.607

Note: Results are based on model (4) of Table 5.3. Calculation of predicted probabilities uses the observed value approach (Hanmer & Kalkan 2013).

TABLE 5.A.5. *Marginal effects for logistic models of Table 5.4 of choice between decrees and statutes, Argentina post-Alfonsín Era*

Variable	Average marginal effects			
	(1)		(2)	
	Effect	P	Effect	p
High	0.3424	<0.001	0.3172	<0.001
Low	0.2041	<0.001	0.1861	<0.001
Excluded CDA	−0.0496	<0.05	−0.0568	<0.05
Constitutional Reform 1994	0.0353	<0.05	−0.0459	
Bicameral Committee	−0.0536	<0.05	−0.0611	
Economic Package	−		0.1065	<0.01
Inflation (% Change)	−		−0.0001	<0.001
Commodity Index	−		−0.0056	<0.001
Public Expenditure	−		0.0001	<0.05
Divided Government	−		−0.0655	<0.1
President Popularity	−		0.0022	<0.05
Honeymoon Effect	−		0.0082	
Days to Election	−		0.0046	<0.1
Menem	−		0.0388	
De La Rúa	−		−0.0765	
Duhalde	−		0.3203	<0.01
Kirchner	−		0.2509	<0.05

Note: Results are average partial effects. For dichotomous variables it is the partial change from 0 to 1.

TABLE 5.A.6. *Predicted probabilites for logistic model (2) of choice between decrees and statutes, Argentina post-Alfonsín Era*

Variables	Minimum	Predicted probability at min.	Maximum	Predicted probability at max.	Difference in probability
High	0	0.103	1	0.419	0.316
Low	0	0.151	1	0.338	0.187
Excluded from CDA	0	0.209	1	0.153	−0.056
Const Reform 1994	0	0.235	1	0.191	−0.044
Bicameral Committee	0	0.209	1	0.149	−0.06
Economic Package	0	0.167	1	0.272	0.105
Inflation	−1.8	0.224	4923.6	0.006	−0.218
Commodity Index	75.39	0.345	145.97	0.042	−0.303
Public Expenditure	31065	0.16	63768	0.325	0.165
Divided Government	0	0.262	1	0.197	−0.065
Presidential Popularity	8	0.148	84	0.323	0.175
Honeymoon Effect	0	0.204	1	0.205	0.001
Days to Election	0.02	0.167	21.73	0.269	0.102
Menem	0	0.192	1	0.231	0.039
De La Rúa	0	0.213	1	0.138	−0.075
Duhalde	0	0.177	1	0.499	0.322
Kirchner	0	0.164	1	0.42	0.256

Note: Results are based on model (2) of Table 5.4. Calculation of predicted probabilities uses the observed value approach (Hanmer & Kalkan 2013).

TABLE 5.A.7. *Marginal effects for logistic models of Table 5.5 of choice decrees and statutes, Argentina pre and post-Constitutional Reform of 1994*

						Average marginal effects				
	(1)		(2)		(3)		(4)		(5)	
Variable	Effect	p	Effect	p	Effect	p	Effect	p	Effect	p
High	0.048		0.386	<0.001	0.140	<0.01	0.369	<0.001	0.361	<0.001
Low	−0.005		0.239	<0.001	0.083	<0.1	0.223	<0.001	0.219	<0.001
Excluded CDA	0.132	<0.001	−0.156	<0.001	0.129	<0.001	−0.161	<0.001	−0.160	<0.001
Bicameral Committee	—		−0.054	<0.05	—		−0.016		−0.069	<0.1
Economic Package	—		—		0.032		−0.034		−0.055	
Inflation2 (% Change)	—		—		−0.007	<0.05	0.051		−0.026	
Commodity Index	—		—		−0.002		−0.004	<0.01	−0.006	<0.001
Public Expenditure	—		—		−0.004	<0.001	−0.001	<0.001	0.001	<0.1
Divided Government	—		—		—		−0.090	<0.05	−0.081	<0.05
President Popularity	—		—		−0.001	<0.1	0.002		0.002	<0.1

(continued)

TABLE 5.A.7 (continued)

Variable	Average marginal effects									
	(1)		(2)		(3)		(4)		(5)	
	Effect	p	Effect	p	Effect	p	Effect	p	Effect	p
Honeymoon Effect	–		–		0.553	<0.001	0.038		–0.013	
Days to Election	–		–		–0.005		–0.007	<0.01	0.003	<0.01
Menem	–		–		–		–0.150	<0.001	–0.275	<0.001
De La Rúa	–		–		–		–		–0.211	<0.001
Duhalde	–		–		–		–		0.068	
Kirchner	–		–		–		–		–0.106	

Note: Results are average partial effects. For dichotomous variables it is the partial change from 0 to 1.

6

The Choice of Legislative Paths in Comparative Perspective

6.1 INTRODUCTION

Most of the literature analyzing presidential systems comparatively, and Latin American presidentialism in particular, has purported a fairly homogeneous picture of presidents as powerful agenda-setters who govern relatively unchecked – a picture that students of legislatures have striven to refute. The puzzle presented by the variation in the extent to which polities rely on decree authority, as this chapter shows, provides a point of entry to analyze the issue comparatively.

Chapters 4 and 5 were devoted to analyzing variations in the choice of decrees versus statutes within Brazil and Argentina, countries with identical hurdle factors but different levels of institutional commitment. This chapter presents evidence regarding the variation in levels of institutional commitment across countries, and it tests the effect of such variation on the choice to enact decrees versus statutes. The current chapter analyzes levels of reliance on decrees through a pooled sample of seven countries during the period 1994–2009. These are seven out of ten Latin American countries with CDA for which sufficient information was available such that a balanced sample could be put together. The findings reveal that politicians' level of institutional commitment effectively explains *levels of reliance on decree authority*,[1] even as partisan and economic crises, the main explanatory contenders, break out, and resolve.

---

[1] This chapter operationalizes the choice between decrees and statutes through the notion of reliance on decree authority, which is the extent to which decrees are preferred as a legislative instrument. Measurement details are presented in Section 6.3.

The chapter proceeds as follows. Section 6.2 provides the comparative framework for empirical analysis, discussing the theoretical aspects of institutional commitment and hurdle factors for a cross-country analysis of reliance on decrees. Section 6.3 outlines the countries analyzed in this chapter (different than Argentina and Brazil), emphasizing their institutional setup and the main aspects related to the legislative process and the control of constitutional decree authority. Section 6.4 describes the operationalization of the variables used in this chapter and the empirical strategy (times-series-cross-section analysis) used to estimate the effect of institutional commitment on decree reliance. Finally, Section 6.5 summarizes the results of the quantitative analysis and discusses implications.

6.2 HURDLE FACTORS AND INSTITUTIONAL COMMITMENT IN COMPARATIVE PERSPECTIVE

Recall that the theory presented in Chapter 2 claims that the choice to adopt policies by decree or statutes is determined by three factors: (I.) *constitutional rules*, (II.) the *valuation that interest groups assign to policies*, and (III.) *politicians' valuation of their decision rights*, which I refer to as institutional commitment. This chapter focuses on the first and third of these factors, which in the previous chapters were held constant by design.

Regarding the rules, I have pointed out that these establish which actors have the right to make policy decisions and how those decisions can be made, so in this sense they determine which actor's agents should approach when pursuing policies, and the costs they confront in that endeavor. As explained, following Diermeier and Myerson (1999), this book operationalizes those rules as hurdle factors, which provide synthetic information regarding the decision-making rules that are in place at a given time, with higher values representing more difficulty to reach decisions. Variation in hurdle factors occurs across actors (the executive, members of congress, supreme court justices), decisions (passage of a law, override of a veto, impeachment), and countries. The rules are an important theoretical factor, and they are to be taken into account both theoretically and empirically, yet inspection of the evidence reveals that while variation in the rules exists, it is minimal.[2]

In Chapter 3 this book claims that this lack of variation in rules paired with interesting variation in terms of reliance on decrees confirms that

---

[2] In spite of the small variation, this factor cannot be left aside. It is not a constant, either; variation exists and may cause effects in the outcome.

decision rights *per se* reveal little of the workings of many polities, and we need to probe further. Importantly, we must ask whether rights on paper are guarded *de facto* – a problem I tackle through the notion of institutional commitment. Institutional commitment is higher when the gains expected from the possession of decision rights are higher. Thus, institutional commitment is a function of the elements that can affect those gains in expectation: (I.) the factors affecting politicians' time horizon,[3] and (II.) the factors affecting external contributions. I return to this when presenting the empirical approach taken to the measurement of institutional commitment. But, before doing so, a note on the limits imposed on CDA already made in Chapter 2 is worth repeating here.

Constitutions that provide executive decree authority usually establish conditions for its use. Most commonly, they restrict enactment of decrees to urgent, exceptional circumstances of national emergency. Additionally, some constitutions exclude certain subject matters from decree authority.[4] This chapter argues, importantly, that while these boundaries fare well in theory, their effects vary in practice. What the evidence shows is that despite limitations on the conditions under which CDA may be used, presidents issue decrees that are *not* in compliance with those established rules (and in that sense, are unconstitutional or illegal decrees). Legislators and the courts may confront these situations, and sometimes they do, while other times they do not.[5] A central claim in this chapter is that variation in this practice is a function of politicians' institutional commitment.

6.2.1 Institutional Commitment across Countries

To explain the different levels of reliance on decrees across countries, we must take into account different levels of *institutional commitment*, determined by politicians' time horizon in their current jobs and their broader career goals. Explaining the determinants of existing levels of institutional commitment exceeds the purpose of this study. Rather, I base my assessment of each country's situation on uncontroversial facts about each and on well-established expectations of behavior resulting from specific institutional arrangements. Career ambition, the electoral

[3] Longer time horizons lead to higher institutional commitment.
[4] True in Latin America, but also in Russia and other post-Soviet countries (Remington 2014: 83).
[5] The number and frequency of decrees issued in most countries suggests that they cannot all be urgent (Figure 6.1); closer inspection of their subjects confirms it.

connection, and progressive ambition have been singled out as guiding principles of politicians' behavior (Schlesinger 1966; Mayhew 1974; Samuels 2002; Jones et al. 2002). The extent to which different institutions affect turnover gives way to a host of behavioral expectations. I rely on those predictions to infer levels of institutional commitment.

Where politicians (legislators and supreme court justices) expect to maintain their positions for extended periods of time, they face incentives to forego gains in the present to maximize their gains in the long run. Because decision rights are their key to those gains, politicians who expect to stay in their current jobs have the motivation to defend them against encroachment by other actors. It follows that politicians who expect to be out the door soon will maximize the gains they can extract from the position today and will make decisions that, if anything, will improve their chances to obtain their next post.

6.2.2 Levels of Institutional Commitment in Comparative Perspective

In this subsection, first I sketch out brief assessments of cases I have analyzed in depth (Argentina,[6] Brazil,[7] and Chile), along the dimensions highlighted above. I provide these fundamentally as illustrations that justify the proxies used to capture levels of institutional commitment. Second, I present the indicators used as proxies for job security and institutional commitment.

6.2.2.1 *Argentina*

The literature that analyzes institutions and institutional performance in Argentina suggests that levels of institutional commitment might be low. Scholars have repeatedly suggested that Argentine legislators and Supreme Court justices are not committed to the institutions they occupy, but only to their own political survival. The work of Spiller and Tommasi (2007) emphasizes the effects of fragmentation, instability, and institutional design in generating myopic legislators and a Supreme Court that has more often than not yielded to the interests of the executive. Mark Jones, in a series of works (2002a, 2002b; and Jones and Hwang 2005) has documented the motivations guiding Argentine legislators, pointing out that they are in Congress *en route* to other posts. Low reelection rates are largely due to nomination procedures, not voter decisions. The

---

[6] For more details see Chapter 4.
[7] For more details see Chapter 5.

works of Helmke (2002, 2005), Iaryczower, Spiller, and Tommasi (2002), Kim (2007), and Molinelli (1999), among others, focus on the Argentine Supreme Court's instability throughout the twentieth century, which at the very least has affected justices' perceptions of how long they will remain in their job.

6.2.2.2 *Brazil*

The case of Brazil presents a different pattern. Firstly, it reveals higher legislative reelection rates than those in Argentina. Pereira, Leoni, and Rennó (2004) report that in 1998, 80 percent of the legislators in the Lower Chamber ran for reelection (the figure for Argentina in 1997 is 35 percent – and the 1997 figure for Argentina is up by a third with respect to previous election years). Regarding stability of the Supreme Court, there is little doubt that during the period under analysis here, Brazil's Supreme Court has seen none of the abuses that occurred in Argentina or Peru. While Brazil's top court has seen renovation, such changes have not been linked to presidential strategies to control judicial outcomes. The work of Diana Kapiszewski (2012) compares the role of the Argentine and Brazilian Supreme Courts and suggests that the Argentine Supreme Court's profile is of submission to the executive, while in Brazil compromise prevails. These indicators seem to suggest that Brazilian legislators and Supreme Court justices indeed have higher levels of job security than their neighbors, with the corresponding correlation in institutional commitment.

6.2.2.3 *Chile*

The case of Chile stands out within the region, among other things, for having one of the highest legislative reelection rates (second only to Uruguay). Navia (2004) reports that no less than 70 percent of legislators in the Lower Chamber seek reelection at the end of each 4-year term, and over 80 percent of these incumbents are successful. While this still implies that approximately 40 percent of deputies in each legislative period are serving their first term, the figure seems small when compared with the renewal rate in neighboring countries. The Chilean legislature is a place where politicians seek to build a career, which stands in sharp contrast to Argentina and somewhat at odds with the situation in Brazil. Chile's Supreme Court, a conservative enclave with remnants from the Pinochet era, has been immune to political tweaking since the inauguration of democracy in 1990.

In line with the photographs sketched out by the literature, a comparative study by Stein et al. (2006) shows measurements of several indicators regarding congress and the judiciary, which present a picture that resembles the one I seek to provide here. From their summary of measures of legislatures' capabilities, we learn that the average experience of legislators in years is 2.9 in Argentina, 5.2 in Peru, 5.5 in Brazil, and 8.0 in Chile, and that these legislatures' qualifications as places to build a career are low in both Argentina and Peru, and high in Brazil and Chile.

Regarding supreme courts, Henisz (2000) shows, and Stein et al. (2006) emphasize, that supreme court tenure during 1960–1995 was approximately 5 years for Argentine justices, 11 years for Brazilian justices, and 17 years for Chilean justices. Stein et al. (2006) also present two measures of judicial independence, one resulting from a survey by the World Economic Forum (scale 1–7),[8] and a *de facto* judicial independence index developed by Feld and Voigt (2003).[9] On the first measure, Argentina is assigned a mark of 1.8, Brazil 3.9, and Chile 4.6; on the second measure, Argentina gets a 0.33, Brazil 0.49, and Chile 0.58.

Using indicators of the two factors affecting institutional commitment that I have highlighted, legislators' and supreme court justices' job security, I establish proxies for institutional commitment. In the case of legislators, the reelection rate is an aggregate measure of the durability of their careers. If a greater proportion of deputies can remain in their seats after elections, legislators will perceive a longer time horizon for their careers and will seek to maximize their gains in the long run, protecting their decision rights from encroachment by other actors. A similar argument applies to supreme court justices: the book claims that longer tenures, or lower rotation of court members, will increase justices' commitment to their decisions rights. The average tenure and average yearly rotation of the court are good aggregate indicators of justices' job security. As presented in Figure 3.3 (see Chapter 3), these indicators are heterogeneous across countries.

Table 6.1 presents indicators of institutional commitment for the seven countries included in this chapter's statistical analysis.[10] The table shows that Chile has the highest legislative reelection rate and the longest

---

[8] Average response of business executives in each country to the statement "The judiciary in your country is independent from political influence of members of government, citizens, or firms" (1 = no, heavily influenced; 7 = yes, entirely independent).

[9] This index by Feld and Voigt (2003) is based on actual tenure of supreme court justices, deviations from *de jure* tenure, removal of justices before the end of their terms, increase of number of justices on the court, and changes to their budget and to the real income of justices, among other indicators.

[10] Note, however, that the values used in calculations for Table 6.1 are based on all the data available for each country (as cited in Appendix 6.A), while the data used for regression

TABLE 6.1. *Indicators of institutional commitment by country*

Country	Legislative reelection (%)	Mean Supreme Court tenure (years)	Supreme Court rotation (rate)
Argentina	19.13	6.48	0.88
Brazil	43.36	5.48	0.92
Chile	62.54	7.72	0.92
Colombia	34.61	4.16	0.85
Ecuador	14.02	2.56	0.75
Nicaragua	26.63	3.79	0.88
Peru	21.46	4.17	0.79

Source: Calculated from Lara-Borges, Castagnola, and Pérez Liñán (2012) for Supreme Court tenure and rotation, and from multiple sources listed in Appendix 6.A for Legislative reelection.

average supreme court tenure.[11] In the opposite extreme are Ecuador and Nicaragua, which have the highest levels of instability in both realms. In summary, Ecuador and Nicaragua would be assigned relatively low levels of institutional commitment, whereas Chile would receive the highest mark. The remaining countries fall somewhere in between. The prediction stemming from this table and Figure 3.1 in Chapter 3 is that at high levels of institutional commitment, we expect policies to be enacted primarily by statute, and that is precisely the observation in Chile, where only two decrees have been enacted since democracy was re-established in 1990. As levels of institutional commitment fall, reliance on executive decrees grows. To maintain emphasis on the cases discussed above, Argentina presents lower levels of institutional commitment, suggesting that, on average, reliance on decrees should be higher there. We expect Brazil to rely on decrees less heavily than Argentina, based on this simple indicator of institutional commitment. Figure 6.1 presents the annual variation of reliance on decrees[12] in the seven countries for which data is available.[13]

---

[11] analyses spans the period between January 1994 and December 2009, in order to obtain a balanced panel.

[11] The rotation of the judges of the Supreme Court is among the highest. But there are smaller differences among countries in this variable. This feature will be useful later in the construction of an index of institutional commitment.

[12] The level of reliance is measured as a ratio that is equal to zero when no decrees are enacted, and approaches one as the proportion of decrees increases.

[13] Unfortunately, Nicaragua is excluded from the statistical analysis conducted later because of missing data on key explanatory variables.

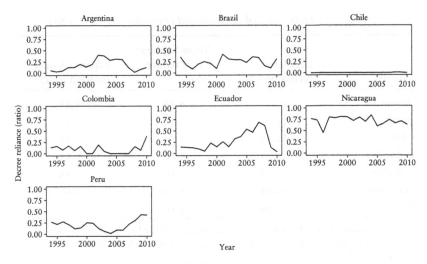

FIGURE 6.1. *Annual reliance on decrees, by country*
Source: Elaborated from multiple sources (See Appendix 6.A for details).

A glance at the levels of reliance on decrees shows sufficient variation such that the puzzle is not a simple one to solve. While Chile nicely meets predictions, other cases are not as straightforward. The questions posed earlier remain: What determines the choice between decrees and statutes at intermediate levels of institutional commitment? Under what conditions should we expect policies to be enacted by statutes if levels of institutional commitment are intermediate? Section 6.3 probes for answers.

6.3 DECREES IN LATIN AMERICA: THE CASES

Chapters 4 and 5 sought to explain the variation within a single country. This chapter carries out a different exercise, which is to explain the difference among countries, beyond any internal variation in each.

Before delving into the quantitative analysis, this section provides a review in broad strokes of the institutional setup and the main features of relevance to the legislative process in Chile, Colombia, Ecuador, Nicaragua and Peru. These five countries, together with Argentina and Brazil, provide the empirical basis for the analyses in this chapter. While Argentina and Brazil received thorough attention in the previous two chapters, this section seeks to provide context on the remaining countries. It intends, among other things, to place the seven countries in comparative perspective.

6.3.1 Chile

The country to which this book devotes most attention after Argentina and Brazil is Chile, which is unique in its minimal use of CDA. Like in the other nine countries where CDA exists, Chile's constitution, enacted in 1980, provides the president with the prerogative to issue decrees in article 32 §22. Chilean presidents, by several accounts the most powerful among Latin American countries (Shugart and Carey 1992; Siavelis 2002; Negretto 2013) have nevertheless resisted the temptation to enact decrees and forego congressional passage of legislation. Between 1990 and 2010, Chile enacted only two decrees of the CDA type. This type of decree is termed in Chile *Decretos Supremos de Emergencia* (Supreme Decrees of Emergency), but commonly referred to as *"el 2% constitucional"* (the constitutional 2 percent, in reference to the 2 percent of the budget that the president can tap into by using these decrees in cases of national emergency). The two decrees, decree N°1178, enacted on September 5, 2008, and decree N°1, enacted on January 5, 2009, were passed under truly extraordinary circumstances. Both were issued to tap into additional resources for the City of Santiago's failing public transportation system (the *Transantiago*, as it is commonly known). Although there has been much political contention around the shortcomings of the public transportation system, neither the public nor the opposition questioned whether the circumstances leading to the decrees were deserving of presidential use of unilateral emergency powers. It seems interesting that Chile, not possessing a particularly strong congress (Siavelis 2000; Siavelis 2002; Palanza and Espinoza 2017) nevertheless shows such restraint in levels of reliance on decrees.

The Chilean president stands with most other Latin American presidents in terms of her concentration of influential legislative powers, which include a broad-reaching prerogative of exclusive proposal rights over legislation (i.e., on an extended number of issues, legislators cannot initiate bills as these are reserved for the president); the prerogative to introduce amendments to bills while these are being discussed in Congress; a particular form of presidential veto that extends the typical package veto to include a form of partial veto that not only can delete but also introduce new content in the form of amendments; and the prerogative to tweak the congressional legislative agenda by designating selected bills urgent, as in Brazil.

Chilean Congress members, however, unlike most legislators in weak congresses, have the longest tenures in Latin America. All members, i.e., the Upper Chamber's thirty-eight senators and the Lower Chamber's one hundred and twenty *diputados*, have been elected in two-member districts since 1989 and until 2017.[14] While single-member districts are expected to generate bipartisan systems, Chilean electoral rules has given way to a system in which two coalitions, each composed of several parties, dominate Congress. Members of Chile's *Tribunal Constitucional* serve nine-year terms, almost twice as long as members of Peru's Constitutional Court. And Supreme Court justices may sit on the court until retirement.

Some authors have argued that low levels of reliance on decrees are due to a particular style of political bargaining that prevails in Chile, which is described as cooperative or non-confrontational (Aninat 2006). This book argues, instead, that the observation of cooperative behavior is an equilibrium outcome. Open confrontation is avoided because political actors are aware of their decision rights and of actors' willingness to enforce them if needed, i.e., should open conflict arise. Legislators' and justices' job security lead to the expectation that in likelihood they will remain in their posts, and this in turn leads to their willingness to enforce their rights over the policymaking process.

6.3.2 Colombia

In Colombia, as in most other Latin American countries, presidents have ample legislative prerogatives. According to Cárdenas, Junguito, and Pachón (2006) the concentration of power in hands of the Colombian president is surpassed only by the Brazilian case. Efforts made by constitution drafters of the 1991 reform, intended to increase checks and balances and strengthen congress and the Constitutional Court vis à vis the president, have not provided noticeable presidential restraint.

Colombia's bicameral Congress is composed of an Upper Chamber with one hundred senators elected in a single nation-wide district, and a Lower Chamber composed of one hundred and sixty-one members elected in districts with magnitudes ranging between 2 and 18 seats (Botero and Rennó 2007). Elections occur in both chambers every four years and seats are all up for renewal using a system of closed list proportional representation in both chambers. As Botero and Rennó (2007) emphasize, closed list proportional representation works in a rather unconventional

---

[14] Proportional representation ballots that are the least proportional a ballot can be without being single-member. The electoral system, however, was recently reformed, with a moderately more proportional system replacing the two-member districts as of the 2017 elections.

way in Colombia. In contrast to the expected effect of closed lists, which is strong partisan control of list composition, the experience in Colombia has led strong intra-party competition to evolve into a system where multiple lists compete, causing typically that only the first candidate on each list makes it into Congress. Work by Botero and Rennó (2007) shows that legislative reelection rates in Colombia are similar to those in Brazil, albeit with very different percentages of legislators willing to run for reelection in each country. In Colombia, the percentage of legislators winning reelection among those who ran between 1994 and 1998 is 69.4 percent, and 60.2 percent among those who ran between 1998 and 2002 (the percentages in Brazil, for identical time periods, are 62.0 and 69.6 percent, respectively). However, those seeking reelection in Colombia are only 52.8 percent (1994–1998) and 51.6 percent (1998–2002). According to Cárdenas, Junguito, and Pachón (2006), constitutional arrangements between 1968 and 1990 endowed presidents with broad-reaching decree powers, lacking time constraints, and with few limits in terms of the policy areas on which decrees could be enacted. The constitutional reform of 1991 significantly reduced executive decree authority by requiring the declaration of urgency, placing time limits, and requiring judicial review before they are enacted, albeit maintaining few limits on the policy areas on which decrees can be enacted and allowing referendums to be called by decree (Cárdenas, Junguito and Pachón 2006). This reform also created a new institution, the Constitutional Court, charged with judicial review. The overall constitutional reduction in decree authority, however, has not held the president back from enacting decrees on a regular basis. Uprimny (2010) shows that judicial review of presidential declarations of "state of exception," which enable the president to enact decrees, has become more severe since 1991. Citing García Villegas (2001), Uprimny claims that while between 1984 and 1991 the Colombian Supreme Court nullified only nine percent of "state of siege" decrees, between 1992 and 1996 the Constitutional Court nullified 34 percent of "internal commotion" decrees (Uprimny 2010, p. 55).

The descriptive information presented here suggests that Colombia stands at intermediate levels of institutional commitment, as Figures 3.2 and 3.3 in Chapter 3 would also lead us to believe. In terms of levels of reliance on decrees, Colombia is the only country, besides Chile, that did not issue decrees in several years. In 2010, the year in which Colombia issued the largest number of decrees, it enacted 37 decrees – only a few more than the 23 enacted in Nicaragua in 1996, when Nicaragua issued the smallest amount of decrees between 1994 and 2010. See Figure 6.1.

6.3.3 Ecuador

Following three decades of executive-legislative confrontation, Ecuador's latest two constitutional reforms have sought to reign in confrontation and strengthen presidential legislative prerogatives (Basabe Serrano 2009). However, Bernabe Serrano (2009) claims that the dis-balance generated by the latest constitution holds the seed to heightened instability. The average legislative reelection rate in Ecuador's Lower House was approximately twenty-seven percent between 1996 and 2002 (Saiegh 2005). Yet, unlike what one might expect in contexts where legislators have high turnover rates, the president has not been able to capitalize on this in his favor in terms of legislative success. Stein et al. (2006) report that in Ecuador presidential success rates passing legislation through congress is forty-two percent between 1979 and 1996 (ranking twelfth of thirteen countries measured), and Mejía Acosta and Polga Hecimovich (2011) claim that the executive's success rate was higher before the constitutional reform of 1998. Saiegh (2010) reports that according to the Latinobarometer, on average the general public has the least favorable view of Congress in Ecuador, Bolivia, and Guatemala.

The constitutional reform of 1998 formally established the *Tribunal Constitucional* (Constitutional Tribunal), with nine members designated by Congress for four-year terms. Despite the short mandate of these justices (compared, for instance, to the nine-year mandate of Chile's *Tribunal Constitucional*, which is still brief when compared to longer-standing Supreme Court justices in Chile and in other countries), between 1996 and 2013 "no individual judge has managed to complete the constitutionally stipulated forty-eight-month term" (Basabe Serrano and Polga Hecimovich 2013: 156). Basabe Serrano, and Polga Hecimovich show that on four occasions the entire court was changed, unconstitutionally, by Congress. And, as suggested above, the Ecuadoran Congress itself is also subject to instability.

Levels of reliance on decrees fluctuate considerably in Ecuador, from a low of 0.03 (0.05 in 1998) (less than 1 percent of laws enacted by decree) in 2010 to a high of 0.7 (approximately 70 percent of laws enacted by decree) in 2007, as Figure 6.1 illustrates (above). This is in line with Ecuador's location at the lower left corner of Figure 3.3 (Chapter 3), which suggests low levels of institutional commitment.

6.3.4 Nicaragua

Latin American presidents in general are known to concentrate extensive legislative powers; in this context, the Nicaraguan president stands out among the weakest in the region (Saiegh 2006). Nicaragua's legislature, in turn, operates mostly as a veto player, as it lacks the organizational resources and staff experience required for a more active and autonomous role (Stein et al. 2006). The legislature has only one chamber, to which its 90 members are elected through proportional representation, 20 in a national district and 60 in departmental districts and the autonomous regions. The legislature includes as members the former president and vice president of Nicaragua (the latter as substitute), and the runners up to the positions of president and vice-president in the latest elections. Legislators are elected for five-year mandates.

There seems to be a consensus that politics in Nicaragua have been straddling the border between a competitive system and one of hegemonic tendencies (Martí i Puig 2013; Martínez Barahona, and Brenes Barahona 2012). These authors also agree that President Daniel Ortega and the *Frente Sandinista de Liberación Nacional* (FSLN) control the judiciary – effectively achieving an unconventional constitutional reform that enabled presidential reelection in Nicaragua, until then forbidden by the Constitution. Regarding reliance on decrees, Marti i Puig speaks of the president's reliance on decrees and his control of the judiciary as his two main tools of domination. In particular, an episode called "el decretazo," the name given to a decree that Ortega enacted on January 9, 2010, extending the mandates of twenty-two government officials that were about to expire, including justices from the *Tribunal Supremo Electoral* (Supreme Electoral Tribunal) and from the Supreme Court, a decision that should have been made by a qualified majority of 60 percent of the votes in the *Asamblea Nacional*, Nicaragua's unicameral congress (Martí i Puig 2013). This decree secured the FSLN's control of then-upcoming elections in 2011 and 2012. As mentioned, Nicaragua issued 132 decrees in 2000, the maximum number of decrees enacted in a one-year period by any of the seven countries analyzed in this book. The average level of reliance on decrees between 1994 and 2014 is 0.72 (the median is 0.73) in Nicaragua – with the lowest level of reliance on decrees at 0.45. Hence, Nicaragua has made extensive use of decree authority, not only in terms of their impact, but also in quantitative terms.

6.3.5 Peru

In Peru, the 1990s brought a clear-cut example of delegative democracy at the hands of Alberto Fujimori, even as most other countries in the region had transitioned or were in the middle of their transition to democracy. After having been elected in an apparently clean electoral process, Alberto Fujimori reverted to authoritarian rule by means of a self-coup, only to win elections again in 1995.[15] The rule of law was reinstated after ousting Fujimori, in 2000, when Alejandro Toledo took office after his electoral victory and following a brief transition term served by Valentín Paniagua. The Peruvian Congress is unicameral, composed of 130 members (120 until 2016) elected by closed list proportional representation through preferential vote (lists are closed and not blocked). Between 1980 and 1993, the Peruvian Congress had two chambers and 240 members (Morón and Sanborn 2005), downsized by the constitutional reform of 1993. Legislators' ties to parties are highly volatile, many of them switching parties between elections. According to Meléndez and Villa García, the Peruvian Congress is one of the least prestigious institutions in the country (Meléndez and Sosa Villagarcia 2013). Rotation is high in the Peruvian Congress[16]: only 22 legislators participated in all three consecutive Congresses between 1980 and 1992, and the average reelection rate between 1995 and 2016 was 21 percent, the lowest, after Bolivia, of the seven countries analyzed in this book.

In line with this, we expect levels of institutional commitment to be relatively low, which would, in turn, lead us to expect high levels of reliance on decrees. Enactment of decrees was highest in 2009, a year in which 121 decrees were passed. While this is a very high incidence of decrees in one year (only surpassed by Nicaragua in 2000 and by Brazil in 2001[17]), reliance on decrees that year marks only 42 percent, as Peru is also characterized by passing statutes in large numbers (and that year Congress passed 163 statutes).[18]

6.4 RELIANCE ON DECREES: EMPIRICAL ANALYSIS

The empirical exercise undertaken in this section stems from the predictions derived in Chapter 2. Recall that the theory supporting this chapter suggests that when in need of policy enactment, external actors will

---

[15] The analysis in this chapter includes the entire 1994–2010 period for Peru, in an effort to keep the sample balanced. Note, however, that the 1994 data is qualitatively not different from the years under democratic rule.

[16] An interesting analysis is advanced in work by Gallardo and Muñiz (2004), "Análisis de la carrera legislativa en el Perú: estrategias para permanecer en el cargo," an unpublished manuscript at the Centro de Investigación de la Universidad del Pacífico, Perú.

[17] A highly irregular year in Brazil as it is the year of Constitutional Amendment 32, which abolished the indefinite re-issuing of decrees, and led to transition arrangements that increased the number of MPVs that year.

[18] As decree reliance is the number of decrees divided by the sum of decrees and statutes.

approach politicians (legislators, the executive, the supreme court) to seek their support in the process. They know that policy may be enacted by congressional statutes but also by decree, and they will estimate the odds that policy will be upheld by the branches. Because legislators oppose legislation by decree at higher levels of institutional commitment, that is, when they value their prerogatives enough that they are willing to act against encroachment by the executive, we should expect lower levels of reliance on decrees where institutional commitment is higher. Recall Figure 3.2 (Chapter 3), which graphs the inverse relationship between institutional commitment and reliance on decrees.

Following the predictions in Chapter 2, this chapter presents two fundamental hypotheses:

H1: Institutional commitment affects reliance on decrees inversely, i.e., at lower levels of institutional commitment we expect more reliance on decrees.

H2: At high levels of institutional commitment we should observe no decrees.

This section is devoted to the analysis of levels of institutional commitment in Latin America, where 10 of 18 countries endow their presidents with CDA. The theory presented predicts that while at sufficiently high levels of institutional commitment we are to observe the enactment of policy by statutes only, and that at extremely low levels we expect to see the enactment of all policies by decree, there is an interesting middle ground where we expect to see a mix of decrees and statutes. In the cross-country comparison that follows I estimate the effect of institutional commitment on the choice between decrees and statutes. The empirical analysis presented in this section is the first to approach the issue of reliance on decrees across countries, and the dataset was collected especially for this purpose. The analysis is conducted using a pooled sample of seven countries during the period 1994–2009.[19]

6.4.1 Data and Variables

The data collected for this analysis includes all decrees enacted in each of the seven countries under analysis as its centerpiece. To estimate the

---

[19] Table 6.A.1 in Appendix 6.A shows which countries in Latin America have adopted CDA. Descriptive statistics of all variables used in the chapter are included in Table 6.A.2 in Appendix 6.A. The exact sample sizes used in regressions are presented with each specification.

significance of decree enactment as a legislative tool in each country, the data is evaluated alongside the number of statutes enacted in each of the countries during the same years, as graphed in Figure 6.1. Difficulties with data collection in specific countries explain why some countries with CDA are not included in the sample used for regressions (Bolivia, Guatemala, and Honduras).

The choice between decrees and statutes is captured through levels of reliance on decrees, measured as the proportion of all policy that is enacted by decree. The dependent variable, for this purpose, is denominated DECREE RELIANCE, a continuous variable defined as $DR = d/(d+s)$, where d is the number of decrees enacted and s is the number of statutes.[20] In this, I follow earlier work that has taken the same approach (Pereira, Power, and Rennó 2005, 2008). The variable takes values between zero and one.[21] For this reason I implement OLS regressions and control for sources of heterogeneity (across countries and through time) following recommendations on the time-series-cross-sectional (TSCS) analysis literature initiated by Beck and Katz (1995).

6.4.2 Independent Variables

6.4.2.1 A Proxy for Institutional Commitment Across Cases

We are unable to observe variations in institutional commitment directly. I have argued that we can infer politicians' overall levels of institutional commitment in each country by looking at indirect measures, such as reelection rates and other factors affecting job security, and I have explained why job security is relevant to levels of institutional commitment. Hence, I propose the variables LEGISLATIVE REELECTION and SUPREME COURT ROTATION or SUPREME COURT TENURE as proxies for the variation in institutional commitment across countries. LEGISLATIVE REELECTION is measured as the percentage of legislators in a given period who were also legislators in the immediately preceding period. In turn, SUPREME COURT TENURE measures the average tenure of all justices on the Supreme Court

---

[20] All statutes are included, regardless of origin. I include bills that were successful only. The alternative to take into account solely statutes initiated by the president would miss an essential component of the problem as I have construed it. The choice of policy instrument is not the president's alone; it includes other actors.

[21] It is calculated monthly for regressions, although the yearly ratio is used for the elaboration of figures where noted.

or Constitutional Tribunal[22] in years, and is measured each year. Finally, SUPREME COURT ROTATION measures the proportion of justices that are removed on a yearly basis.

Later in the chapter, I present different models that test the effect of these two proxies. I also created an INSTITUTIONAL COMMITMENT INDEX (ICI), which provides a convenient aggregate way to estimate the joint effect of institutional commitment playing out through the two branches of government charged with checking the executive. The index provides for a simple interpretation of the results. To create the index, first I rescaled the variables measuring LEGISLATIVE REELECTION and SUPREME COURT ROTATION into a common range so that they both take values between 0 and 50. Second, I added the value of each of the two variables, such that the resulting variable ranges from 0 to 100.

ICI = Legislative Reelection (rescaled) + Supreme Court Rotation (rescaled)

6.4.2.2 *Institutional Variation*

Regarding the effect of institutional arrangements, the main insight of this chapter is that outcomes vary considerably among Latin American countries despite the practically identical institutional rules affecting the legislative process. In the cases under analysis here, the hurdle factor is 2, and it is identical for Argentina, Brazil, Colombia, Ecuador, Nicaragua, and Peru. The only country with a different (lower) hurdle factor is Chile, where it is 1.5. The variable HURDLE FACTOR is constructed following Diermeier and Meyerson (1999) by taking into account the quotient needed for bill approval: $r = 1/(1-Q)$ where r represents the hurdle factor and Q the quotient.

6.4.2.3 *Economic Context Variables*

At least from O'Donnell (1993, 1994) onward, the concentration of power in executive hands in Latin America has been associated with mayhem in the economic realm. A prominent approach to the analysis of decree authority in Latin America has focused on the economy and factors related to the urgency imposed by economic crises, so I assess the effect of such factors here. Power, Pereira, and Rennó (2008), when analyzing the

---

[22] The term supreme court is used for simplicity, but this variable refers to tenure of supreme court justices as well as justices on constitutional tribunals. It captures tenure in the organization deciding the constitutionality of acts by the other branches (i.e., decree enactment). Countries place this responsibility with the supreme court or with a constitutional tribunal.

determinants of levels of reliance on decree authority in Brazil, find that although the economic context affects levels of reliance during specific times, the effect is lost once a longer time period is considered.

In this chapter, to test the effect of economic instability on the choice between decrees and statutes, I include a host of economic variables intended to capture the effect of economic crises on the executive's inclination to use decrees. Despite its problems, I use INFLATION (CPI) to capture contextual economic effects. Other variables tested (results not reported here) include CURRENCY RATE and EFFECTIVE CURRENCY RATE, ACTIVE INTERESTS, and DEPOSIT INTEREST, alternating among them given disparities across countries in the availability of these variables. Due to the inconsistency of effects across specifications and to missing values, I present results using INFLATION alone. In all cases, the economic indicators were taken from the International Financial Statistics data developed by the International Monetary Fund.

6.4.2.4 *Partisan and Political Context Variables*
Theories of delegation, as well as unilateral action theory, have produced persuasive, if contradictory, claims regarding the conditions under which we can expect the executive to take a greater role in the lawmaking process. I include a host of political context variables to account for the effects of parties, popularity, the timing of elections, and other time-specific variables that may explain the variation in the choice between decrees and statutes. The variables used to test these effects are measured identically in all countries in the dataset, and include: COMPETITIVENESS,[23] to capture the proximity between the executive and the legislature in lieu of divided government, which proves to be less informative in multi-party settings[24]; PRESIDENTIAL POPULARITY, measured with as much frequency as sources allow, but predominantly every three to four months (see Appendix 6.A for further detail); and HONEYMOON, which captures the first 100 days of a presidency, during which presidents usually enjoy higher levels of support. Other variables not reported here are those related to the electoral cycle, such as the number of days to the next election and dummies to identify electoral years. As they consistently yield insignificant results and their exclusion does not alter results, I do not include them.

---

[23] As constructed by Pérez Liñán et al. (2011), see Section 6.A.1 of Appendix 6.A for further detail. The variable takes into account parties as well as governing coalitions.

[24] Calvo (2014) claims that plurality-led congresses differ in fundamental ways from majority-led congresses. Given this, to use divided versus unified government in multi-party environments is misleading.

6.4.3 Empirical Testing

The sample of monthly ratios of DECREE RELIANCE analyzed in this chapter includes a total of 1,428 month/year observations, collected for the seven countries compared in the chapter: Argentina, Brazil, Chile, Colombia, Ecuador, Nicaragua, and Peru. Analysis of the data is carried out using standard procedures for time-series-cross-sectional (TSCS) analysis.

Table 6.2 presents eight specifications designed to assess the validity of my main claim regarding the effect of institutional commitment. I use OLS (completely pooled) with Beck and Katz (1995) panel corrected standard errors in these models. Models 1 to 3 differ from models 5 to 7 in the proxy used for supreme court job security in each set of models. Models 1 to 3 use SUPREME COURT TENURE, while models 4 to 6 use SUPREME COURT ROTATION. Models 1 and 4 include only the two institutional commitment proxies (LEGISLATIVE REELECTION with either one or the other used for the judiciary), while models 2 and 5 add the HURDLE FACTOR as an explanatory variable. In models 3 and 6, I analyze if the relation between the proxies is interactive. Complementary statistical tests provide no evidence of a conditional nature of these variables. Finally, model 7 tests the effect of the INSTITUTIONAL COMMITMENT INDEX (ICI).

In Table 6.2 LEGISLATIVE REELECTION stands out in terms of the consistency of its negative effect on levels of reliance on decrees across different specifications. The estimated coefficients for judicial proxies are more heterogeneous, but in general their effect is negative. Secondly, the negative effect of SUPREME COURT ROTATION is more consistent across specifications than is SUPREME COURT TENURE. Altogether, these results lend support to the hypothesis that as institutional commitment increases reliance on decrees diminishes. Finally, model 7 presented provides preliminary evidence of the utility of the INSTITUTIONAL COMMITMENT INDEX.

Also interesting is the confirmation that hurdle factors do matter. However, because variation on this variable is minimal (in temporal and comparative terms), from here on I exclude it from most specifications. In methodological terms, hurdle factor is a time-invariant variable, so it cannot be included in models with fixed country effects.[25]

---

[25] When unit fixed effects are used, the variance between units is not taken into account and only the within-unit variance is used for the estimation (Wooldridge 2010). In other words, given that a fixed-effects model (FEM) is equivalent to a Least Squares Dummy Variables (LSDV), the time-invariant variable is perfectly collinear with country effects (Wilson and Butler 2007, Shor et al. 2007), precluding the estimation of the coefficient.

TABLE 6.2. *Linear analysis of decree reliance in Latin America 1994–2009, baseline OLS*

			Dependent variable: Decree reliance				
	(1)	(2)	(3)	(4)	(5)	(6)	(7)
Legislative Reelection	-0.007***	-0.001*	-0.009***	-0.007***	-0.001	-0.00001	
	(0.0003)	(0.001)	(0.001)	(0.0003)	(0.001)	(0.001)	
SC Tenure	0.0004	0.001*	-0.007***				
	(0.001)	(0.001)	(0.002)				
SC Rotation				-0.032	-0.137***	-0.285***	
				(0.049)	(0.049)	(0.085)	
Hurdle Factor		0.394***	0.255***		0.435***	0.435***	0.384***
		(0.053)	(0.061)		(0.054)	(0.054)	(0.041)
SC Tenure × Reelection			0.0004***				
			(0.0001)				
SC Rotation × Reelection						0.006***	
						(0.002)	
ICI							-0.002***
							(0.001)
Constant	0.478***	-0.534***	-0.083	0.480***	-0.620***	-0.640***	-0.394***
	(0.022)	(0.122)	(0.153)	(0.017)	(0.125)	(0.126)	(0.117)
Observations	1342	1150	1150	1342	1150	1150	1150
Adjusted R²	0.116	0.106	0.139	0.116	0.112	0.115	0.111

Models include observations from Argentina, Brazil, Chile, Colombia, Ecuador, Nicaragua (only in the models without hurdle factor) and Peru.
Note: Panel corrected standard errors in parenthesis; *$p < 0.1$; **$p < 0.05$; ***$p < 0.01$.

Table 6.3, below, presents six models that add variables to the baseline models presented in Table 6.2 to test the effect of contextual factors on the choice between decrees and statutes. At the same time, these models present variations in the modeling strategy. The country fixed effects (Models 1, 2, and 5) are not a universal solution to the unit heterogeneity problem (Wilson and Butler 2007), so I analyzed two other alternatives: pooled (Models 3 and 4) and two-ways[26] (unit and time, Model 6) fixed effects.[27] Following standard recommendations in the literature on TSCS analysis, the specifications in Table 6.3 include the dependent variable lagged one period.

These models provide additional support regarding the effect of career related variables. Model 1 is the only specification in which the two variables used as proxies of politicians' job security are included as separate measures. In models 2 through 6, the INSTITUTIONAL COMMITMENT INDEX is used instead – as explained above, this index is created from those two variables to provide a better measurement of their joint effect. Models 3–6, which are less restrictive as they include variables accounting for the political and economic context, confirm the negative effect of the ICI on DECREE RELIANCE, but note that the effect of ICI holds even in model 2, the most restrictive version. In all the models in Table 6.3, the INSTITUTIONAL COMMITMENT INDEX has a negative effect on DECREE RELIANCE.

On the other hand, the lagged dependent variable is highly significant in all models. As Plümper, Troeger, and Manow (2005) argue, the inclusion of unit fixed effects along with a lagged dependent variable absorbs parts of cross-sectional and temporal variance associated with other independent variables. Acknowledging these shortcomings, Keele and Kelly (2006) show that the lagged dependent variable is appropriate for many common dynamic processes, and tests to explore this aspect support this choice. My theory does not posit any particular temporal process for my explanatory variables, so I test alternative versions of an autoregressive distributed lag model for modelling dynamics (Beck and Katz 2011). The results provide evidence of the utility of a lagged dependent variable. In summary, the empirical adjustment of decree reliance is very quick (short-term effects) and more complicated models with differing adjustments of independent variables don't contribute relevant additional explanatory power.

---

[26] While arguably some of the cross-national source of variation in the data is accounted for through independent variables included in the model, variation due to the panel structure of the data is not.

[27] Models with random effects are tested and yield similar conclusions. Given that these models imply stronger assumptions, their results are not shown.

TABLE 6.3. *Time-series cross-sectional analysis of decree reliance in Latin America 1994–2009*

Dependent variable: Decree reliance

	(1) Country FE	(2) Country FE	(3) Pooled OLS	(4) Pooled OLS	(5) Country FE	(6) Country & Time FE
Legislative Reelection	−0.002 (0.001)					
SC Rotation	−0.064 (0.047)					
ICI		−0.001* (0.001)	−0.001** (0.001)	−0.003*** (0.001)	−0.002* (0.001)	−0.002* (0.001)
Hurdle Factor			0.229*** (0.044)			
Decree Reliance (lag)	0.307*** (0.031)	0.307*** (0.031)	0.398*** (0.033)	0.423*** (0.032)	0.301*** (0.031)	0.282*** (0.031)
Competitiveness			0.079 (0.062)	0.020 (0.058)	−0.140* (0.073)	−0.201*** (0.074)
Honeymoon			0.067** (0.032)	0.072** (0.033)	0.073** (0.029)	0.038 (0.030)
Presidential Popularity			−0.00001 (0.0004)	−0.0003 (0.0004)		
Inflation			0.003 (0.003)	0.004 (0.003)		0.002 (0.003)
Constant			−0.292** (0.138)	0.286*** (0.049)		
Observations	1336	1336	1113	1113	1336	1336
R2	0.099	0.099	0.264	0.251	0.106	0.100

Note: Models include observations from Argentina, Brazil, Chile, Colombia, Ecuador, Nicaragua (only in the models without hurdle factor) and Peru. Panel Corrected Standard Errors in parenthesis; * $p < 0.1$; ** $p < 0.05$; *** $p < 0.01$.

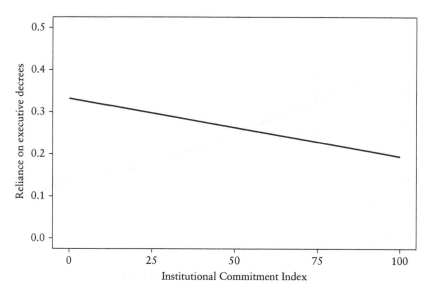

FIGURE 6.2. *Predicted decree reliance based on institutional commitment index*
Note: Based on Model 2 of Table 6.3.

Of the other variables, the HONEYMOON period seems to affect DECREE RELIANCE positively (with varying levels of statistical significance across models), suggesting that honeymoons lead to greater reliance on decrees. The effect of COMPETITIVENESS, which varies in direction, quite reasonably becomes significant only when time fixed effects are included in the model (and PRESIDENTIAL POPULARITY is excluded). PRESIDENTIAL POPULARITY and INFLATION do not appear to affect the choice between decrees and statutes.

Figure 6.2 presents the predicted value of DECREE RELIANCE for the range of values of the INSTITUTIONAL COMMITMENT INDEX, based on Model 3 of Table 6.2. The predicted values of the models are in the observed ranges of DECREE RELIANCE, with no cases outside of the interval [0,1]. However, it may be argued that the effect of institutional commitment is nonlinear, in which case OLS would not necessarily be the best estimator to analyze this relationship given the nature of my dependent variable. To deal with this possibility, I estimate a fractional response logistic model (Wooldridge, 2010).[28] While the results from

---

[28] Simply stated, this modeling strategy is specifically designed for the analysis of proportions as dependent variables, where values range between 0 and 1 (the conditional mean of the dependent variable given some covariates is examined with a link function that restricts the predicted values to the unitary interval without using a linear functional form).

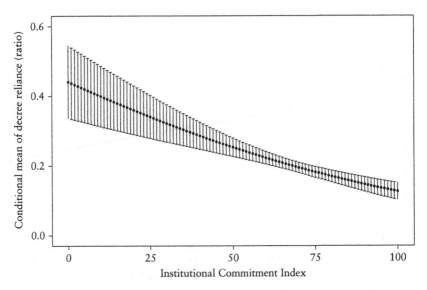

FIGURE 6.3. *Predictive margins of institutional commitment index*
over decree reliance
Note: Based on Model 5 of Table 6.A.3. Predictive margins with
95% confidence intervals.

that analysis are presented in the Appendix of this chapter (Table 6.A.3), Figure 6.3 graphs the marginal effects predicted for the whole range of possible values of the INSTITUTIONAL COMMITMENT INDEX, with 95% confidence intervals. This figure works as a robustness check, showing that the negative effect of the INSTITUTIONAL COMMITMENT INDEX is not dependent on the functional form used to model it.

As I mention earlier, there is heterogeneity among countries. Among the countries included in the regressions, Chile stands out as an outlier on several dimensions, and there are reasons to believe that this case could be driving the results. Figure 6.4 calculates the predicted values of decree reliance by country, based on model 5 in Table 6.3 (linear model with country fixed-effects). I include a dashed line to indicate the observed average value of the INSTITUTIONAL COMMITMENT INDEX in each country[29]. As expected, the differences by country are substantive: Chile is an outlier in the observed value of the INSTITUTIONAL COMMITMENT INDEX (93.56 with a maximum value of 100) and in the predicted values with a low country intercept.

It is fair to ask whether the effects of the main explanatory variables related to this book's theory are merely a function of the exceptionality of Chile. To assess whether this is the case, i.e., that regression results are

[29] The average is also presented in Figure 6.4 (μ).

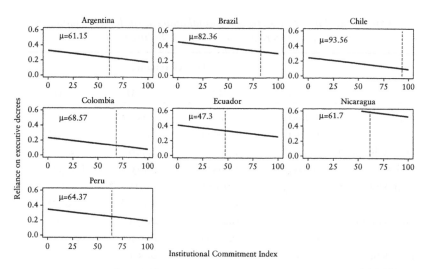

FIGURE 6.4. *Predicted decree reliance based on institutional commitment index by country*
Note 1: Based on Model 5 of Table 6.3.
Note 2: The dashed lined reflects the mean observed value of the Index by country.

led by the inclusion of Chile, the sample used for regressions in Table 6.4 excludes this country. If my main independent variables carry explanatory weight, we should expect effects to hold when Chile is excluded from the sample. As in previous models, I used panel corrected standard errors and include the dependent variable lagged one period. Models 1 and 2 and 5 consider country fixed effects; model 6 adds time fixed effects.

Exclusion of Chile from the sample reinforces the empirical findings of this chapter by showing that the effect of institutional commitment on levels of reliance on decrees is present even when Chile, the case with the highest level of institutional commitment as measured by the proxies presented here, is excluded from the analysis. The results in Table 6.4 do not show substantial variation with respect to those in Table 6.3, and are included only to control that the effect of institutional commitment holds across the sample even when Chile is not part of the sample.

6.5 CONCLUSIONS

The evidence presented in this chapter fills a long-sustained vacuum, given the ongoing concern regarding the concentration of power in executive hands in democracies new and old around the globe, and the shortcomings of the theories that have set out to explain encroachment

TABLE 6.4. *Time-series cross-sectional analysis of decree reliance in Latin America 1994–2009 excluding Chile*

	Decree reliance			
	(1)	(2)	(3)	(4)
ICI	−0.002	−0.002*	−0.002*	−0.002*
	(0.001)	(0.001)	(0.001)	(0.001)
Decree Reliance	0.325***	0.300***	0.306***	0.275***
(Lag)	(0.034)	(0.031)	(0.037)	(0.032)
Competitiveness	−0.115	−0.142*	−0.194**	−0.232***
	(0.073)	(0.074)	(0.079)	(0.077)
Honeymoon	0.072**	0.083**	0.033	0.039
	(0.036)	(0.033)	(0.039)	(0.035)
Presidential	0.001		0.001	
Popularity	(0.001)		(0.001)	
Inflation	0.002		0.001	
	(0.003)		(0.003)	
Country Fixed	Yes	Yes	Yes	Yes
Effects				
Time Fixed			Yes	Yes
Effects				
Observations	923	1146	923	1146
R²	0.128	0.108	0.121	0.101

Models include Argentina, Brazil, Colombia, Ecuador, Nicaragua, and Peru.
Note: Panel Corrected Standard Errors in parenthesis; *p < 0.1; **p < 0.05; ***p < 0.01.

of prerogatives. While the chapter tests implications applied to the analysis across cases that could not be addressed in the previous empirical chapters, it also serves as a fundamental test of the theory that carries it beyond the analysis of those cases that played an important role in the inception of the theory.

This chapter tests the validity of its claims across seven Latin American cases in which rules allocated similarly along the legislative process provide varying levels of reliance on decrees. We know that the country with the highest level of institutional commitment, Chile, rarely enacts policies by decree. Other countries do so very frequently. The empirical analysis conducted in this chapter suggests that variation in the variables used as proxies of institutional commitment, SUPREME COURT ROTATION and

LEGISLATIVE REELECTION, affect levels of reliance on decrees in a systematic manner. It also suggests that this finding is robust to different operationalizations of the key independent variables. The INSTITUTIONAL COMMITMENT INDEX, created from those variables, has a systematic negative effect over DECREE RELIANCE. Additional robustness checks support this conclusion.

While the consensus has been that any and all constraints come from party and coalitional determinants, this chapter emphasizes that the main determinant may *not* be organizational or contextual, but derived from institutions and the incentives they put forth in terms of institutional commitment. By defending the legislative prerogatives that give politicians continued access to the resources that ensure their long-term goals, politicians (legislators, justices) may effectively limit encroachment by the executive and strengthen legislative institutions in the process.

This strong support for the main theoretical proposal of this book, which speaks directly to challenges facing the inter-branch relations in separation of powers systems, has implications for the extent to which presidents overstep their constitutional roles. The two basic components of stability in each of the branches charged with checking the executive, legislative reelection and supreme court tenure, are indeed associated to lower levels of reliance on decrees within the Latin American context. In other words, stable, longer-lived players within the judicial and legislative branches, charged with checking the executive, effectively lead to higher levels of enforcement of the rules that impose limits on the encroachment of legislative decision rights by presidents. The next chapter develops the conclusions derived from the cross-country analysis further and places them in broader perspective.

6.A APPENDIX: COMPLEMENTARY ANALYSIS AND SOURCES

6.A.1 Variables and Sources

DECREE RELIANCE: ratio of decrees to total legislation, calculated according to the following equation: $dr = (decrees/(decrees + statutes))$.
SOURCES BY COUNTRY:
ARGENTINA: DIP, Cámara de Diputados, HCN;
BRAZIL: SICON, Senado Federal http://legis.senado.gov.br/sicon/#/basica
CHILE: Biblioteca del Congreso Nacional www.leychile.cl/Consulta/homebasico

COLOMBIA: www.presidencia.gov.co/prensa_new/decretoslinea/   y
http://web.presidencia.gov.co/leyes/archivo.htm;

ECUADOR: www.lexis.com.ec/website/content/servicio/esilec.aspx

NICARAGUA: www.asamblea.gob.ni/index.php?option=com_wrapper
&view=wrapper&Itemid=360;   Perú: www.congreso.gob.pe/ntley/Ley
NumePP.htm

HURDLE FACTOR: following Diermeier and Myerson (1999), the hurdle factor here is calculated as $r = 1/(1-Q)$, where Q is the majority requirement, that is, the fraction Q that needs to support a bill for it to pass. Higher values represent more parties involved in the legislative process, and imply more difficulty in passing bills.

SOURCES: Databases at Georgetown University and at Biblioteca Virtual Miguel de Cervantes, http://pdba.georgetown.edu/Constitutions/constitutions.html and www.cervantesvirtual.com/portales/constituciones_hispanoamericanas/

LEGISLATIVE REELECTION: percentage of re-elected legislators in the Lower Chamber, calculated after elections.

SOURCES BY COUNTRY:

ARGENTINA: www.diputados.gov.ar/

BOLIVIA: www.oep.org.bo/ Tribunal Supremo Electoral 1997–2002 and 2002–2005, http://americo.usal.es/oir/legislatina/ for the period 2005–2010 and www.diputados.bo/ for the period 2010–2015.

BRAZIL: www2.camara.leg.br/deputados/pesquisa and checked against Legislatina

CHILE: www.elecciones.gov/.cl/ and www.camara.cl/

COLOMBIA: http://web.registraduria.gov.co/;   www.congresovisible
.org/ and www.camara.gov.co/portal2011/

GUATEMALA: http://americo.usal.es/oir/legislatina/;   www.congreso
.gob.gt/ and http://200.12.63.122/gt/diputados.asp

HONDURAS: http://americo.usal.es/oir/legislatina/;   www.congreso
nacional.hn/;www.revistazo.com/ene/doc1.html/andhttp://voselsoberano
.com/index.php?option=com_content&view=article&id=1940:diputados-
iotra-vez&catid=1:noticias-generales;

NICARAGUA: http://americo.usal.es/oir/legislatina/ and www.asamblea
.gob.ni/

PERÚ: http://americo.usal.es/oir/legislatina/ and www.congreso.gob
.pe/; www.jne.gob.pe/; http://blog.pucp.edu.pe/fernandotuesta/files/
2000-2001%20Congresistas.pdf .

Sc TENURE: Annual average tenure of Supreme Court or Constitutional Tribunal.

SOURCE: Lara-Borges, Castagnola and Pérez Liñán (2012).

Sc ROTATION: Annual rotation rate of Supreme Court or Constitutional Tribunal justices. Source: Lara-Borges, Castagnola and Pérez Liñán (2012)

INFLATION: Monthly percentage change in consumer price index. SOURCE: International Financial Statistics, IMF.

PRESIDENTIAL POPULARITY: percentage of positive appraisal of presidential performance, replicating the measure used in Pereira, Power, and Rennó (2008). Multiple sources in order to achieve the greatest temporal variability.

SOURCE BY COUNTRY:

ARGENTINA: Data from Nueva Mayoría Poliarquía (pollster company).

BRAZIL: DataFolha (1988–2008), Vox Populi/Sensus (1995–2008), CNI/Ibope (1995–2010). Dataset provided by Fernando Rodrigues, UOL.

CHILE: Encuesta Mensual Adimark Gfk (pollster company). Data obtained from Adimark Gfk and Fundación Futuro repository.

COLOMBIA: Encuesta Gallup Colombia. Dataset provided by Mónica Pachón.

ECUADOR: CEDATOS - Gallup Ecuador (pollster company). Document of Presidential Approval in Democratic Period 1979–2011.

PERÚ: IPSOS Perú (pollster company).

COMPETITIVENESS: Altman and Peréz-Liñán (2002) created this index to measure the level of competitiveness in the Lower Chamber of each Congress. The competitiveness index is calculated as $C = \left|\dfrac{G - 0}{100}\right|$, where G stands for government ($G = \dfrac{\sum g_i^2}{\sum g_i}$, g_i is the share of seats for the i-th party in government), and O for opposition ($O = \dfrac{\sum o_i^2}{\sum o_i}$, o_i is the share of seats for the i-th opposition party). Values of C vary between 1 and 0, and "the value of C tends to zero whenever the government (or the opposition) controls the whole legislature, and to one if there is balance between government and opposition with values closer to 1, implying higher levels of competition" (Altman and Pérez-Liñán, 2002: 89–90).

SOURCE:

HONEYMOON: Indicator equal to 1 during the first three months in office of each president inaugurated during the period analyzed in this chapter.

SOURCE: Elaborated from information available on Inter-Branch Crises in Latin America (ICLA) Dataset. Elaborated by Gretchen Helmke. Available on www.gretchenhelmke.com/data.html

6.A.2 Complementary Analysis

TABLE 6.A.1. *Adoption of CDA in Latin America*

Country	CDA?	Inclusion of CDA	Article/s
Argentina	Yes	Reform, 1994	Art. 99
Bolivia	Yes	Constitution 2009	Art. 172, §8
Brazil	Yes	Constitution 1988	Art. 62
		Reform 2001 (restricts)	Art. 62
Chile	Yes	Constitution 1980	Art. 32 §22
Colombia	Yes	Reform 1958 (at least)	Art. 118 §8
		Constitution 1991 (restricts)	Art. 150§10 & Art. 213
Costa Rica	No	–	–
Ecuador	Yes	Constitution 1979	Art. 65
		Constitution 1998 (under state of emergency[a])	Art.155 &156; Art.181
		Constitution 2008 (under state of exception[a])	Art. 164
El Salvador[b]	No	–	–
Guatemala	Yes	Constitution 1987 (w/ amendments to 1995)[c]	Art. 183 §f
Honduras	Yes	Constitution 1982 (w/ amendments to 2005)	Art. 245 §20
Mexico	No	–	–
Nicaragua	Yes	Constitution 1987 (w/ amendments to 2005)[d]	Art. 150
Panama	No	–	–
Paraguay	No	–	–
Peru	Yes	Constitution, 1993	Art. 118 § 19
Uruguay	No	–	–
Venezuela	No	–	–

[a]The constitution of Ecuador (1998) requires the declaration of state of emergency to enable the enactment of more than one decreto-ley simultaneously.
[b]The constitution of El Salvador (1983, amended in 2000) explicitly excludes CDA.
[c]Guatemala's Constitution of 1966 included CDA through art. 189.
[d]Nicaragua's Constitution of 1950 included CDA through art. 191
Source: Country constitutions and reforms, in http://pdba.georgetown.edu/ Constitutions/constudies.html, and www.cervantesvirtual.com/portales/ constituciones_hispanoamericanas/catalogo_paises/

TABLE 6.A.2. *Summary statistics cross country dataset*

Variable	Obs	Freq = 0	Freq = 1	Min	Max	Range	Median	Mean	Standard deviation
Argentina	1428	85.71	14.29	–	–	–	–	–	–
Brazil	1428	85.71	14.29	–	–	–	–	–	–
Chile	1428	85.71	14.29	–	–	–	–	–	–
Colombia	1428	85.71	14.29	–	–	–	–	–	–
Ecuador	1428	85.71	14.29	–	–	–	–	–	–
Nicaragua	1428	85.71	14.29	–	–	–	–	–	–
Peru	1428	85.71	14.29	–	–	–	–	–	–
Decree Reliance	1428	–	–	0	1	1	0.14	0.28	0.33
Hurdle Factor (Q)	1224	–	–	1.5	2	0.5	2	1.92	0.19
Hurdle Factor (R)	1224	–	–	0.67	1	0.33	1	0.95	0.12
Leg Reelection	1426	–	–	0	64	64	29	31.21	16.97
SC Tenure	1344	–	–	0.93	11.78	10.84	4.95	5.3	2.34
SC Tenure (Adj)	1344	–	–	0.93	11.78	10.84	4.79	5.21	2.36
SC Rotation	1344	–	–	0	1.05	1.05	0.06	0.12	0.17
S.C. Rotation (Adj)	1344	–	–	0	1.05	1.05	0.06	0.13	0.18
Competitiveness	1423	–	–	0.46	0.98	0.52	0.88	0.83	0.14
Pres Popularity	1190	–	–	7	85	78	40	41.03	17.83
Honeymoon	1428	–	–	0	1	1	0	0.06	0.24
Months to Election	1428	–	–	0	71	71	25	25.86	16.45
Inflation	1428	–	–	-1.91	47.43	49.34	0.48	0.89	2.97

TABLE 6.A.3. *Fractional logistic regression of decree reliance in Latin America 1994–2009*

	Dependent variable: Decree reliance (ratio)				
	(1)	(2)	(3)	(4)	(5)
ICI	-0.031***			-0.019***	-0.019***
	(0.003)			(0.003)	(0.003)
Hurdle Factor (Q)		12.48***			
		(1.448)			
Decree Reliance (Lag)			2.839**	2.258***	2.695***
			(0.136)	(0.178)	(0.144)
Competitiveness				0.218	
				(0.012)	
Honeymoon				0.482*	0.340
				(0.205)	(0.182)
Presidential Popularity				-0.004	-0.140*
				(0.003)	(0.073)
Constant	1.142***	-26.03***	-1.881***	-0.555	-0.572*
	(0.206)	(2.893)	(0.066)	(0.367)	(0.236)
Number of Observations	1342	1224	1421	1113	1336
Pseudo R²	0.0432	0.0837	0.1471	0.1155	0.1657

Models include observations from Argentina, Brazil, Chile, Colombia, Ecuador, Nicaragua (only in the models without hurdle factor) and Peru.

Note: Robust standard errors in parenthesis; *p < 0.1; **p < 0.05; ***p < 0.01

7

Conclusions

Rules, Institutional Commitment, and Checks on Presidents

This book was motivated by a concern with overextended presidents who seem to decide on policy without much regard for the opinion of congress and the constituencies legislators represent. This is a long-held preoccupation in Latin America, a region characterized over three decades ago as breeding delegative democracies. Executive reliance on decrees is at the heart of this concern, and it has been analyzed as a problematic trait of presidential systems well beyond the Latin American context.

Understanding the determinants of decree authority is important for different reasons, which this book has tried to highlight. Mainstream approaches to the policymaking process have seen policy as emerging from the interaction of a set of veto players. For instance, the influential work of Tsebelis (2002) has suggested that policy stability is determined by the preferences of veto players. This book has shown that which actors are veto players is not established by constitutions, but by actors' willingness to enforce constitutional rules. In this sense, one may see this book's contribution as complementary to that of Tsebelis (2002) and other authors who highlight the importance of veto players. This book provides guidelines to help establish which actors are *effectively* veto players, and, in turn, understand the ways in which that set of actors, however specified, contributes to policy and policy stability. Which players stand behind decrees? What can be said of policy stability if policies are enacted by decree?

A long-held belief suggests that policy enacted by decree is less stable than policy enacted by congressional statute, given the breadth of the support backing congressional statutes. Through the theory presented in Chapter 2 and the evidence in Chapters 4, 5, and 6, this book provides support for those claims: the number of players involved and the resources invested in passing bills through congress is indeed greater and suggests we can expect those policies to be more stable.

If policy enacted by decree is less stable, it is in no way trivial to take a close look at levels of reliance on decrees both within and across countries. As this book argues, we can infer the health of separation of powers systems from variations in the ways in which countries enact their legislation, in particular, their choices in terms of legislative instruments and legislative tools.

7.1 VARIATION IN RELIANCE ON DECREES

The single most interesting fact regarding executive decree authority in presidential democracies, however, is the scope of variation in its use. It is fairly uncontroversial that Latin American presidents, especially those of the Southern Cone, are powerful actors with command over internal politics and strong legislative prerogatives. Most of these executives are endowed with constitutional decree authority. The puzzle addressed by this book is presented by how decree authority is exercised: Presidents use this authority to varying degrees. There is no question that executive decree authority, present across a number of presidential democracies, has turned law enactment into a fairly simple process in many countries. This simplification of lawmaking appeals to those worried about institutional paralysis. However, it comes at a cost, as the majoritarian bias of decrees raises serious concerns of a different nature. The cost of deciding policy by decree is ultimately borne by democracy itself.

By relying on executive decree authority, Argentine President Mauricio Macri, as well as his recent predecessors, was able to pass influential pieces of legislation without consulting the Argentine Congress. So was ousted Brazilian President Dilma Rousseff, her successor Michel Temer, and their predecessors since 1989, as well as the presidents of Colombia, Ecuador, Nicaragua, and Peru. Some presidents, however, regularly choose not to use their constitutionally granted decree authority, as is the case of Chilean presidents since 1990. Beyond Latin America, it is well known that Russian presidents have made extensive use of decrees, as have other presidents in Eastern Europe (Protsyk 2004).

This book has striven to provide an explanation of the variations we observe in levels of reliance on decrees, with the conviction that by understanding the determinants of this process we take steps to understand the mechanisms underlying unilateral action by presidents. This book attributes presidential encroachment of legislative attributes mainly to quiescence on the part of the actors charged with checking presidential actions and contributing to the enforcement of checks and balances in separation of powers systems.

By analyzing the choice to enact policy through congressional statutes or executive decrees, we gain insight to the motivations facing actors involved in the process, allowing us to grasp the microfoundations of encroachment of decision rights, as well as their enforcement. The checks and balances that stand at the core of separation of powers systems depend crucially on this enforcement. This book has identified three factors that explain why sometimes we see policy enacted by decree, and sometimes we do not. Those three factors – institutions, external interests, and institutional commitment – explain variations of levels of reliance on decrees across countries, and also variation within each country.

7.2 INSTITUTIONAL COMMITMENT AND THE ENFORCEMENT OF CHECKS ON THE EXECUTIVE

Chapter 2 presented a theory of the choice of legislative instruments that has implications both for domestic politics and the comparative level of analysis. It argues that the choice of decrees versus statutes is determined by the rules that allocate decision rights, politicians' valuation of those rights, and external agents' interest in specific policies. The theory has implications that allow us to understand the enforcement of checks on the executive both within countries and across.

Regarding differences across countries, the theory explains why some presidents never resort to decrees, even when the rules enable them to do so, and even when partisan and economic factors might seem favorable to the adoption of policies by decree. Likewise, it explains why other presidents choose to issue decrees even when congressional statutes may seem the most reasonable, stable, or ultimately the most democratic route to take.

Far from arguments that highlight presidential self-restraint or cultural traits of respect for institutional provisions, this book places institutional commitment, born of self-interested behavior by legislators and supreme court justices, as the factor standing at the center of the enforcement of checks on the executive. Institutional commitment speaks of politicians' appreciation for the provisions that make them influential actors in the legislative process, their decision rights. I argue that when levels of institutional commitment are higher, politicians are more likely to stand in defense of their decision rights. Consequently, as the evidence analyzed in Chapter 6 confirms, where levels of institutional commitment are higher, presidents tend to rely less on decrees.

Given the weight granted to institutional commitment in enforcing decision rights and consequentially checking the more expansive branches in separation of powers systems, it is reasonable to ask what makes it thrive or decline. Chapters 1, 2, and 3 claim that job security is a key determinant of institutional commitment. While it is reasonable not to care about the devaluation of a job and the privileges it entails if one's expectation is to hold the job very briefly, incentives change when the expectation is to maintain it for some time. Legislators' and supreme court justices' expectation that they will continue to hold their jobs motivates them to defend their privileges in the form of decision rights, i.e., to enforce where other actors' limits lie.

Regarding variations in levels of reliance on decrees within countries, the puzzle is slightly different. We know some countries rely more heavily on decrees than do others. But what explains the choice to enact a specific policy by decree, and yet another one through a congressional statute? Again, the answer depends on levels of institutional commitment. On one end of the continuum, where institutional commitment is at its highest, we expect decrees to be enacted under truly extraordinary circumstances, very sparingly. At the opposite end of the continuum one might find decrees taking over.

Most countries, however, have levels of institutional commitment such that decrees are chosen often yet not always. In these cases, whatever level of institutional commitment politicians of one branch have in a given country interacts with their valuation of what is at stake in that case, surrounding that specific policy on a specific issue. The claim is that different policy issues vary in the stakes they raise. So, in one country it may be the case that labor policy or energy policy is high stakes, while agricultural policy or health policy is low stakes, and this may be different in a neighboring country.

The book argues that the level of resources that an issue commands (votes, organizational capacities, ability for mobilization, and economic resources, among others) affects the stakes around that issue. Further, whether the stakes are high or low does not say anything about the importance of the issue. Instead, it tells us whether the issue attracts attention from resourceful agents on more than a single side of the debate surrounding it. If it does, the stakes increase; if it does not, they tend to be low. When the stakes are high for a certain issue, agents that are confronted in terms of the policy they support invest their resources to further their positions. Politicians are interested in capturing precisely those resources for their own political benefit. Therefore, this book claims that politicians will be more willing to enforce their decision rights and bring issues to be decided within their domain when the stakes are higher, i.e., when they have more to gain. All else equal, they will care less if the executive decides on low-stakes issues by herself. This choice stands at the root of the choice between decrees and statutes within a given country, especially at intermediate levels of institutional commitment.

How all this plays into the theory was the topic of Chapter 3, which explained why we might see variation in levels of institutional commitment across countries and apparently also within countries, and how all this can be measured. Importantly, that chapter establishes (a) that levels of institutional commitment are fixed within specific countries, and (b) that commitment to the enforcement of their prerogatives is activated to different extents by different policy areas. It also set up the empirical approach that was carried out in Chapters 4–6. When conducting country-specific analyses, we hold the level of institutional commitment fixed, while allowing for variation in the extent to which this commitment is triggered. Cross-country analysis requires, instead, analysis of the variation on the institutionally derived dimension.

Chapters 4, 5, and 6 provide empirical support to the theoretical claims made in Chapters 2 and 3. Furthermore, Chapter 6 tests the core of the theory systematically, analyzing the determinants of levels of reliance on decrees across seven countries. Chapters 4 and 5 analyze Brazil and Argentina, respectively, delving into the choice of decrees versus statutes within each of those countries. Based on the evidence shown in Chapter 3, Figure 3.3, the book posits that politicians in Brazil have higher levels of institutional commitment than do politicians in Argentina, such that we should expect more initiative to block the enactment of decrees in Brazil than in Argentina, *ceteris paribus*. Related, the main claim that is tested in these chapters is the one regarding the interaction between levels of institutional commitment and the stakes surrounding policy, as the theory associates institutional commitment to politicians' self-interested behavior in promotion of their careers.

Together, the chapters show that at higher levels of institutional commitment, as in Brazil, we can expect high-stakes policies to be enacted by statutes, whereas low-stakes policies are more likely to be enacted by decree. When levels of institutional commitment are lower, as in Argentina, the stakes surrounding policies may not be enough of a pull to affect the likelihood of decrees, and more policy seems to be enacted by decree overall. The evidence provided by the case of Chile, where only two decrees were enacted during the entire period under analysis (see Figure 3.1 in Chapter 3), suggests that at sufficiently high levels of institutional commitment the stakes surrounding policies may also become irrelevant – fewer decrees are enacted overall.

7.2.1 Parties and the Economy

Until now, theories seeking to explain the determinants of reliance on decrees had focused on the effect of economic shocks and on the partisan composition of government. Guillermo O'Donnell (1993, 1994) suggested that the economic instability that has characterized Latin America played a key role in providing a justification for the delegation of decision rights to presidents, ultimately leading to a diminished type of democracy. In the decades that followed, students of Latin American democracies with an eye to presidential reliance on decree authority continued to consider the economy and partisan ties the most likely determinants of encroachment by the executive. In turn, partisan support played a role in explanations in one of two forms. Some have suggested that presidents are more inclined to issue decrees when they lack support in congress, out of their need to get things done; others, instead, have argued that when presidents have control of congress, it is more likely that legislators will be willing to delegate to the president, making decrees more likely.

This book has shown that economic and partisan factors are not sufficient to explain the variation in reliance on decrees within and across countries. While economic factors may contribute to the enactment of decrees under very specific conditions, and partisan ties may at times facilitate building coalitions to back decrees under specific circumstances, this book claims that variations in the economic context and in partisan support for the president in congress simply cannot explain the ongoing use of decrees in certain countries nor the resistance to issue decrees in others. These variations cannot explain why statutes would be enacted at all under certain circumstances, nor why what we observe most regularly is a mix of decrees and statutes (see Figure 6.2 in Chapter 6).

7.3 CHECKING PRESIDENTS

This book has striven to show that the fundamental factor underlying the use of decrees is not contextual. Institutional commitment, which is derived from job security, in turn stemming from the motivations and incentives displayed by different institutional settings, is at the heart of why decision rights may be encroached upon. One might claim, therefore, that any country vested in increasing levels of institutional commitment may ultimately improve its capacity to check the president. To acknowledge this implies that the allocation of decision rights carried out at the constitutional level, while important, cannot ensure the effectiveness of the checks and balances that are desirable in separation of powers systems. Additionally, it signals that the preservation of any institutional order relies on the will of politicians to uphold that order. The notion of institutional commitment seeks to shed light on the valuation of institutions that ultimately moves politicians to defend them, and, in doing so, preserve the foundations of their capacity to influence politics through their actions.

In his recent book, Gary Cox insists that executive constraint will be only as strong as the weakest link in the chain of veto players. But that constraining the executive is important for a number of reasons, of which a top concern of his is achieving good budgetary institutions and state economic growth (Cox, 2016). Just as he does, we must ask whether achieving these good institutions, or what this book denominates commitment to institutions, is easy.

7.3.1 Why are High Levels of Institutional Commitment Rare?

The sample considered in this book certainly suggests that high levels of institutional commitment are not prevalent in Latin America. A legacy of regime instability has played into this situation, even when the results in this book depend solely on data from current-day democracies born out of the latest wave of democratization in the region. The book has suggested that job stability in top political jobs, fundamentally in the supreme court and the legislature, are fundamental determinants of levels of institutional commitment. Clearly, stability is not easily attained.

The strong association between the enforcement of decision rights and job security, the latter linked to longer tenures in the supreme court and in congress, does suggest that supreme courts that are longer lived and legislators who create careers within congress are more inclined to check presidents with a propensity to overstep their bounds. Different polities range anywhere between banning reelection to legislative jobs and establishing fixed-term short-lived supreme court benches, to placing no limits on reelection and establishing indefinite tenure in the supreme court. And we know that these rules are not alone in determining tenure, other rules not considered here may also play a role.

This book tells us that higher levels of institutional commitment are desirable, that they are associated to the enforcement of decision rights and that this makes checking executives more likely. It shows how higher levels of institutional commitment are linked to higher levels of job security. Yet countries adopt institutions often in response to problems they confronted in their recent (and not-so-recent) history, and in combination with other institutional traits and political dynamics that are specific to each country. So, no evaluation of the effects of specific institutions can be done in isolation of those conditions.

7.3.2 Can Countries Strengthen Institutional Commitment?

One would be inclined to believe that by inducing longer tenures in the supreme court and legislatures, levels of institutional commitment would rise. If so, it might be interesting to understand how, in what way, can such a process be brought about. How can longer tenures be achieved? Unfortunately, establishing rules that provide for unlimited reelection to congress or indefinite tenure in the supreme court will not do the trick – at least not alone. Changes in these rules will not necessarily bring rises in levels of institutional commitment, because the connection is not direct. These rules are not the sole determinants of longer tenures, as the abundant literature cited in Chapters 1, 4, and 5 has pointed out. Countries with unlimited reelection to congress and indefinite supreme court tenure may, in practice, experience high levels of rotation in both spheres due to other incentives that weigh upon decisions to stay on. Factors ranging from the structure of party lists in systems of proportional representation to intimidation to leave the bench can affect tenure, as research cited earlier in this book has shown.

To be certain, it is not reasonable to expect changes in levels of institutional commitment in short periods of time. Its strengthening, as much as its deterioration, is a process that involves looking forward in time, and occurs over the long term. Levels of institutional commitment are determined by the current institutional setting and by inter-temporal calculations, as explained in Chapter 3. This is also why levels will not deteriorate quickly.

Consider the case of the United States of America. Levels of institutional commitment there are certainly at the higher end of the spectrum. Recent events in US politics, such as the executive order signed by President D. Trump on 27 January 2017, a travel ban "Protecting the Nation from foreign terrorist entry into the United States," provides a glimpse into how the dynamics emphasized by this book come to play. In this specific case, those who claim that partisan support in congress enables the executive to issue decrees certainly have a point. The partisan majority held by republicans in Congress stood still while an expansive ban was placed on travel into the USA, countering established policy in this realm. Yet, given that this ban violates constitutional rights, the judiciary was able to step in and revert it. To be sure, the judiciary in the USA has the capacity to counter the decisions of a standing president because there is a history of judicial independence, and it is difficult to imagine that a standing judge would face losing her job as a consequence of her decisions.

Clearly, this is not always the case outside of the United States. Most interestingly, it may not always be the case in the United States: a few weeks into the Trump presidency observers were already wondering whether job security in the judiciary will remain as strong as it has been. But the point is that other countries already face the reality of low levels of institutional commitment, and its strengthening requires a multifaceted approach that can lead to longer tenures.

The utility, therefore, to both legislators and other actors, of enforcing decision rights, is beyond question. Yet a fundamental point made in this book is that the degree to which actors enforce their decision rights is affected by the incentives that they face more broadly. This lies at the heart of the explanation of why career incentives are not easily altered. The public utility of enforcing decision rights is not always aligned with the individual utility of legislators and other politicians. When the two are aligned, higher levels of institutional commitment benefit the public by providing checks and balances to the system. When they are not, unfortunately, the cycle that results is difficult to break.

Politicians are not naïve regarding these choices. The powerful actors of today feed off of the current incentive structure, so to expect that they make changes in the direction of strengthening actors that will then limit discretion or constrain them simply does not seem reasonable. Such changes require a good dosage of statesmanship, with a dash of altruism. They require a firm conviction by a majority of the actors involved that the strengthening of the branches, which comes hand in hand with the imposition of constraints on the executive, has the power to bring about long-term benefits to the entire polity.

How likely is it that a handful of actors, perhaps a few key legislators with longer tenures in congress, may see it in their interest to generate changes that may strengthen the institution in the long term? It is undoubtedly these politicians who hold the key – if there is one – to affect the utility of being a legislator. Admittedly, incentive structures are in place for a reason, so to expect actions that go against equilibrium behavior does not seem sensible – but such is the magic of agency, as history has taught us over and over, and it is not to be discounted altogether.

Bibliography

Achen, C. 2000. "Why lagged dependent variables can suppress the explanatory power of other independent variables". Paper presented at the Annual Meeting of the Methodology Section of the American Political Science Association, Los Angeles, July 20–22, 2000.

Acuña, C. 1995. "Algunas notas sobre los juegos, las gallinas y la lógica política de los pactos constitucionales (reflexiones a partir del pacto constitucional en la Argentina)" in Acuña, Carlos, ed., *La Nueva Matriz Política Argentina*, Editorial Nueva Visión

Alemán, E. and E. Calvo. 2010. "Unified Government, Bill Approval, and the Legislative Weight of the President." *Comparative Political Studies* 43(4): 511–534.

Alemán, E., and M. Pachón. 2008. "Las Comisiones de conciliación en los procesos legislativos de Chile y Colombia." *Política y Gobierno* 15(1): 3–34.

Altman, D., and A. Pérez Liñán. 2002. "Assessing the Quality of Democracy: Freedom, Competitiveness and Participation in Eighteen Latin American Countries." *Democratization* 9(2): 85–100.

Amorim Neto, O. 2002. "Presidential Cabinets, Electoral Cycles, and Coalition Discipline in Brazil." In Morgenstern, Scott and Benito Nacif, eds., *Legislative Politics in Latin America*. Cambridge University Press.

Amorim Neto, O. 2006. "The Presidential Calculus. Executive Policy Making and Cabinet Formation in the Americas." *Comparative Political Studies* 39(4): 415–440.

Amorim Neto, O., and P. Tafner. 2002. "Governos de Coalizão e Mecanismos de Alarme de Incêndio no Controle Legislativo das Medidas Provisórias." *DADOS–Revista de Ciências Sociais* 45(1): 5–38.

Amorim Neto, O., G. Cox, and M. McCubbins. 2003. "Agenda Power in Brazil's Câmara dos Deputados, 1989 to 1998." *World Politics* 55(4): 550–578.

Aninat. C. 2006. "Balance de Poderes Legislativos en Chile ¿Presidencialismo exagerado o base de un Sistema politico cooperativo? *Revista Política* 47: 127–148.

Archer, R., and M. Shugart. 1997. "The Unrealized Potential of Presidential Dominance in Colombia." In S. Mainwaring and M. S. Shugart, eds., *Presidentialism and Democracy in Latin America*. Cambridge University Press.

Arnold, R. D. 1990. *The Logic of Congressional Action*, Yale University Press.

Baltagi, B. 2001. *Econometric Analysis of Panel Data*. Wiley and Sons.

Basabe Serrano, S. 2009. "Ecuador: Reforma constitucional, nuevos actores políticos y viejas prácticas partidistas." *Revista de Ciencia Política* 29(2): 381–406.

Basabe Serrano, S., and J. Polga Hecimovich. 2013. "Legislative Coalitions and Judicial Turnover under Political Uncertainty: The Case of Ecuador." *Political Research Quarterly* 66(1): 154–166.

Beck, N. 2001. "Time-Series-Cross-Section Data: What have We Learned in the Past Few Years?" *Annual Review of Political Science* 4: 271–293.

Beck, N., and J. Katz. 1995. "What To Do (and Not To Do) with Time-Series Cross Section Data." *The American Political Science Review* 89(3): 634–647.

1996. "Nuisance Versus Substance: Specifying and Estimating Time-Series-Cross-Section Models". *Political Analysis* 6: 1–36.

2011. "Modeling Dynamics in Time-Series-Cross-Section Political Economy Data". *Annual Review of Political Science* 14: 331–352.

Biblioteca del Congreso Nacional de la República de Chile. 2017. Buscador de Leyes. Available in website: www.leychile.cl/Consulta/homebasico/.

Botero, F., and L. Rennó. 2007. "Career Choice and Legislative Reelection: Evidence from Brazil and Colombia." *Brazilian Political Science Review* 1: 102–124.

Bronfman Vargas, A., and J. Martinez Estay. 2005. *Constitución Política de la República de Chile*. Editorial Lexis Nexis. 5ª Edición.

Calvo, E. 2007. "The Responsive Legislature: Public Opinion and Law Making in Highly Disciplined Legislature." *British Journal of Political Science* 37(2): 263–280.

2014. *Legislator Success in Fragmented Congresses in Argentina. Plurality Cartels, Minority Presidents, and Lawmaking*. Cambridge University Press.

Câmara dos Deputados da República Federativa do Brasil. 2017. Pesquisa Projetos de Lei e Outras Proposicões. Available in website: www.camara.leg .br/buscaProposicoesWeb/pesquisaAvancada/

2005. *Constituição 1988 com alterações adotadas pelas Emendas Constitucionais* (23ª Edição).

Cámara de Diputados de la República Argentina. 2017. Dirección de Información Parlamentaria. Available in website www.hcdn.gov.ar/.

Cameron, C. 2000. *Veto Bargaining: Presidents and the Politics of Negative Power*. Cambridge University Press.

Canes Wrone, B. 2001. "The President's Legislative Influence from Public Appeals." *American Journal of Political Science* 45(2): 313–329.

Canes Wrone, B., W. Howell, and D. Lewis. 2008. "Toward a Broader Understanding of Presidential Power: A Reevaluation of the Two Presidencies Thesis." *The Journal of Politics* 70(1): 1–16.

Cárdenas, M., R. Junguito, and M. Pachón. 2006. "Political Institutions and Policy Outcomes in Colombia: The Effects of the 1991 Constitution." (IADB Working Paper R-508). Retrieved from Inter-American Development Bank website: https://publications.iadb.org/.

2008. "Political Institutions and Policy Outcomes in Colombia: The Effects of the 1991 Constitution." In E. Stein and M. Tommasi, eds., *Policymaking in Latin America: How Politics Shapes Policies*. IDB-Harvard University Press.

Carey, J., and M. Shugart, eds. 1998. *Executive Decree Authority*. Cambridge University Press.

Casa Civil da Presidência da República, www4.planalto.gov.br/legislacao/ portal-legis/legislacao-1/medidas-provisorias, and www4.planalto.gov.br/ legislacao/portal-legis/legislacao-1/leis-ordinarias

Chasquetti, D., and J. Micozzi. 2014. "The Subnational Connection in Unitary Regimes: progressive Ambition and Legislative Behavior in Uruguay." *Legislative Studies Quarterly* 39(1): 87–112.

Chavez, R. 2003. "The Construction of the Rule of Law in Argentina: A Tale of Two Provinces". *Comparative Politics* 35(4): 417–437.

Cheibub, J. 2007. *Presidentialism, Parliamentarism, and Democracy*. Cambridge University Press.

Clark, T. 2010. *The Limits of Judicial Independence*. Cambridge University Press.

de Abreu Junior, D. A. 2002. Medidas provisórias: o poder quase absoluto. *Câmara dos Deputados, Centro de Documentação e Informação (CEDI)*, Coordenação de Publicações.

Merlin Clève, C., 2000. Atividade legislativa do poder executivo. Editora Revista dos Tribunais, 2da Edição.

Congreso de la Nación Perú. 2017. Archivo Digital de la Legislación en el Perú. Available in website www.leyes.congreso.gob.pe/.

Cox, G. 2016. *Marketing Sovereign Promises. Monopoly Brokerage and the Growth of the English State*. Cambridge University Press.

Cox, G., and M. McCubbins. 1993. *Legislative Leviathan: Party Government in the House*. University of California Press.

Cox, G., and S. Morgenstern. 2001. "Latin America's Reactive Assemblies and Proactive Presidents". *Comparative Politics* 33(2): 171–189.

Cox, G. and S. Morgenstern. 2002. "Epilogue: Latin America's Reactive Assemblies and Proactive Presidents." In Morgenstern, Scott and Benito Nacif, eds., *Legislative Politics in Latin America*. Cambridge University Press.

Dargent, E., and M. Urteaga. 2016. "Respuesta estatal por presiones externas: los determinantes del fortalecimiento estatal frente al boom de oro en el Perú (2004–2015)." *Revista de Ciencia Política* 36(3): 655–677.

De Moraes, A. 2006. *Constituição do Brasil Interpretada*. Editora Atlas.

Desposato, S. 2006. "Parties for Rent? Ambition, Ideology, and Party Switching in Brazil's Chamber of Deputies." *American Journal of Political Science* 50(1): 62–80.

Diario Oficial de la República de Chile. 2005. *Colección de Índices de Leyes, Decretos con Fuerza de Ley y Decretos Leyes, 1979–2004*.

Diermeier D., and R. Myerson. 1999. "Bicameralism and Its Consequences for the Internal Organization of Legislatures." *The American Economic Review* 89(5): 1182–1196.

Epstein, D., and S. O'Halloran. 1999. *Delegating Powers: A Transaction Cost Politics Approach to Policy Making under Separate Powers*. Cambridge University Press.

Epstein, L., and J. Knight. 1998. *The Choices Justices Make.* Congressional Quarterly Press.

Epstein, L., and J. Segal. 2005. *Advice and Consent: The Politics of Judicial Appointments.* Oxford University Press.

Etchemendy, S., and V. Palermo. 1998. "Conflicto y concertación. Gobierno, Congreso y organizaciones de interés en la reforma laboral del primer gobierno de Menem (1989–1995)." *Desarrollo Económico* 37(148): 559–590.

Feld, L., and S. Voigt. 2003. "Economic Growth and Judicial Independence: Cross-Country Evidence Using a New Set of Indicators." *European Journal of Political Economy* 19(3): 497–527.

Ferejohn, J., and C. Shipan. 1990. "Congressional Influence on Bureaucracy." *Journal of Law, Economics and Organization* 6(Especial Issue): 1–20.

Ferreira Rubio, D., and M. Goretti. 1998. "When the President Governs Alone: The Decretazo in Argentina, 1989–93." In J. Carey and M. Shugart, eds., *Executive Decree Authority.* Cambridge University Press.

Figueiredo, A., and F. Limongi. 1997. "O Congresso e as medidas provisórias: abdicação ou delegação?" *Novos Estudos-CEBRAP* 47: 127–154.

Figueiredo, A., and F. Limongi. 2000. "Presidential Power, Legislative Organization, and Party Behavior in Brazil." *Comparative Politics* 32(2): 151–170.

García Villegas, M. 2001. "Constitucionalismo perverso, normalidad y anormalidad constitucional en Colombia: 1957–1997." In B. de Sousa Santos and M. García Villegas, eds., *El Caleidoscopio de la Justicia Colombiana.* Uniandes Siglo del Hombre.

Gallardo, C. y D. Muñiz. 2004. *Análisis de la Carrera Legislativa en el Perú: Estrategias para permanecer en el cargo,"* typescript, Universidad del Pacífico, Perú.

Gely, R., and P. Spiller. 1990. "A Rational Choice Theory of Supreme Court Statutory Decisions with Applications to the 'State Farm' and 'Grove City' Cases". *Journal of Law, Economics and Organization* 6(2): 263–300.

González-Ocantos, E., C. de Jonge, C. Meléndez, and D. Nickerson. 2012. "Vote Buying and Social Desirability Bias: Experimental Evidence from Nicaragua." *American Journal of Political Science* 56(1): 202–217.

Groseclose, T., S. Levitt, and J. Snyder. 1999. "Comparing Interest Group Scores across Time and Chambers: Adjusted ADA Scores for the U.S. Congress." *The American Political Science Review* 93(1): 33–50.

Groseclose, T., and N. McCarty. 1996. *Presidential Vetoes: Bargaining, Blame-Game, and Gridlock.* (Unpublished Manuscript). Department of Political Science, Ohio State University.

2001. "The Politics of Blame: Bargaining before an Audience." *American Journal of Political Science* 45(1): 100–119.

Groseclose, T., and J. Snyder. 1996. "Buying Supermajorities." *The American Political Science Review* 90(2): 303–315.

Gross, O., and R. Wagner. 1950. "*A Continuous Colonel Blotto Game.*" Research Memorandum 408 RAND Corporation.

Hanmer, M. and K. O. Kalkan. 2013. "Behind the Curve: Clarifying the Best Approach to Calculating Predicted Probabilities and Marginal Effects from Limited Dependent Variable Models." *American Journal of Political Science* 57(1): 263–277.

Helmke, G. and J. Ríos Figueroa. 2011. *Courts in Latin America*. Cambridge University Press.

Helmke, G. 2002. "The Logic of Strategic Defection: Court-Executive Relations in Argentina under Dictatorship and Democracy." *The American Political Science Review* 96(2): 291–303.

2005. *Courts under Constraints. Judges, Generals, and Presidents in Argentina*. Cambridge University Press.

Henisz, W. 2000. "The Institutional Environment of Economic Growth." *Economics and Politics* 12(1): 1–31.

Hiroi, T. 2005. *Bicameral Politics: The Dynamics of Lawmaking in Brazil*. (Ph.D. Dissertation). University of Pittsburgh.

Howell, W. 2003. *Power without Persuasion: The Politics of Direct Presidential Action*. Princeton University Press.

Howell, W., and D. Lewis. 2002. "Agencies by Presidential Design." *The Journal of Politics* 64(4): 1095–1114.

Huber, J., and C. Shipan. 2002. *Deliberative Dicretion? The Institutional Foundations of Bureaucratic Autonomy*. Cambridge University Press.

Iaryczower, M., P. Spiller, and M. Tommasi. 2002. "Judicial Independence in Unstable Environments, Argentina 1935–1998." *American Journal of Political Science* 46(4): 699–716.

Indridason, I. 2011. "Executive Veto Power and Credit Claiming: Comparing the Effects of the Line-item Veto and the Package Veto." *Public Choice* 146(3/4): 375–394.

Jones, M. 2002a. "Explaining the High Levels of Party Discipline in the Argentine Congress." In S. Morgenstern and B. Nacif, eds., *Legislative Politics in Latin America*. Cambridge University Press.

2002b. "Legislator Behavior and Executive-Legislative Relations in Latin America." *Latin American Research Review* 37(3): 176–188.

2005. "The Role of Parties and Party Systems in the Policymaking Process." *Paper presented at the workshop of State Reform, Public Policies, and Policymaking Processes*, Inter-American Development Bank, Washington DC, February 28–March 2, 2005.

Jones, M., S. Saiegh, P. Spiller, and M. Tommasi. 2002. "Amateur Legislators – Professional Politicians: The Consequences of Party-Centered Electoral Rules in a Federal System." *American Journal of Political Science* 46(3): 656–669.

Jones, M. and W. Hwang. 2005. "Party Government in Presidential Democracies: Extending Cartel Theory beyond the U.S. Congress." *American Journal of Political Science* 49(2): 267–282.

Jones, M. and S. Saiegh. 2007. "Congress, Political Careers, and the Provincial Connection." In P. Spiller and M. Tommasi, eds., *The Institutional Foundations of Public Policy in Argentina*. Cambridge University Press.

Kapiszewski, D. 2005. *Challenging Decisions: High Courts and Economic Governance in Argentina and Brazil*. (Ph.D. Dissertation). University of California, Berkeley.

2012. *High Courts and Economic Governance in Argentina and Brazil*. Cambridge University Press.

Keele, L. and N. Kelly. 2006. "Dynamic Models for Dynamic Theories: The Ins and Outs of Lagged Dependent Variables." *Political Analysis* 14(2): 186–205.

Kiewiet, D., and M. McCubbins. 1991. *The Logic of Delegation: Congressional Parties and the Appropriations Process*. University of Chicago Press.

Kim, J. 2006. "Institutional Constraints on Presidential Lawmaking Power: Analysis of Necessity and Urgency Decrees in Argentina from 1916 to 2004." Paper presented at the Annual Meeting of the Southern Political Science Association, Atlanta, January 5-7, 2006.

2007. *Constrained Unilateralism: Comparing Institutional Foundations of Executive Decrees in Presidential Democracies*. (Ph.D.) Dissertation, Columbia University.

Krehbiel, K. 1992. *Information and Legislative Organization*. University of Michigan Press.

1998. *Pivotal Politics. A Theory of U.S. Lawmaking*. University of Chicago Press.

2000. "Party Discipline and Measures of Partisanship." *American Journal of Political Science* 44(2): 212–227.

Landa Arroyo, C., and A. Velazco Lozada. 2005. *Constitución Política del Perú 1993*. Fondo Editorial de la Pontificia Universidad Católica del Perú.

La Nación. (2008, March, 19). "El paro agropecuario se extenderá una semana más." In Sección Economía, La Nación. Retrieved from: www.lanacion.com.ar

(2008, October, 23). "El gobierno ya decidió la expropiación de Aerolíneas." In Sección Economía, La Nación. Retrieved from: www.lanacion.com.ar

Lara-Borges, O., A. Castagnola, and A. Pérez Liñán. 2012. "Diseño Constitucional y Estabilidad Judicial en América Latina, 1900–2009". *Política y Gobierno* 19(1): 3–40.

Leoni, E., C. Pereira, and L. Renno. 2004. "Political Survival Strategies: Political Career Decisions in the Brazilian Chamber of Deputies." *Journal of Latin American Studies* 36(1): 109–130.

Levitsky, S., and M. Murillo. 2005. *Argentine Democracy: The Politics of Institutional Weakness*. Pennsylvania State University Press.

Lewis, D. 2003. *Presidents and the Politics of Agency Design: Political Insulation in the United States Government Bureaucracy, 1946–1997*. Stanford University Press.

Llanos, M. 1998. "El Presidente, el Congreso y la Política de Privatizaciones en la Argentina (1989–1997)." *Desarrollo Económico* 38(151): 743–770.

2002. *Privatization and democracy in Argentina: An Analysis of President-Congress Relations*. Palgrave Macmillan.

Limongi, F., and A. Figueiredo. 1998. "Bases institucionais do presidencialismo de coalizão". *Lua Nova* 44: 81–106.

Londregan, J. 2000. *Legislative Institutions and Ideology in Chile*. Cambridge University Press.

Londregan, J., and C. Aninat. 2006. "Measuring Spatial Aspects of Legislative Delay: Evidence from the Chilean Congress." (CI&G Working Paper N° 26). Retrieved from Center for Institutions and Governance, University of California, Berkeley website: http://igov.berkeley.edu/sites/default/files/N026_Londregan.pdf.

Machado, F., C. Scartascini, and M. Tommasi. 2011. "Political Institutions and Street Protests in Latin America." *Journal of Conflict Resolution* 55(3): 340–365.

Magar, E. 2001. "The Elusive Authority of Argentina's Congress: Decrees, Statutes, and Veto Incidence, 1983–1994." Paper presented at the Annual Meeting of the American Political Science Association, San Francisco, August 30–September 2, 2001.

Martí I Puig, S. 2009. "Nicaragua 2008: Polarización y Pactos." *Revista de Ciencia Política* 29(2): 515–531.

———. 2013. "Nicaragua 2008: La Consolidación de un Régimen Híbrido." *Revista de Ciencia Política* 33(1): 269–286.

Martínez, E., and A. Brenes. 2012. "Y volver, volver, voler..." Un Análisis de los Casos de Intervención de las Cortes Supremas en la Reelección Presidencial en Centroamérica." *Anuario de Estudios Centroamericanos* 38: 109–136.

Maurich, M., and G. Liendo. 1998. "La Argentina de Alfonsín y Menem: ¿Estilo decisionista o estrategia decretista de Gobierno?" In E. Kvaternik, ed., *Elementos para el Análisis Político. La Argentina y el Cono Sur en los `90.* Editorial Paidós.

Maurich, Mario and Gabriela Liendo. 1998. "¿La Argentina de Alfonsín y Menem: Estilo decisionista de Gobierno o Estrategia decretista de Gobierno (1983–1995)?." In Kvaternik, Eugenio (Ed.) *Elementos para el Análisis Político. La Argentina y el Cono Sur en los '90.* Editorial Paidos, pp. 371–394.

Mayer, K. 2001. *With the Stroke of a Pen. Executive Orders and Presidential Power.* Princeton University Press.

Mayhew, D. 1974. *Congress: The Electoral Connection.* Yale University Press.

———. 1991. *Divided We Govern: Party control, lawmaking, and investigations, 1946–1990.* Yale University Press.

McCarty, N. 2000. "Proposal Rights, Veto Rights, and Political Bargaining." *American Journal of Political Science* 44(3):506–522.

McCarty, N., K. Poole, and H. Rosenthal. 2001. "The Hunt for Party Discipline in Congress." *The American Political Science Review* 95(3): 673–687.

McCubbins, M., R. Noll, and B. Weingast. 1989. "Structure and Process. Politics and Policy: Administrative Arrangements and the Political Control of Agencies." *Virginia Law Review* 75(2): 431–482.

McCubbins, M. and T. Schwartz. 1984. "Congressional Oversight Overlooked: Police Patrols versus Fire Alarms." *American Journal of Political Science* 28(1): 165–179.

Mejía Acosta, A., and J. Polga Hecimovich. 2010. "Parliamentary Solutions to Presidential Crises in Ecuador." In M. Llanos, and L. Marsteintredet, eds., *Presidential Breakdowns in Latin America: Causes and Outcomes of Executive Instability in Developing Democracies.* Palgrave Macmillan.

———. 2011. "Coalition Erosion and Presidential Instability in Ecuador." *Latin American Politics and Society* 53(2): 87–111.

Meléndez, C. and C. León. 2010. "Perú 2009: Los Legados del Autoritarismo." *Revista de Ciencia Política* 30(2): 451–477.

Meléndez, C. and P. Sosa Villagarcia. 2013. "Perú 2012: ¿Atrapados por la Historia?" *Revista de Ciencia Política* 33(1): 325–350.

Micozzi, J. P. 2013. "Does Electoral Accountability Make a Difference? Direct Elections, Career Ambition, and Legislative Performance in the Argentine Senate." *The Journal of Politics* 75(1): 137–149.

2014. "From House to Home: Strategic Bill Drafting in Multilevel Systems with Non-static Ambition," *The Journal of Legislative Studies* 20(3): 265–284

Ministerio de Economía y Finanzas Públicas de Argentina. 2017. Dirección de Análisis de Gasto Público y Programas Sociales. Available in website www .economia.gob.ar/peconomica/basehome/gastosocial.html/.

Mittal, S. and B. R. Weingast. 2013. "Self-Enforcing Constitutions: With an Application to Democratic Stability In America's First Century," *The Journal of Law, Economics, and Organization*, 29(2): 278–302.

Moe, T., and W. Howell. 1999. "The Presidential Power of Unilateral Action." *Journal of Law, Economics, and Organization* 15(1): 132–179.

Molinelli, G. 1999. "La Corte Suprema de Justicia de la Nación frente a los poderes politicos, a través del control de constitucionalidad, 1983–1998." (Mimeo). *Instituto de Investigaciones Ambrosio Gioja*. Facultad de Derecho Universidad de Buenos Aires.

Molinelli, G., V. Palanza, and G. Sin. 1999. *Congreso, Presidencia y Justicia en Argentina. Materiales para su estudio*. Editorial Temas.

Morgenstern, S. and B. Nacif, eds. 2002. *Legislative Politics in Latin America.* Cambridge University Press.

Morón, E. A. and C. Sanborn. 2006. "The Pitfalls of Policymaking in Peru: Actors, Institutions and Rules of the Game," IDB Working Paper No. 206. Available at SSRN: https://ssrn.com/abstract=1814760 or http://dx.doi .org/10.2139/ssrn.1814760.

Murphy, W. 1964. *Elements of Judicial Strategy*. Chicago University Press.

Mustapic, A. 2002. "Oscillating Relations: President and Congress in Argentina." In S. Morgenstern and B. Nacif, eds., *Legislative Politics in Latin America.* Cambridge University Press.

Navia, P. 2004. "*Legislative Candidate Selection in Chile*." Paper presented at the Symposium Pathways to Power: Political Recruitment and Democracy in Latin America, Winston-Salem, April 3–4, 2004.

Negretto, G. 2000. "Does the President Govern Alone? Legislative Decree Authority and Institutional Design in Brazil and Argentina." Paper presented at Universidad Torcuato Di Tella, Buenos Aires, December 13, 2000.

2004. "Government Capacities and Policy Making by Decree in Latin America: The Cases of Brazil and Argentina." *Comparative Political Studies* 37(5): 531–562.

2009. "Political Parties and Institutional Design: Explaining Constitutional Choice in Latin America." *British Journal of Political Science* 39(1): 117–139.

2013. *Making Constitutions. Presidents, Parties, and Institutional Choice in Latin America.* Cambridge University Press.

Núcleo de Estudos Comparados e Internacionais. 2017. Banco de Dados Legislativos CEBRAP [Dataset]. Available from http://neci.fflch.usp.br/node/506/.

O'Donnell, G. 1993. "On the State, Democratization and some conceptual problems: A Latin American View with Glances at some Post-Communist Countries." *World Development* 21(8): 1355–1369.

1994. "Delegative Democracy" *Journal of Democracy* 15(1): 55–69.

Osborne, M. J. 2004. *An Introduction to Game Theory*. Oxford University Press.

Palanza, V. 2020. "Variations on the Veto Prerogative: Evidence from Chile," *Latin American Research Review* 55(2).

Palanza, V., and G. Sin. 1997. "Partidos Provinciales y Gobierno Nacional en el Congreso (1983–1995)" *Boletín de la Sociedad Argentina de Análisis Político* 5: 46–94.

Palanza, V. and R. Espinoza. 2017. "El locus del Congreso en el sistema político chileno," in J. P. Luna and R. Mardones, eds., *La Columna Vertebral Fracturada: Revisitando Intermediarios Políticos en Chile*. Santiago: RIL Editores

Palanza, V., C. Scartascini and M. Tommasi. 2016. "Congressional Institutionalization: A Cross-National Comparison." *Legislative Studies Quarterly* 41(1): 7–34.

Palanza, V., and G. Sin. 2013. "Item Vetoes and Attempts to Override Them in Multiparty Legislatures." *Journal of Politics in Latin America* 5(1): 37–66.

2014. "Veto Bargaining and the Legislative Process in Multiparty Presidential Systems." *Comparative Political Studies* 47(5): 766–792.

Pereira, C., and A. Mejía Acosta. 2010. "Policymaking in Multiparty Presidential Regimes: A Comparison between Brazil and Ecuador." *Governance* 23(4): 641–666.

Pereira, C., and B. Mueller. 2002. "Comportamento Estratégico em Presidencialismo de Coalizão: As Relações entre Executivo e Legislativo na Elaboração do Orçamento Brasileiro." *DADOS–Revista de Ciências Sociais* 45(2): 265–301.

2004. "The Cost of Governing. Strategic Behavior of the President and Legislators in Brazil Budgetary Process." *Comparative Political Studies* 37(7): 781–815.

Pereira, C., and T. Power, and L. Rennó. 2005. "Under what Conditions do Presidents Resort to Decree Power? Theory and Evidence from the Brazilian Case." *Journal of Politics* 67(1): 178–200.

2008. "Agenda Power, Executive Decree Authority, and the Mixed Results of Reform in the Brazilian Congress." *Legislative Studies Quarterly* 33(1): 5–33.

Pérez Liñán, A. (Coord.). 2011. "Legislatures in Latin America." Unpublished dataset, University of Pittsburgh.

2011. "Replication data for Diseño Constitucional y Estabilidad Judicial en América Latina, 1900–2009". Harvard Dataverse V1, hdl:1902.1/15801 UNF:5:LZ954jtaZVCahdjwpWgllw==.

Plümper, T., V. Troeger, and P. Manow. 2005. "Panel Data Analysis in Comparative Politics. Linking Method to Theory." *European Journal of Political Research* 44(2): 327–354.

Polga Hecimovich, J. 2013. "Ecuador: Estabilidad Institucional y la Consolidación de poder de Rafael Correa." *Revista de Ciencia Política* 33(1): 135–160.

Polsby, N. 1968. "The Institutionalization of the U.S. House of Representatives." *The American Political Science Review* 62(1): 144–168.

Posdeley, C. 2016. "Apuntes sobre el rol y las funciones de control de la Comisión Bicameral de Trámite Legislativo." In Asociación de Docentes de la Facultad de Derecho y Ciencias Sociales, eds., *El Control de la Actividad Estatal: Discrecionalidad, División de Poderes y Control Extrajudicial.* Universidad de Buenos Aires.

Power, T. 1998. "The Pen is Mightier than the Congress: Presidential Decree Power in Brazil." In J. Carey and M. Shugart, eds., *Executive Decree Authority.* Cambridge University Press.

Protsyk, O. 2004. "Ruling with Decrees: Presidential Decree Making in Russia and Ukraine." *Europe-Asia Studies* 56(5): 637–660.

Quinzio, J. 2003. *Tratado de Derecho Constitucional* (Vol. 1 & 2). Editorial Lexis Nexis.

Remington, T. 2014. *Presidential Decree in Russia. A Comparative Perspective.* Cambridge University Press.

Rohde, D. 1979. "Risk-Bearing and Progressive Ambition: The Case of Members of the United States House of Representatives." *American Journal of Political Science* 23(1): 1–26.

Sabsay, D. and J. Onaindia, eds. 1995. *La Constitución de los Argentinos.* Errepar.

Saiegh, S. 2005. "The Role of Legislatures in the Policymaking Process." Paper presented at the workshop of State Reform, Public Policies, and Policymaking Processes, Inter-American Development Bank, Washington DC, February 28–March 2, 2005.

2010. "Active Players or Rubber Stamps? An Evaluation of the Policymaking Role of Latin American Legislature." In C. Scartascini, E. Stein and M. Tommasi, eds., *How Democracy Works.* Inter-American Development Bank – David Rockefeller Center for Latin American Studies, Harvard University.

2011. *Ruling by Statute. How Uncertainty and Vote Buying Shape Lawmaking.* Cambridge University Press.

Samuels, D. 2002. *Progressive Ambition, Federalism, and Pork-Barreling in Brazil.* Cambridge University Press.

Scartascini, C., E. Stein and M. Tommasi, eds. 2010. *How Democracy Works.* Inter-American Development Bank – David Rockefeller Center for Latin American Studies, Harvard University.

Scartascini, C., P. Spiller, E. Stein, and M. Tommasi, eds. 2011. *El Juego Político en América Latina: ¿Cómo se deciden las políticas públicas?* Banco Interamericano de Desarrollo – Mayol Ediciones.

Schickler, E., and A. Rich. 1997a. "Controlling the Floor: Parties as Procedural Coalitions in the House." *American Journal of Political Science* 41(4): 1340–1375.

1997b. "Party Government in the House Reconsidered: A Response to Cox and McCubbins." *American Journal of Political Science* 41(4): 1387–1394.

Schlesinger, J. 1966. *Ambition and Politics: Political Careers in the United States.* Rand McNally.

Schmidt, G. 1998. "Presidential Usurpation or Congressional Preference? The Evolution of Executive Decree Authority in Peru." In J. Carey and M. Shugart, eds., *Executive Decree Authority.* Cambridge University Press.

2000. "Delegative Democracy in Peru? Fujimori's 1995 Landslide and the Prospects for 2000." *Journal of Interamerican Studies and World Affairs* 42(1): 99–132.

Shor, B., J. Bafumi, L. Keele, and D. Park. 2007. "A Bayesian Multilevel Modeling Approach to Time-Series Cross-Sectional Data." *Political Analysis* 15(2): 165–181.

Scribner, D. 2002. "Executive Accountability: Juridical Control of Presidential Decree Authority in Chile." Paper presented at the 61st Midwest Political Science Association Annual Conference, Chicago, April 27–30, 2002.

2004. Limiting Presidential Power: Supreme Court-Executive Relations in Argentina and Chile." (Ph.D. Dissertation). University of California, San Diego.

2007. "Courts under Constraints: Judges, Generals, and Presidents in Argentina (Review)." *Latin American Politics and Society* 49(4): 202–205.

Secretaria-Geral da Mesa do Senado in Brazil, www25.senado.leg.br/web/atividade/legislacao

Segal, J. 1997. "Separation of Powers Games in the Positive Theory of Congress and Courts." *The American Political Science Review* 91(1): 28–44.

Shepsle, K., and B. Weingast. 1987. "The Institutional Foundations of Committee Power." *The American Political Science Review* 81(1): 85–104.

Shugart, M., and J. Carey. 1992. *Presidents and Assemblies. Constitutional Design and Electoral Dynamics.* Cambridge University Press.

Siavelis, P. 2000. *The President and Congress in Postauthoritarian Chile. Institutional Constraints to Democratic Consolidation.* Pennsylvania State University Press.

2002. "Exaggerated Presidentialism and Moderate Presidents: Executive-Legislative Relations in Chile." In S. Morgenstern and B. Nacif, eds., *Legislative Politics in Latin America.* Cambridge University Press.

Siavelis, Peter. 2006. "Electoral Reform Doesn't Matter – or Does it?: A Moderate PR System for Chile." *Revista de Ciencia Política* 26(1): 216–225.

Sin, G. 2015. *Separation of Powers and Legislative Organization: The President, the Senate, and Political Parties in the Making of House Rules.* Cambridge University Press.

SICON. Sistema de Informações do Congresso http://legis.senado.gov.br/sicon/#/basica

Smulovitz, C. 1995. "Reforma y Constitución en la Argentina: del Consenso Negativo al Acuerdo." *Revista Uruguaya de Ciencia Política* 8: 69–84.

Snyder, J., and T. Groseclose. 2001. Estimating Party Influence on Roll Call Voting: Regression Coefficients versus Classification Success." *The American Political Science Review* 95(3): 689–698.

Sonnleitner, W. 2010. "Las últimas elecciones en América Central: ¿el Quiebre de la Tercera Ola de Democratizaciones?" *Foro Internacional* 50, 3/4(201/202): 808–849.

Spiller, P., and R. Gely. 1992. "Congressional Control or Judicial Independence: The Determinants of U.S. Supreme Court Labor-Relations Decisions, 1949–1988." *The RAND Journal of Economics* 23(4): 463–492.

Spiller, P., and S. Liao. 2006. "Buy, Lobby or Sue: Interest Groups' Participation in Policy Making – A Selective Survey." (NBER Working Paper N° 12209). Retrieved from The National Bureau of Economic Research website: www .nber.org/papers/w12209.

Spiller, P., and M. Tommasi. 2000. *Los Determinantes Institucionales del Desarrollo Argentino. Hacia una Agenda Institucional.* Centro de Estudios para el Desarrollo Institucional (Fundación Gobierno y Sociedad) and United Nations Program for Development. EUDEBA.

2007. *The Institutional Foundations of Public Policy in Argentina: A Transactions Cost Approach.* Cambridge University Press.

Stein, E., M. Tommasi, K. Echebarría, E. Lora, and M. Payne (Coords.) 2006. *The Politics of Policies. Economic and Social Progress in Latin America (2006 Report).* Inter-American Development Bank – David Rockefeller Center for Latin American Studies, Harvard University.

Stein, E., M. Tommasi, and C. Scartascini, eds. 2008. *Policymaking in Latin America: How Politics Shapes Policies.* Inter-American Development Bank – David Rockefeller Center for Latin American Studies, Harvard University.

Stinga, L. 2008. "Revisiting Governance by Decree in Argentina: Political Culture or Structure?" *Paper presented at the ECPR Graduate Conference in Barcelona*, August 24–26, 2008.

Tsebelis, G. 2002. *Veto Players. How Political Institutions Work.* Princeton University Press.

Tsebelis, G., and E. Alemán. 2005. "Presidential Conditional Agenda Setting in Latin America." *World Politics* 57(3): 396–420.

Tsebelis, G. and E. Alemán (Eds.). 2016. *Legislative Institutions and Lawmaking in Latin America, Oxford Studies in Democratization.* Oxford University Press.

Uprimny, R. 2010. "The Constitutional Court and Control of Presidential Extraordinary Powers in Colombia." *Democratization* 10(4): 46–69.

Walker, L. 2009. "Delegative Democratic Attitudes and Institutional Support in Central America." *Comparative Politics* 42(1): 83–101.

Weingast, B. 1989. "The Political Institutions of Representative Government: Legislatures." *Journal of Institutional and Theoretical Economics* 145(4): 693–703.

Weingast, B. 2005. "*Self-Enforcing Constitutions: With an Application to Democratic Stability in America's First Century,*" typescript Stanford University, copy available at http://ssrn.com/abstract=1153527.

Wiesehomeier, N. and K. Benoit. 2009. "Presidents, Parties, and Policy Competition." *The Journal of Politics* 71(4): 1435–1447.

Wilson, S., and D. Butler. 2007. "A Lot More to do: the Sensitivity of Time-Series Cross-Section Analyses to Simple Alternative Specifications." *Political Analysis* 15(2): 101–123.

Wooldridge, J. 2010. *Econometric Analysis of Cross Section and Panel Data*. MIT Press.

Zavalía, R. 2001. *Constitución de la Nación Argentina*. Editorial Zavalía.

Zucco, C. 2009. "Ideology or What? Legislative Behavior in Multiparty Presidential Settings." *The Journal of Politics* 71(3): 1076–1092.

———. 2013. "When Payouts Pay Off: Conditional Cash Transfers and Voting Behavior in Brazil, 2002–2010." *American Journal of Political Science* 57(4): 810–822.

Zucco, C., and B. Lauderdale. 2011. "Distinguishing between Influences on Brazilian Legislative Behavior." *Legislative Studies Quarterly* 36(3): 363–396.

Zucco, C., and T. Power. 2013. "Bolsa Familia and the Shift in Lula's Electoral Base, 2002–2006: A Reply to Bohn." *Latin American Research Review* 48(2): 3–24.

Zuñiga, F. (Coord.). 2005. *Reforma Constitucional*. Editorial Lexis Nexis.

Index